Contents

Third Edition

GREAT JOBS

FOR

Criminal Justice Majors

Stephen Lambert and Debra Regan

Mc
Graw
Hill

New York   Chicago   San Francisco   Lisbon   London   Madrid   Mexico City
Milan   New Delhi   San Juan   Seoul   Singapore   Sydney   Toronto

The McGraw-Hill Companies

Library of Congress Cataloging-in-Publication Data

Lambert, Stephen E.
    Great jobs for criminal justice majors / by Stephen Lambert and Debra Regan. — 2nd ed.
       p.   cm
    Includes index.
    ISBN 0-07-147613-X (pbk. : alk. paper)
      1. Law enforcement—Vocational guidance—United States.   2. College graduates—
Employment—United States.   3. Job hunting—United States.   I. Regan, Debra.   II. Title.

    HV8143.L335   2007
    364.973023—dc22   2006050567

2 3 4 5 6 7 8 9 10 11 12 13 14 15 16 17 18 19 20 21   DOC/DOC 0 9

ISBN-13: 978-0-07-147613-3
ISBN-10:   0-07-147613-X

McGraw-Hill books are available at special quantity discounts to use as premiums and sales promotions, or for use in corporate training programs. For more information, please write to the Director of Special Sales, Professional Publishing, McGraw-Hill, Two Penn Plaza, New York, NY 10121-2298. Or contact your local bookstore.

This book is printed on acid-free paper.

Acknowledgments

The following individuals contributed greatly to the writing of this book. To Captain Art Walker of the Keene, New Hampshire, Police Department; Dr. Lynda Pintrich, professor of criminal justice, Middlesex Community College; David Collum, former chief of police, Rindge, New Hampshire; and John E. Clark, chief of security/campus police, Plymouth State College, thank you for sharing your time, experiences, observations, and expertise with us and for leading us in the right direction. Your combined input provided the foundation for *Great Jobs for Criminal Justice Majors*. To our colleagues Rosemary Nichols, director of career planning and placement, Franklin Pierce College, Rindge, New Hampshire, and Sam Allen, director of career services, Saint Anselm College, Manchester, New Hampshire, thank you for providing us with your resources, contacts, and insights into the criminal justice major. To Karen Fuller, public information coordinator, American Probation and Parole Association, and Anne Skove, knowledge management analyst, National Center for State Courts, we extend our appreciation for your quick response to our requests for information. The information you sent was exactly what we needed.

The editors would like to thank Josephine Scanlon for revising this edition.

Introduction

Investigate the Opportunities

It's difficult to generalize about the field of criminal justice. Some observers may say, "It's harsh!" Criminal justice majors will remind you of the compassionate and deeply feeling role of juvenile counselors and the impact and difference that their caring, listening skills, and empathy can mean in positively redirecting a young life. Others may say, "It's black-and-white, no room for gray!" Criminal justice majors will tell you that's not entirely true, either. In fact, although the Justice Department announced in 2000 that arrests were up nationwide, over the past decade we have seen a 30 percent decline in the likelihood of convicted criminals going to prison. Why? The American justice system has increased the numbers of offenders receiving probation for drug offenses and drunken driving convictions through specific treatment plans, community supervision, and supervised rehabilitation.

Generalizations are often not fair, and they are particularly hard to make about criminal justice jobs and careers. However, one generalization we can confidently make about criminal justice careers is that they hold breadth and depth for the graduates of these programs. The five career paths outlined in this book demonstrate the remarkable range of occupations available to the graduate today.

Perhaps no criminal justice career typifies the changes in our systems of justice administration more than law enforcement. You've seen reports in newspapers and on television news programs that document these changes: hiring more women and minorities, increased cultural sensitivity, a greater focus on community policing, and awareness that law enforcement officials are members of the communities in which they work. You may know, as well, that the educational backgrounds of law enforcement officials have never been so high and that they're getting higher! Entry-level applicants with bachelor's degrees are competing with each other for jobs that before might have gone

to associate degree recipients or even high school graduates. Today the supply of job applicants with four-year degrees far outnumbers the positions, so
employers can select the "cream of the crop" and fill positions that may not
strictly require a bachelor's degree with bachelor's degree candidates.

And once you're on the job, your education is hardly over. Those state
trooper vehicles passing you on the highway are more likely than not to contain officers who have passed the bar exam and are licensed attorneys. In management and administration, you'll find that the number of personnel with
master's degrees in criminal justice, business management, or other social science fields is on the rise. Law enforcement these days is about brains, not
brawn, and law enforcement employers want smart people who have the motivation and self-discipline to continue their education.

Still, all these wonderful changes in professionalism and educational standards, however important to you, are only symptoms of the deeper change
going on in law enforcement and the criminal justice system in general. These
deeper changes have to do with a new emphasis on legitimacy in law enforcement, and you'll find that emphasized throughout your entry period, during
training, and in the daily practice of your career. Here are some of the ways
in which law enforcement is working to enhance its own legitimacy:

Law enforcement officials are mandated to have high-quality "ordinary"
interactions with the public, not just to respond during those times when we
depend on law enforcement to provide needed services. Your encounters with
the public must now be more than obligatory; they must be ordinary, every-
day, common, and consistent occurrences.

No matter which law enforcement organization you choose to work for,
be it the local police, the FBI, or some branch of state law enforcement, you'll
discover a new emphasis on making that organization more visible and more
open to public scrutiny, which can be intense. Gone are the days when law
enforcement ruled by fiat. The public is interested in being assured that policies, practices, and organizational structures are appropriate.

More and more, law enforcement is asking the public to realize that common citizens have a vital role to play in crime control and criminal justice
operations. Law enforcement increasingly works alongside and in partnership
with citizens for the goals of order and justice.

In the field of corrections, opportunities have never been more dynamic.
The number of people under correctional supervision stands at an all-time
high of 6.6 million at the time of this book's publication. Of this number,
nearly 5 million are adult men and women on probation or parole; the rest
are literally behind bars. The scope and numbers of people involved with the
criminal justice system have increased substantially over the past twenty

years. From just a little over 1 percent of the population in 1980, the offender total has climbed to its current record level of more than 3 percent of all adults. That's one out of every thirty-two men and women.

These probation and parole facts, however, do not mean that prisons are not also working with higher populations. They are. More aggressive and longer sentencing that began in the 1990s means overcrowded conditions in many states, with complicated repercussions. Some states have been forced to move prisoners to other states, raising a public outcry from family members, who say these distant sites of incarceration are yet another form of inhumane punishment. In a case in Connecticut in which two prisoners who had been transferred to Virginia died (one a suicide, one of natural causes following a struggle with a guard), the volume of criticism rose to new decibel levels.

These few telling statistics underlie the correspondingly high employment demands of the correctional system. Correctional officers specialize in many areas beyond the obvious category of security. They can develop specialized skills in registration and other administrative procedures, in structured vocational activities, in counseling (both individual and group) and recreation, and—as our statistics for parolees and probationers indicate—in the all-important field of specialized aftercare and treatment programs for reentry into society.

The field of corrections offers wonderful growth and personal development along its varied career tracks. At the working apex of these promotional ladders is the role of warden, filled now by capable men and women whose careers in corrections and whose continuing education in the areas of criminal justice, business management, sociology, and psychology have qualified them for these demanding administrative executive positions. Beyond the job of warden lie many state and regional correctional facility management and commission positions for those who are looking for a career path with true growth and personal potential.

The potential for the role of our courts in the justice system is incalculable. It's the arena in which we sort out what has happened and how we will redress any injustice that has been done. It's both an active place and a thoughtful one. This book presents a full range of possible occupations within the courts—some available to you immediately upon graduation, others requiring some additional education and training—and, as in every career path, includes details on more advanced career positions to which you may aspire.

Sadly, the American public receives a false impression of most criminal justice activity through the media. Television dramas, movies, novels, and stories often portray every aspect of the system in a heightened and overly sensationalized manner. For those of us who have actually witnessed courtroom proceedings, the difference between fiction and reality is stunningly obvious! Court processes are methodical and reflective—and surprisingly, not very loud or dramatic in most cases. They are, however, terribly complex and seldom black-and-white.

You know from your sociology and psychology course work that people are motivated by any number of stimuli and that those are different for each of us, ranging from our genetic makeup to our psychological and sociological conditioning. Experts have yet to categorize good and evil as absolutes. Even the "good" person can commit a crime, and the "bad" person is capable of goodness. So, courts aren't about good and bad as much as they are about people and about people coming into conflict with one another. The court's job is to sort it out and determine a fair and equitable resolution.

Courts today, like every other facet of the justice system, are trying hard to change. They've been subject to the same exponential growth that has affected the correctional system. Former Chief Justice Warren Burger once said, "The entire legal profession—lawyers, judges, law teachers—has become so mesmerized with the stimulation of the courtroom contest that we forget that we ought to be healers of conflict." And that's where the changes are occurring today, as we see pilot projects such as neighborhood justice centers or pretrial settlement conferences. This is an exciting time to think about working in the court system.

As with every career path featured in Chapters 6 through 10, your degree in criminal justice gives you enormous scope for your options in the courts. There's good work in court security as either a court security officer or bailiff, and both of these jobs have many interesting duties in addition to their principal charge to maintain the integrity of the courtroom. Like most other employees in the court system, you are very much part of a team in the work you do and the role you play.

Several administrative positions are highlighted as well, some very active and visible and others more behind-the-scenes and less obvious. Chief among these are the jobs of clerk of court and court administrator. These are critical administrative functions that organize and regularize the schedules and work of the court. People in both positions, depending on the size and location of the court, may hear and resolve some disputes themselves. They are significant positions and hold the promise of careers full of constant learning. You'll discover continuing career interest and wonderful possibilities for personal growth and professional development either by moving up from a clerk position to a senior court administrator or by moving to a larger court or into the federal system.

We all are aware of the role of court reporters, who are visible in any depiction, real or fictionalized, of the court. A skilled, demanding, and highly responsible position with excellent financial rewards and career stability, this is an attractive option for many criminal justice majors who are interested in adding to their degrees with the specific training that the position requires. Other attractive features of this work are the distinct possibilities of freelancing with these skills and the ability to be mobile. Both of those are especially attractive options in a society in which many of us move several times in a career and want to be able to find work in our field quickly or need to "stop out" of work or work part-time for personal or family reasons. The work of court reporting makes that possible.

Behind the scenes and not well known to many outside the court are the legal research positions that support the judicial staff and court legal staff through their work in law libraries and on the computer (frequently using database skills or purchased CD-ROM information-database software). They provide the legal definitions, history, precedents, and background that underpin the administration of justice in the courts. If you are fascinated by the law, enjoy reading and problem solving, and have good detective skills, every day on this job will bring you a new set of interesting cases to pursue as you track down the relevant information. It's a quieter type of excitement and challenge, but it's infinitely varied and always surprising.

The final two positions featured in the courts career path, each requiring its own additional education and training, are those of paralegal and lawyer. Each has a natural career relationship to your criminal justice education, is highly visible in the courts, and is apt to set you thinking about the career possibilities. Each is thus attractive in its own way and for its own reasons.

Paralegals are the workhorses of the law profession. Frequently specializing and often paired with a particular attorney, they do the complex and vital research and administrative paperwork for the legal case that the attorney is preparing. Researching items such as past opinions, precedents, and exceptions for multiple cases is demanding, exciting, and always different. While there are certifications and professional standards for paralegals, there are also many possible routes to this job. Some criminal justice majors may simply begin work with on-the-job training in a law office and develop their skills as they go, gaining expertise through additional professional development seminars or short courses along the way. Others, depending on geography or setting, earn a certificate through a formal program or school to qualify for these jobs.

This career choice can be ideal if you are proficient in research and writing. Paralegal jobs are highly stable and can be very lucrative; most important, you are recognized as being an integral part of the organization. Your work is valued by others, and for you, the rewards include increased competency, professionalism, and income as you grow in the profession.

This growing expertise leads many paralegals to enter law school and become attorneys. We include lawyers in this career path because they are active participants in the court process, and the law degree is hardly a stranger to those with a criminal justice undergraduate degree—and not just in the court setting, either. Many criminal justice professionals in corrections and law enforcement pursue graduate studies in law for the J.D. (Juris Doctor) and the ability to practice law. Likewise, many paralegals find that they are doing work so closely akin to that of the more highly paid attorneys that it becomes important to them to become attorneys themselves. The opportunities that unfold with a law degree are a volume unto themselves!

The issues (and as a result, the careers) surrounding juvenile justice and serious and violent juvenile (SVJ) offenses focus on prevention rather than punishment. Much has been learned from studies of serious and violent juvenile crime. For example:

- A distinct group of offenders who start early and continue throughout their youth is responsible for a disproportionately high percentage of all juvenile crime. Consequently, if juvenile justice specialists can reach this group, the chances of breaking that cycle would be significantly greater.
- Most offenders younger than twelve are not routinely processed in juvenile court, and services in the community are unfortunately fragmented. Juvenile justice experts must work with other mental health, social welfare, and school officials to redirect these potential offenders.
- The development of delinquent behavior in boys takes place in an orderly fashion, progressing from less serious problems to more significant crimes. Boys tend to progress from conflict with authority to covert actions to overt actions. Once they reach these aggressive stages, it is more difficult to habituate them to healthier behaviors.

Your work may be in a detention center, within the juvenile court system, or in a residential facility for delinquent youth. Regardless of the locale, the work remains the same: inhibiting inappropriate behavior and redirecting it into healthier and more productive channels. Your job will involve either reducing the risk factors that promote bad behavior (such as in a residential facility) or helping to change the way a child responds to these risks (by increasing the child's resilience). Ultimately your work is about promoting positive behavior, health and well-being, and personal success. In addition to resilience, the protective factors you will help to place within the young person's reach will include positive adult and peer relationships that promote bonding. You'll also work to enhance healthy beliefs and clear standards. No pressure!

In all seriousness, can there be more challenging and yet more rewarding work? Nevertheless, you must also be aware that the pressures on those who work in this field, who must serve as daily, hourly, and minute-by-minute role models, are unrelenting. You are not expected to be perfect, but you must be careful, thoughtful, appropriate, empathetic, and infinitely patient—which means that this area of criminal justice is certainly not for everyone. It's a special area of jobs for special people.

The final chapter in this book only hints at the unlimited career horizons possible in allied business with your criminal justice degree. Private security and the growing field of cybercrime both place the criminal justice degree high on their lists of qualifications. Each of these fields offers personal rewards and professional development and allows you the advantage of staying within your degree field of knowledge but exercising a range of other skills and talents that you may have and want to use.

Contrary to popular belief, private security may be the world's oldest profession! There has always been a need for additional security or investigative work outside of public agencies. Sometimes, that has been the result of public law enforcement agencies being too busy or burdened to provide the necessary resources in a situation (especially older, evidentially weaker cases). Other times, it is simply a matter of the client wanting the extra measure of security, discretion, and privacy that these services ensure. Of even more importance to people considering this work is that they can be assured that the future is bright—although the technological demands of the investigative side of the profession will certainly increase along with its usefulness to the industry.

Private security is really a reflection of our culture. The growing number of secure, gated communities with their own security forces, the increasing emphasis on corporate security and integrity of office buildings and headquarters, and the continuing need for private investigative work and personal bodyguards assure the entrepreneurial criminal justice major of an incredibly full menu from which to choose the endeavors that best fit your particular skills, aptitudes, and work needs.

Detective services also fill a niche for customers that cannot be met by public practitioners of the law. Private detective services came about and have remained in the marketplace because they fill an important void in criminal justice services. The individuals and organizations who buy private detective services from providers are hoping for discretion, efficiency, and tact as they seek investigative and other services for issues that concern them.

The final area of criminal justice discussed in this career path is cybercrime. If you enjoy computers and perhaps are graduating with some significant computer expertise in addition to your criminal justice degree, you may find the area of cybercrime to be just what you're looking for. A criminal justice education, strong computer skills (and an equally strong desire to learn and know more of this technology), and basic business acumen are what you need to get your foot in the door of an employer that specializes in investigating and uncovering incidents of computer crime.

The impact of computer viruses is not to be underestimated, and their swift detection and, even more important, internal defenses against them are critical. But a virus is only one kind of computer terrorism. So-called computer hackers and crackers have threatened organizations by breaking through password-protected sites and infiltrating supposedly secure computer domains—domains that may contain huge amounts of personal and privileged information. Even the relatively easily solved problems of jamming corporate Internet accounts with enough queries or messages to effect a shutdown can cost businesses (and ultimately consumers) millions of dollars.

Internal issues abound, too. The field of cybercrime may have you investigating employee crimes involving misuse of computers for illegal purposes such as pornography or stealing computer time for processing of personal materials. It may involve employees stealing data to use themselves or to sell to a competitor. Increasingly, firms have also been subjected to incidents of personal vandalism during layoffs or discharge procedures that have caused significant damage to the business operation.

These few examples do not begin to do justice to the investigative adventure that cybercrime situations present, nor can this book predict what new criminal endeavors may be prompted by technological advances. It is that very inability to predict the future, the ignorance of what may be around the corner both in computer development and in crimes that seek to take illegal advantage of that technology, that you may find exciting.

However exciting cybercrime may appear to you, it would be too easy and, in fact, wrong to label this the "new frontier" of criminal justice. These are, after all, machines—machines made by people—and what is more infinitely complex than the mind of a man or woman? Without question, cybercrime represents a new and as yet undeveloped area of investigation and criminal activity. But the innovation and dramatic changes going on in law enforcement, in the courts, in the field of juvenile justice, and in corrections are equally dramatic and sometimes startling. If you're seeking a career highly charged with almost a volatile level of change, any of the areas of criminal justice set forth in these pages will fit the bill nicely!

The simple reason for this is that justice is an abstract concept, as are the ideas of good and evil. On television and in comic books, good is rewarded and evil punished. But is that how it really is? No, sometimes in the real world, evil goes unpunished, and very bad things can happen to good people. Or good people conflict with good people, or evil conflicts with evil, because intents are different or perceptions vary. The result is the same. It is not the comic-book good and evil with which you will deal in your career but the harsh truths of the real world—and seeking justice here is far more complicated, frustrating, and mystifying than any fiction.

It is these complexities of human nature, their infinite variety and form, which make the careers in criminal justice so demanding. Cybercrime may be "new," but it joins a long list of social crises that we have yet to solve—including poverty, racism, and organized crime—despite dramatic developmental progress on many fronts. So, it stands to reason that as the challenges proliferate, so do the demands on those who would do battle against these threats to law and order. The careers in criminal justice demand the best people—the smartest, the most creative, the most curious—people who are interested in people. Above all, the careers of criminal justice need people who will work hard against significant obstacles in order to make a true difference in the world for each and every one of us.

PART ONE

THE JOB SEARCH

I

The Self-Assessment

Self-assessment is the process by which you begin to acknowledge your own particular blend of education, experiences, values, needs, and goals. It provides the foundation for career planning and the entire job search process. Self-assessment involves looking inward and asking yourself what can sometimes prove to be difficult questions. This self-examination should lead to an intimate understanding of your personal traits and values, consumption patterns and economic needs, longer-term goals, skill base, preferred skills, and underdeveloped skills.

You come to the self-assessment process knowing yourself well in some of these areas, but you may still be uncertain about other aspects. You may be well aware of your consumption patterns, but have you spent much time specifically identifying your longer-term goals or your personal values as they relate to work? No matter what level of self-assessment you have undertaken to date, it is now time to clarify all of these issues and questions as they relate to the job search.

The knowledge you gain in the self-assessment process will guide the rest of your job search. In this book, you will learn about all of the following tasks:

- Writing résumés and cover letters
- Researching careers and networking
- Interviewing and job offer considerations

In each of these steps, you will rely on and often return to the understanding gained through your self-assessment. Any individual seeking employment must be able and willing to express these facets of his or her personality to recruiters and interviewers throughout the job search. This communication allows you to show the world who you are so that together with employers you can determine whether there will be a workable match with a given job or career path.

How to Conduct a Self-Assessment

The self-assessment process goes on naturally all the time. People ask you to clarify what you mean, you make a purchasing decision, or you begin a new relationship. You react to the world and the world reacts to you. How you understand these interactions and any changes you might make because of them are part of the natural process of self-discovery. There is, however, a more comprehensive and efficient way to approach self-assessment with regard to employment.

Because self-assessment can become a complex exercise, we have distilled it into a seven-step process that provides an effective basis for undertaking a job search. The seven steps include the following:

1. Understanding your personal traits
2. Identifying your personal values
3. Calculating your economic needs
4. Exploring your longer-term goals
5. Enumerating your skill base
6. Recognizing your preferred skills
7. Assessing skills needing further development

As you work through your self-assessment, you might want to create a worksheet similar to the one shown in Exhibit 1.1, starting on the following page. Or you might want to keep a journal of the thoughts you have as you undergo this process. There will be many opportunities to revise your self-assessment as you start down the path of seeking a career.

Step 1   Understand Your Personal Traits
Each person has a unique personality that he or she brings to the job search process. Gaining a better understanding of your personal traits can help you evaluate job and career choices. Identifying these traits and then finding employment that allows you to draw on at least some of them can create a rewarding and fulfilling work experience. If potential employment doesn't allow you to use these preferred traits, it is important to decide whether you

Exhibit 1.1
SELF-ASSESSMENT WORKSHEET

Step 1. Understand Your Personal Traits
The personal traits that describe me are
(Include all of the words that describe you.)
The ten personal traits that most accurately describe me are
(List these ten traits.)

Step 2. Identify Your Personal Values
Working conditions that are important to me include
(List working conditions that would have to exist for you to accept a position.)
The values that go along with my working conditions are
(Write down the values that correspond to each working condition.)
Some additional values I've decided to include are
(List those values you identify as you conduct this job search.)

Step 3. Calculate Your Economic Needs
My estimated minimum annual salary requirement is
(Write the salary you have calculated based on your budget.)
Starting salaries for the positions I'm considering are
(List the name of each job you are considering and the associated starting salary.)

Step 4. Explore Your Longer-Term Goals
My thoughts on longer-term goals right now are
(Jot down some of your longer-term goals as you know them right now.)

Step 5. Enumerate Your Skill Base
The general skills I possess are
(List the skills that underlie tasks you are able to complete.)
The specific skills I possess are
(List more technical or specific skills that you possess, and indicate your level of expertise.)
General and specific skills that I want to promote to employers for the jobs I'm considering are
(List general and specific skills for each type of job you are considering.)

continued

Step 6. Recognize Your Preferred Skills

Skills that I would like to use on the job include

(List skills that you hope to use on the job, and indicate how often you'd like to use them.)

Step 7. Assess Skills Needing Further Development

Some skills that I'll need to acquire for the jobs I'm considering include

(Write down skills listed in job advertisements or job descriptions that you don't currently possess.)

I believe I can build these skills by

(Describe how you plan to acquire these skills.)

---

can find other ways to express them or whether you would be better off not considering this type of job. Interests and hobbies pursued outside of work hours can be one way to use personal traits you don't have an opportunity to draw on in your work. For example, if you consider yourself an outgoing person and the kinds of jobs you are examining allow little contact with other people, you may be able to achieve the level of interaction that is comfortable for you outside of your work setting. If such a compromise seems impractical or otherwise unsatisfactory, you probably should explore only jobs that provide the interaction you want and need on the job.

Many young adults who are not very confident about their employability will downplay their need for income. They will say, "Money is not all that important if I love my work." But if you begin to document exactly what you need for housing, transportation, insurance, clothing, food, and utilities, you will begin to understand that some jobs cannot meet your financial needs and it doesn't matter how wonderful the job is. If you have to worry each payday about bills and other financial obligations, you won't be very effective on the job. Begin now to be honest with yourself about your needs.

Begin the self-assessment process by creating an inventory of your personal traits. Make a list of as many words as possible to describe yourself. Words like *accurate, creative, future-oriented, relaxed,* or *structured* are just a few examples. In addition, you might ask people who know you well how they might describe you.

Focus on Selected Personal Traits. Of all the traits you identified, select the ten you believe most accurately describe you. Keep track of these ten traits.

Consider Your Personal Traits in the Job Search Process. As you begin exploring jobs and careers, watch for matches between your personal traits and the job descriptions you read. Some jobs will require many personal traits you know you possess, and others will not seem to match those traits.

The work of a victim advocate, for instance, requires a high level of sensitivity combined with a solid knowledge of the programs and services that are available to help the client. Listening skills are essential because you will be interacting with clients in highly emotional states who depend on you for guidance. This work can be emotionally demanding, and it is important to be able to put your own feelings aside to do the best job possible.

Your ability to respond to changing conditions, your decision-making ability, productivity, creativity, and verbal skills all have a bearing on your success in and enjoyment of your work life. To better guarantee success, be sure to take the time needed to understand these traits in yourself.

Step 2   Identify Your Personal Values

Your personal values affect every aspect of your life, including employment, and they develop and change as you move through life. Values can be defined as principles that we hold in high regard, qualities that are important and desirable to us. Some values aren't ordinarily connected to work (love, beauty, color, light, relationships, family, or religion), and others are (autonomy, cooperation, effectiveness, achievement, knowledge, and security). Our values determine, in part, the level of satisfaction we feel in a particular job.

Define Acceptable Working Conditions. One facet of employment is the set of working conditions that must exist for someone to consider taking a job.

Each of us would probably create a unique list of acceptable working conditions, but items that might be included on many people's lists are the amount of money you would need to be paid, how far you are willing to drive or travel, the amount of freedom you want in determining your own schedule, whether you would be working with people or data or things, and the types of tasks you would be willing to do. Your conditions might include statements of working conditions you will *not* accept; for example, you might not be willing to work at night or on weekends or holidays.

If you were offered a job tomorrow, what conditions would have to exist for you to realistically consider accepting the position? Take some time and make a list of these conditions.

Realize Associated Values. Your list of working conditions can be used to create an inventory of your values relating to jobs and careers you are exploring. For example, if one of your conditions stated that you wanted to earn at least $30,000 per year, the associated value would be *financial gain*. If another condition was that you wanted to work with a friendly group of people, the value that went along with that might be belonging or interaction with people.

Relate Your Values to the World of Work. As you read the job descriptions you come across either in this book, in newspapers and magazines, or online, think about the values associated with each position.

For example, the responsibilities of a parole officer include interviewing clients, counseling, establishing a position of authority, and referring clients to appropriate community resources for services. Values associated with the job include openness, responsiveness, and networking ability.

At least some of the associated values in the field you're exploring should match those you extracted from your list of working conditions. Take a second look at any values that don't match up. How important are they to you? What will happen if they are not satisfied on the job? Can you incorporate those personal values elsewhere? Your answers need to be brutally honest. As you continue your exploration, be sure to add to your list any additional values that occur to you.

Step 3   Calculate Your Economic Needs

Each of us grew up in an environment that provided for certain basic needs, such as food and shelter, and, to varying degrees, other needs that we now consider basic, such as cable television, e-mail, or an automobile. Needs such as privacy, space, and quiet, which at first glance may not appear to be monetary needs, may add to housing expenses and so should be considered as you examine your economic needs. For example, if you place a high value on a large, open living space for yourself, it would be difficult to satisfy that need without an associated high housing cost, especially in a densely populated city environment.

As you prepare to move into the world of work and become responsible for meeting your own basic needs, it is important to consider the salary you will need to be able to afford a satisfying standard of living. The three-step process outlined here will help you plan a budget, which in turn will allow you to evaluate the various career choices and geographic locations you are considering. The steps include (1) develop a realistic budget, (2) examine starting salaries, and (3) use a cost-of-living index.

Develop a Realistic Budget. Each of us has certain expectations for the kind of lifestyle we want to maintain. To begin the process of defining your economic needs, it will be helpful to determine what you expect to spend on routine monthly expenses. These expenses include housing, food, transportation, entertainment, utilities, loan repayments, and revolving charge accounts. You may not currently spend anything for certain items, but you probably will have to once you begin supporting yourself. As you develop this budget, be generous in your estimates, but keep in mind any items that could be reduced or eliminated. If you are not sure about the cost of a certain item, talk with family or friends who would be able to give you a realistic estimate.

If this is new or difficult for you, start to keep a log of expenses right now. You may be surprised at how much you actually spend each month for food or stamps or magazines. Household expenses and personal grooming items can often loom very large in a budget, as can auto repairs or home maintenance.

Income taxes must also be taken into consideration when examining salary requirements. State and local taxes vary, so it is difficult to calculate exactly the effect of taxes on the amount of income you need to generate. To roughly estimate the gross income necessary to generate your minimum annual salary requirement, multiply the minimum salary you have calculated by a factor of 1.35. The resulting figure will be an approximation of what your gross income would need to be, given your estimated expenses.

Examine Starting Salaries. Starting salaries for each of the career tracks are provided throughout this book. These salary figures can be used in conjunction with the cost-of-living index (discussed in the next section) to determine whether you would be able to meet your basic economic needs in a given geographic location.

Use a Cost-of-Living Index. If you are thinking about trying to get a job in a geographic region other than the one where you now live, understanding differences in the cost of living will help you come to a more informed decision about making a move. By using a cost-of-living index, you can compare salaries offered and the cost of living in different locations with what you know about the salaries offered and the cost of living in your present location.

Many variables are used to calculate the cost-of-living index. Often included are housing, groceries, utilities, transportation, health care, clothing, and entertainment expenses. Right now you do not need to worry about the details associated with calculating a given index. The main purpose of this exercise is to help you understand that pay ranges for entry-level positions may not vary greatly, but the cost of living in different locations *can* vary tremendously.

For example, if you live in Pittsburgh, Pennsylvania, and are interested in working as a police officer, you would plan to earn $45,576 annually, based on average police patrol officer salaries in that city. But, let's say you're also thinking about moving to Oakland, California; Burlington, Vermont; or Little Rock, Arkansas. You know you can live on $45,576 in Pittsburgh, but you'll want to be able to afford the same lifestyle in the other locations you're considering. How much will you have to earn in those cities to do this? Determining the cost of living for each city will show you.

Many websites can assist you in your research. Enter the search term *cost-of-living index* into any search engine, and several choices will appear. Choose a site, and look for options such as cost-of-living analysis or cost-of-living comparator. Some sites will ask you to register and pay for the information, but most are free. Following the instructions, you'll be able to create a table of information like the one shown here.

At the time this comparison was done, you would have needed to earn $79,643 in Oakland, $47,867 in Burlington, and $36,559 in Little Rock to match the buying power of $45,576 in Pittsburgh.

JOB: POLICE PATROL OFFICER		
City	**Base Amount**	**Equivalent Salary**
Pittsburgh, PA	$45,576	
Oakland, CA		$79,643
Burlington, VT		$47,867
Little Rock, AR		$36,559

If you'd like to determine whether it's financially worthwhile to make any of these moves, you'll need one more piece of information: the salaries of police patrol officers in these other cities. One website that contains brief job descriptions and salary information is Salary.com. The "Salary Wizard" will provide you with salary comparisons by city, along with links to additional resources. Salary.com reports the following average salaries for a police patrol officer in your selected cities:

City	Actual Salary	Equivalent Salary Needed	Change in Buying Power
Oakland	$52,774	$79,643	−$26,869
Burlington	$44,985	$47,867	−$2,882
Little Rock	$42,029	$36,559	+$5,470

If you moved to Oakland and found employment as a police patrol officer, you would not be able to maintain the same lifestyle that you would have in Pittsburgh because your annual salary would be worth $26,869 less in buying power! Likewise, Burlington would present a less drastic but still negative result, leaving you with $2,882 less than you'd need. However, if you moved to Little Rock, you'd have an additional $5,470 with which to enhance your lifestyle, even though your salary would be $10,745 less than it would be in Pittsburgh. Remember, though, that these figures change all time, so be sure to do your own research to find the most current information.

You can work through a similar exercise for any type of job you are considering and for many locations when current salary information is available. It will be worth your time to undertake this analysis if you are seriously considering a relocation. By doing so you will be able to make an informed choice.

Step 4   Explore Your Longer-Term Goals

There is no question that when we first begin working, our goals are to use our skills and education in a job that will reward us with employment, income, and status relative to the preparation we brought with us to this position. If we are not being paid as much as we feel we should for our level of education or if job demands don't provide the intellectual stimulation we had hoped for, we experience unhappiness and as a result often seek other employment.

Most jobs we consider "good" are those that fulfill our basic "lower-level" needs of security, food, clothing, shelter, income, and productive work. But even when our basic needs are met and our jobs are secure and productive, we as individuals are constantly changing. As we change, the demands and expectations we place on our jobs may change. Fortunately, some jobs grow and change with us, and this explains why some people are happy throughout many years in a job.

But more often people are bigger than the jobs they fill. We have more goals and needs than any job could satisfy. These are "higher-level" needs of self-esteem, companionship, affection, and an increasing desire to feel we are employing ourselves in the most effective way possible. Not all of these higher-level needs can be met through employment, but for as long as we are employed, we increasingly demand that our jobs play their part in moving us along the path to fulfillment.

Another obvious but important fact is that we change as we mature. Although our jobs also have the potential for change, they may not change as frequently or as markedly as we do. There are increasingly fewer one-job, one-employer careers; we must think about a work future that may involve voluntary or forced moves from employer to employer. Because of that very real possibility, we need to take advantage of the opportunities in each position we hold. Acquiring the skills and competencies associated with each position will keep us viable and attractive as employees. This is particularly true in a job market that not only is technology/computer dependent, but also is populated with more and more small, self-transforming organizations rather than the large, seemingly stable organizations of the past.

For example, if you live in Pittsburgh, Pennsylvania, and are interested in working as a city police officer, you would plan to earn $45,576 annually, based on average police patrol officer salaries in that city. Speaking with people who work in the field you're most interested in—or in a variety of fields if you're still unsure—can be extremely helpful. A patrol officer, counselor, case manager, detention officer, and program director will all have unique perspectives and different values and priorities.

Step 5   Enumerate Your Skill Base

In terms of the job search, skills can be thought of as capabilities that can be developed in school, at work, or by volunteering and then used in specific job settings. Many studies have documented the kinds of skills that employers seek in entry-level applicants. For example, some of the most desired skills for individuals interested in the teaching profession are the ability to interact effectively with students one on one, to manage a classroom, to adapt to varying situations as necessary, and to get involved in school activities. Business employers have also identified important qualities, including enthusiasm for the employer's product or service, a businesslike mind, the ability to follow written or oral instructions, the ability to demonstrate self-control, the confidence to suggest new ideas, the ability to communicate with all members of a group, an awareness of cultural differences, and loyalty, to name just a few. You will find that many of these skills are also in the repertoire of qualities demanded in your college major.

To be successful in obtaining any given job, you must be able to demonstrate that you possess a certain mix of skills that will allow you to carry out the duties required by that job. This skill mix will vary a great deal from job to job; to determine the skills necessary for the jobs you are seeking, you can read job advertisements or more generic job descriptions, such as those found later in this book. If you want to be effective in the job search, you must directly show employers that you possess the skills needed to be successful in filling the position. These skills will initially be described on your résumé and then discussed again during the interview process.

Skills are either general or specific. To develop a list of skills relevant to employers, you must first identify the general skills you possess, then list specific skills you have to offer, and, finally, examine which of these skills employers are seeking.

Identify Your General Skills. Because you possess or will possess a college degree, employers will assume that you can read and write, perform certain basic computations, think critically, and communicate effectively. Employers will want to see that you have acquired these skills, and they will want to know which additional general skills you possess.

One way to begin identifying skills is to write an experiential diary. An experiential diary lists all the tasks you were responsible for completing for each job you've held and then outlines the skills required to do those tasks. You may list several skills for any given task. This diary allows you to distinguish between the tasks you performed and the underlying skills required to complete those tasks. Here's an example:

Tasks	Skills
Answering telephone	Effective use of language, clear diction, ability to direct inquiries, ability to solve problems
Waiting on tables	Poise under conditions of time and pressure, speed, accuracy, good memory, simultaneous completion of tasks, sales skills

For each job or experience you have participated in, develop a worksheet based on the example shown here. On a résumé, you may want to describe these skills rather than simply listing tasks. Skills are easier for the employer to appreciate, especially when your experience is very different from the employment you are seeking. In addition to helping you identify general skills, this experiential diary will prepare you to speak more effectively in an interview about the qualifications you possess.

Identify Your Specific Skills. It may be easier to identify your specific skills because you can definitely say whether you can speak other languages, program a computer, draft a map or diagram, or edit a document using appropriate symbols and terminology.

Using your experiential diary, identify the points in your history where you learned how to do something very specific, and decide whether you have a beginning, intermediate, or advanced knowledge of how to use that particular skill. Right now, be sure to list *every* specific skill you have, and don't consider whether you like using the skill. Write down a list of specific skills you have acquired and the level of competence you possess—beginning, intermediate, or advanced.

Relate Your Skills to Employers. You probably have thought about a couple of different jobs you might be interested in obtaining, and one way to begin relating the general and specific skills you possess to a potential employer's needs is to read actual advertisements for these types of positions (see Part Two for resources listing actual job openings).

For example, you may be interested in working as a youth counselor in a residential facility. A typical job listing may read, "Responsible for the supervision of juveniles during all aspects of daily living, including education and treatment. Provide daily structure and discipline. Assist teachers in the classroom. Responsible for the safety and security of residents. Implement intervention strategies and prepare reports as necessary." Using this ad in combination with other general sources of information about the career field of youth counselor, you will find pertinent information about the position and other job requirements.

Begin building a comprehensive list of required skills as soon as you start reading job descriptions. You will find common skills that are necessary for the job you desire. In building your list, include both general and specific job skills.

Following is a sample list of skills needed for success as a youth counselor. These were taken from general resources and actual job listings:

JOB: YOUTH COUNSELOR

General Skills	Specific Skills
Work in a sometimes-stressful environment	Maintain behavior log
Supervise activities	Mediate disputes
Discipline inappropriate behavior	Write incident reports
Adjust to changing shift schedules	Design activities
Use a computer	Facilitate groups
Work outdoors and indoors	Develop discharge plans
Maintain order	Teach personal grooming
Model appropriate behaviors	Provide counseling
Ensure safety	Issue instructions and procedures
Supervise housing maintenance	Implement intervention strategies
Provide structure	Assist with academics

On a separate sheet of paper, try to assemble a comprehensive list of the required skills for at least one of the jobs you're considering.

The list of general skills that you create for one career path will be valuable for a number of jobs for which you might apply, and many skills will be transferable to other types of positions.

For example, both youth counselors and parole officers need the skills necessary to develop discharge plans.

Step 6 Recognize Your Preferred Skills

In the previous section you developed a comprehensive list of skills that relate to particular career paths that are of interest to you. You can now relate these to skills that you prefer to use. We all use a wide range of skills (some researchers say individuals have a repertoire of about five hundred skills), but we may not particularly be interested in using all of them in our work. There may be some skills that come to us more naturally or that we use successfully time and time again and that we want to continue to use; these are best described as our preferred skills. For this exercise use the list of skills that you created for the previous section, and decide which of them you are *most interested in using* in future work and how often you would like to use them. You might be interested in using some skills only occasionally, while others you would like to use more regularly. You probably also have skills that you hope you can use constantly.

As you examine job announcements, look for matches between this list of preferred skills and the qualifications described in the advertisements. These skills should be highlighted on your résumé and discussed in job interviews.

Step 7 Assess Skills Needing Further Development

Previously you compiled a list of general and specific skills required for given positions. You already possess some of these skills; those that remain to be developed are your underdeveloped skills.

If you are just beginning the job search, there may be gaps between the qualifications required for some of the jobs you're considering and the skills you possess. The thought of having to admit to and talk about these underdeveloped skills, especially in a job interview, is a frightening one. One way to put a healthy perspective on this subject is to target and relate your exploration of underdeveloped skills to the types of positions you are seeking. Recognizing these shortcomings and planning to overcome them with either on-the-job training or additional formal education can be a positive way to address the concept of underdeveloped skills.

On your worksheet or in your journal, make a list of up to five general or specific skills required for the positions you're interested in that you *don't currently possess*. For each item list an idea you have for specific action you could take to acquire that skill. Do some brainstorming to come up with possible actions. If you have a hard time generating ideas, talk to people currently working in this type of position, professionals in your college career services office, trusted friends, family members, or members of related professional associations.

In the chapter on interviewing, we will discuss in detail how to effectively address questions about underdeveloped skills. Generally speaking, though, employers want genuine answers to these types of questions. They want you to reveal "the real you," and they also want to see how you answer difficult questions. In taking the positive, targeted approach discussed previously, you show the employer that you are willing to continue to learn and that you have a plan for strengthening your job qualifications.

Use Your Self-Assessment

Exploring entry-level career options can be an exciting experience if you have good resources available and will take the time to use them. Can you effectively complete the following tasks?

1. Understand your personality traits and relate them to career choices
2. Define your personal values
3. Determine your economic needs
4. Explore longer-term goals
5. Understand your skill base
6. Recognize your preferred skills
7. Express a willingness to improve on your underdeveloped skills

If so, then you can more meaningfully participate in the job search process by writing a more effective résumé, finding job titles that represent work you are interested in doing, locating job sites that will provide the opportunity for you to use your strengths and skills, networking in an informed way, participating in focused interviews, getting the most out of follow-up contacts, and evaluating job offers to find those that create a good match between you and the employer. The remaining chapters in Part One guide you through these next steps in the job search process. For many job seekers, this process can take anywhere from three months to a year to implement. The time you will need to put into your job search will depend on the type of job you want and the geographic location where you'd like to work. Think of your effort as a job in itself, requiring you to set aside time each week to complete the needed work. Carefully undertaken efforts may reduce the time you need for your job search.

The Résumé and Cover Letter

The task of writing a résumé may seem overwhelming if you are unfamiliar with this type of document, but there are some easily understood techniques that can and should be used. This section was written to help you understand the purpose of the résumé, the different types of formats available, and how to write the sections that contain information traditionally found on a résumé. We will present examples and explanations that address questions frequently posed by people writing their first résumé or updating an old one.

Even within the formats and suggestions given, however, there are infinite variations. True, most follow one of the outlines suggested, but you should feel free to adjust the résumé to suit your needs and make it expressive of your life and experience.

Why Write a Résumé?

The purpose of a résumé is to convince an employer that you should be interviewed. Whether you're mailing, faxing, or e-mailing this document, you'll want to present enough information to show that you can make an immediate and valuable contribution to an organization. A résumé is not an in-depth historical or legal document; later in the job search process you may be asked to document your entire work history on an application form and attest to its validity. The résumé should, instead, highlight relevant information pertaining directly to the organization that will receive the document or to the type of position you are seeking.

We will discuss the chronological and digital résumés in detail here. Functional and targeted résumés, which are used much less often, are briefly discussed. The reasons for using one type of résumé over another and the typical format for each are addressed in the following sections.

The Chronological Résumé

The chronological résumé is the most common of the various résumé formats and therefore the format that employers are most used to receiving. This type of résumé is easy to read and understand because it details the chronological progression of jobs you have held. (See Exhibit 2.1.) It begins with your most recent employment and works back in time. If you have a solid work history or have experience that provided growth and development in your duties and responsibilities, a chronological résumé will highlight these achievements. The typical elements of a chronological résumé include the heading, a career objective, educational background, employment experience, activities, and references.

The Heading
The heading consists of your name, address, telephone number, and other means of contact. This may include a fax number, e-mail address, and your home-page address. If you are using a shared e-mail account or a parent's business fax, be sure to let others who use these systems know that you may receive important professional correspondence via these systems. You wouldn't want to miss a vital e-mail or fax! Likewise, if your résumé directs readers to a personal home page on the Web, be certain it's a professional personal home page designed to be viewed and appreciated by a prospective employer. This may mean making substantial changes in the home page you currently mount on the Web.

The Objective
Without a doubt the objective statement is the most challenging part of the résumé for most writers. Even for individuals who have decided on a career path, it can be difficult to encapsulate all they want to say in one or two brief sentences. For job seekers who are unfocused or unclear about their intentions, trying to write this section can inhibit the entire résumé writing process.

Keep the objective as short as possible and no longer than two short sentences.

Exhibit 2.1
CHRONOLOGICAL RÉSUMÉ

SARAH O'NEILL

Bardwell Hall	14 Flamingo Street
University of Massachusetts–Amherst	Key West, FL 98766
Amherst, MA 01851	305-555-5555
413-555-5555	
soneill@xxx.com	
(until May 2007)	

OBJECTIVE
To obtain a position as Victim Services Specialist

EDUCATION
Bachelor of Science in Criminal Justice
University of Massachusetts–Amherst
May 2007
Minor: Human Relations

HONORS/AWARDS
Chancellor's Scholar, Spring/Fall Semesters, 2006
Who's Who Among Universities and Colleges, 2005–2006
Chapel Hill Rotary Award—Student of the Year, 2004

RELATED COURSES

Investigative Procedures	Report Writing
Police Operations	Juvenile Psychology

EXPERIENCE
Internship: Rosie's Place, Boston, Massachusetts, 2005–2006

A credit-granting, structured academic internship at a long-established shelter for homeless women. Provided counseling to indigent women, and developed contacts among several area social service agencies for referrals. Designed and implemented "Rosie's Closet"—a new program to

continued

provide clean, attractive clothing to promote self-esteem and a renewed interest in personal appearance. Arranged for local stores to donate cosmetics.

Nursing Home Aide: Pleasant View Home for the Aged, Billerica, Massachusetts, 2003–2004

Performed general aide duties, including assisting residents in feeding and personal grooming. Delivered meals, changed bed linen, and did light housekeeping. Assisted ambulatory patients with daily exercise, read to patients, and contributed to general therapeutic atmosphere.

Waitress: Captain John's Seafood Restaurant, Key West, Florida, 2001–2002
Summer employment in a prominent restaurant. Fast-paced, high-turnover restaurant that targeted tourists. Provided quality customer service, resolved disputes, and scheduled day staff.

ACTIVITIES
Center for Gender Resources—student staff volunteer for three years.
Peer Tutor—paid position at college academic resource center. Provided tutoring and assistance in study skills for criminal justice majors.

REFERENCES
Available upon request.

Choose one of the following types of objective statement:

I. General Objective Statement

- An entry-level educational programming coordinator position

2. Position-Focused Objective

- To obtain the position of conference coordinator at State College

3. Industry-Focused Objective

- To begin a career as a sales representative in the cruise line industry

4. *Summary of Qualifications Statement*

A degree in criminal justice, combined with four years of increasing job responsibility in the telecommunications industry, have prepared me to enter the field of computer crime analysis in a proprietary security firm that values dedication and hard work.

Support Your Objective. A résumé that contains any one of these types of objective statements should then go on to demonstrate why you are qualified to get the position. Listing academic degrees can be one way to indicate qualifications. Another demonstration would be in the way previous experiences, both volunteer and paid, are described. Without this kind of documentation in the body of the résumé, the objective looks unsupported. Think of the résumé as telling a connected story about you. All the elements should work together to form a coherent picture that ideally should relate to your statement of objective.

Education

This section of your résumé should indicate the exact name of the degree you will receive or have received, spelled out completely with no abbreviations. The degree is generally listed after the objective, followed by the institution name and location, and then the month and year of graduation. This section could also include your academic minor, grade point average (GPA), and appearance on the Dean's List or President's List.

If you have enough space, you might want to include a section listing courses related to the field in which you are seeking work. The best use of a "related courses" section would be to list some course work that is not traditionally associated with the major. Perhaps you took several computer courses outside your degree that will be helpful and related to the job prospects you are entertaining. Several education section examples are shown here:

- Bachelor of Science in Criminology, University of Arizona, Tucson, AZ; May 2006
- Bachelor of Science in Interdisciplinary Studies, a self-designed program concentrating in criminal justice and

computer science, San Diego State University, San Diego, California; May 2007
- Bachelor of Arts in Psychology, State College, Durham, New Hampshire; January 2007; Minor: Criminal Justice

Related Courses
Spanish
Criminology
Courts and Criminal Procedure

Experience

The experience section of your résumé should be the most substantial part and should take up most of the space on the page. Employers want to see what kind of work history you have. They will look at your range of experiences, longevity in jobs, and specific tasks you are able to complete. This section may also be called "work experience," "related experience," "employment history," or "employment." No matter what you call this section, some important points to remember are the following:

1. **Describe your duties** as they relate to the position you are seeking.
2. **Emphasize major responsibilities** and indicate increases in responsibility. Include all relevant employment experiences: summer, part-time, internships, cooperative education, or self-employment.
3. **Emphasize skills**, especially those that transfer from one situation to another. The fact that you coordinated a student organization, chaired meetings, supervised others, and managed a budget leads one to suspect that you could coordinate other things as well.
4. **Use descriptive job titles** that provide information about what you did. A "Student Intern" should be more specifically stated as, for example, "Magazine Operations Intern." "Volunteer" is also too general; a title such as "Peer Writing Tutor" would be more appropriate.
5. **Create word pictures** by using active verbs to start sentences. Describe *results* you have produced in the work you have done.

A limp description would say something such as the following: "My duties included helping with production, proofreading, and editing. I used a design and page layout program." An action statement would be stated as follows: "Coordinated and assisted in the creative marketing of brochures and seminar promotions, becoming proficient in Quark."

Remember, an accomplishment is simply a result, a final measurable product that people can relate to. A duty is not a result; it is an obligation—every job holder has duties. For an effective résumé, list as many results as you can. To make the most of the limited space you have and to give your description impact, carefully select appropriate and accurate descriptors.

Here are some traits that employers tell us they like to see:

- Teamwork
- Energy and motivation
- Learning and using new skills
- Versatility
- Critical thinking
- Understanding how profits are created
- Organizational acumen
- Communicating directly and clearly, in both writing and speaking
- Risk taking
- Willingness to admit mistakes
- High personal standards

Solutions to Frequently Encountered Problems

Repetitive Employment with the Same Employer

EMPLOYMENT: The Foot Locker, Portland, Oregon. Summer 2001, 2002, 2003. Initially employed in high school as salesclerk. Because of successful performance, asked to return next two summers at higher pay with added responsibility. Ranked as the #2 salesperson the first summer and #1 the next two summers. Assisted in arranging eye-catching retail displays; served as manager of other summer workers during owner's absence.

A Large Number of Jobs

EMPLOYMENT: Recent Hospitality Industry Experience: Affiliated with four upscale hotel/restaurant complexes (September 2001–February 2004), where I worked part- and full-time as a waiter, bartender, disc jockey, and bookkeeper to produce income for college.

Several Positions with the Same Employer

EMPLOYMENT: Coca-Cola Bottling Co., Burlington, Vermont, 2001–2004. In four years, I received three promotions, each with increased pay and responsibility.

Summer Sales Coordinator: Promoted to hire, train, and direct efforts of add-on staff of fifteen college-age route salespeople hired to meet summer peak demand for product.

Sales Administrator: Promoted to run home office sales desk, managing accounts and associated delivery schedules for professional sales force of ten people. Intensive phone work, daily interaction with all personnel, and strong knowledge of product line required.

Route Salesperson: Summer employment to travel and tourism industry sites that use Coke products. Met specific schedule demands, used good communication skills with wide variety of customers, and demonstrated strong selling skills. Named salesperson of the month for July and August of that year.

Questions Résumé Writers Often Ask

How Far Back Should I Go in Terms of Listing Past Jobs?

Usually, listing three or four jobs should suffice. If you did something back in high school that has a bearing on your future aspirations for employment, by all means list the job. As you progress through your college career, high school jobs will be replaced on the résumé by college employment.

Should I Differentiate Between Paid and Nonpaid Employment?

Most employers are not initially concerned about how much you were paid. They are eager to know how much responsibility you held in your past employment. There is no need to specify that your work was as a volunteer if you had significant responsibilities.

How Should I Represent My Accomplishments or Work-Related Responsibilities?

Succinctly, but fully. In other words, give the employer enough information to arouse curiosity but not so much detail that you leave nothing to the imagination. Besides, some jobs merit more lengthy explanations than others. Be sure to convey any information that can give an employer a better understanding of the depth of your involvement at work. Did you supervise others? How many? Did your efforts result in a more efficient operation? How much did you increase efficiency? Did you handle a budget? How much? Were you promoted in a short time? Did you work two jobs at once or fifteen hours per week after high school? Where appropriate, quantify.

Should the Work Section Always Follow the Education Section on the Résumé?

Always lead with your strengths. If your education closely relates to the employment you now seek, put this section after the objective. If your education does not closely relate but you have a surplus of good work experiences, consider reversing the order of your sections to lead with employment, followed by education.

How Should I Present My Activities, Honors, Awards, Professional Societies, and Affiliations?

This section of the résumé can add valuable information for an employer to consider if used correctly. The rule of thumb for information in this section is to include only those activities that are in some way relevant to the objective stated on your résumé. If you can draw a valid connection between your activities and your objective, include them; if not, leave them out.

Professional affiliations and honors should all be listed; especially important are those related to your job objective. Social clubs and activities need not be a part of your résumé unless you hold a significant office or you are looking for a position related to your membership. Be aware that most prospective employers' principal concerns are related to your employability, not your social life. If you have any, publications can be included as an addendum to your résumé.

How Should I Handle References?

The use of references is considered a part of the interview process, and they should never be listed on a résumé. You would always provide references to a potential employer if requested to, so it is not even necessary to include this section on the résumé if space does not permit. If space is available, it is acceptable to include the following statement:

- References furnished upon request.

The Functional Résumé

The functional résumé departs from a chronological résumé in that it organizes information by specific accomplishments in various settings: previous jobs, volunteer work, associations, and so forth. This type of résumé permits you to stress the substance of your experiences rather than the position titles you have held. You should consider using a functional résumé if you have held a series of similar jobs that relied on the same skills or abilities. There are many good books in which you can find examples of functional résumés, including *How to Write a Winning Resume* or *Resumes Made Easy.*

The Targeted Résumé

The targeted résumé focuses on specific work-related capabilities you can bring to a given position within an organization. Past achievements are listed to highlight your capabilities and the work history section is abbreviated.

Digital Résumés

Today's employers have to manage an enormous number of résumés. One of the most frequent complaints the writers of this series hear from students is the failure of employers to even acknowledge the receipt of a résumé and cover letter. Frequently, the reason for this poor response or nonresponse is the volume of applications received for every job. In an attempt to better manage the considerable labor investment involved in processing large numbers of résumés, many employers are requiring digital submission of résumés. There are two types of digital résumés: those that can be e-mailed or posted to a website, called *electronic résumés,* and those that can be "read" by a computer, commonly called *scannable résumés.* Though the format may be a bit different from the traditional "paper" résumé, the goal of both types of digital résumés is the same—to get you an interview! These résumés must be designed to be "technologically friendly." What that basically means to you is that they should be free of graphics and fancy formatting. (See Exhibit 2.2.)

Electronic Résumés
Sometimes referred to as plain-text résumés, electronic résumés are designed to be e-mailed to an employer or posted to one of many commercial Internet databases such as CareerMosaic.com, America's Job Bank (ajb.dni.us), or Monster.com.

Exhibit 2.2
DIGITAL RÉSUMÉ

MICHAEL RESNICK   ←——————————————— Put your name at the
234 Palmer Street   top on its own line.
Olathe, KS 66061
913-555-8888   ←——————————————— Put your phone number
mresnick@xxx.com.   on its own line.

                                                              Use a standard-width
                                                              typeface

KEYWORD SUMMARY   Keywords make your
B.S. Criminal Justice, 2006 ←———————————— résumé easier to find in
Law enforcement, Corrections,   a database.
Detention Officer, Jail, Security,
Weapons training, Police officer

EDUCATION ←————————————————————— Capitals letters to
Bachelor of Science, Criminal Justice, 2006   emphasize heading
University of Kansas, Lawrence, Kansas
Minor: Human Behavior
G.P.A.: 3.0

RELATED COURSES   No line should exceed
Criminal Investigation and Evidence ←———————— 65 characters.
Courts and Criminal Procedure
Criminology
Corrections

SKILLS TRAINING
Certified EMT, Lifesaving, First Aid, ←———————— End each line by
CPR, Self-Defense, Triathlete   hitting the ENTER key.

continued

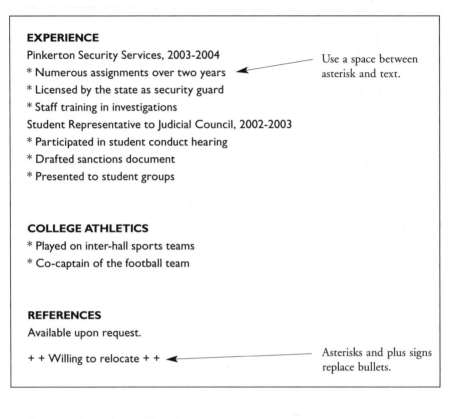

EXPERIENCE

Pinkerton Security Services, 2003-2004
* Numerous assignments over two years ◄———— Use a space between asterisk and text.
* Licensed by the state as security guard
* Staff training in investigations
Student Representative to Judicial Council, 2002-2003
* Participated in student conduct hearing
* Drafted sanctions document
* Presented to student groups

COLLEGE ATHLETICS
* Played on inter-hall sports teams
* Co-captain of the football team

REFERENCES
Available upon request.

+ + Willing to relocate + + ◄———— Asterisks and plus signs replace bullets.

Some technical considerations:

- Electronic résumés must be written in American Standard Code for Information Interchange (ASCII), which is simply a plain-text format. These characters are universally recognized so that every computer can accurately read and understand them. To create an ASCII file of your current résumé, open your document, then save it as a text or ASCII file. This will eliminate all formatting. Edit as needed using your computer's text editor application.
- Use a standard-width typeface. Courier is a good choice because it is the font associated with ASCII in most systems.
- Use a font size of 11 to 14 points. A 12-point font is considered standard.
- Your margin should be left-justified.
- Do not exceed sixty-five characters per line because the word-wrap function doesn't operate in ASCII.
- Do not use boldface, italics, underlining, bullets, or various font sizes. Instead, use asterisks, plus signs, or all capital letters when you want to emphasize something.

- Avoid graphics and shading.
- Use as many "keywords" as you possibly can. These are words or phrases usually relating to skills or experience that either are specifically used in the job announcement or are popular buzzwords in the industry.
- Minimize abbreviations.
- Your name should be the first line of text.
- Conduct a "test run" by e-mailing your résumé to yourself and a friend before you send it to the employer. See how it transmits, and make any changes you need to. Continue to test it until it's exactly how you want it to look.
- Unless an employer specifically requests that you send the résumé in the form of an attachment, don't. Employers can encounter problems opening a document as an attachment, and there are always viruses to consider.
- Don't forget your cover letter. Send it along with your résumé as a single message.

Scannable Résumés

Some companies are relying on technology to narrow the candidate pool for available job openings. Electronic Applicant Tracking uses imaging to scan, sort, and store résumé elements in a database. Then, through OCR (Optical Character Recognition) software, the computer scans the résumés for keywords and phrases. To have the best chance at getting an interview, you want to increase the number of "hits"—matches of your skills, abilities, experience, and education to those the computer is scanning for—your résumé will get. You can see how critical using the right keywords is for this type of résumé.

Technical considerations include:

- Again, do not use boldface (newer systems may be able to read this, but many older ones won't), italics, underlining, bullets, shading, graphics, or multiple font sizes. Instead, for emphasis, use asterisks, plus signs, or all capital letters. Minimize abbreviations.
- Use a popular typeface such as Courier, Helvetica, Ariel, or Palatino. Avoid decorative fonts.
- Font size should be between 11 and 14 points.
- Do not compress the spacing between letters.
- Use horizontal and vertical lines sparingly; the computer may misread them as the letters L or I.
- Left-justify the text.

- Do not use parentheses or brackets around telephone numbers, and be sure your phone number is on its own line of text.
- Your name should be the first line of text and on its own line. If your résumé is longer than one page, be sure to put your name on the top of all pages.
- Use a traditional résumé structure. The chronological format may work best.
- Use nouns that are skill-focused, such as *management, writer,* and *programming.* This is different from traditional paper résumés, which use action-oriented verbs.
- Laser printers produce the finest copies. Avoid dot-matrix printers.
- Use standard, light-colored paper with text on one side only. Since the higher the contrast, the better, your best choice is black ink on white paper.
- Always send original copies. If you must fax, set the fax on fine mode, not standard.
- Do not staple or fold your résumé. This can confuse the computer.
- Before you send your scannable résumé, be certain the employer uses this technology. If you can't determine this, you may want to send two versions (scannable and traditional) to be sure your résumé gets considered.

Résumé Production and Other Tips

An ink-jet printer is the preferred option for printing your résumé. Begin by printing just a few copies. You may find a small error or you may simply want to make some changes, and it is less frustrating and less expensive if you print in small batches.

Résumé paper color should be carefully chosen. You should consider the types of employers who will receive your résumé and the types of positions for which you are applying. Use white or ivory paper for traditional or conservative employers or for higher-level positions.

Black ink on sharp, white paper can be harsh on the reader's eyes. Think about an ivory or cream paper that will provide less contrast and be easier to read. Pink, green, and blue tints should generally be avoided.

Many résumé writers buy packages of matching envelopes and cover sheet stationery that, although not absolutely necessary, help convey a professional impression.

If you'll be producing many cover letters at home, be sure you have high-quality printing equipment. Learn standard envelope formats for business, and retain a copy of every cover letter you send out. You can use the copies to take notes of any telephone conversations that may occur.

If attending a job fair, either carry a briefcase or place your résumé in a nicely covered legal-size pad holder.

The Cover Letter

The cover letter provides you with the opportunity to tailor your résumé by telling the prospective employer how you can be a benefit to the organization. It allows you to highlight aspects of your background that are not already discussed in your résumé and that might be especially relevant to the organization you are contacting or to the position you are seeking. Every résumé should have a cover letter enclosed when you send it out. Unlike the résumé, which may be mass-produced, a cover letter is most effective when it is individually prepared and focused on the particular requirements of the organization in question.

A good cover letter should supplement the résumé and motivate the reader to review the résumé. The format shown in Exhibit 2.3 (see page 34) is only a suggestion to help you decide what information to include in a cover letter.

Begin the cover letter with your street address six lines down from the top. Leave three to five lines between the date and the name of the person to whom you are addressing the cover letter. Make sure you leave one blank line between the salutation and the body of the letter and between paragraphs. After typing "Sincerely," leave four blank lines and type your name. This should leave plenty of room for your signature. A sample cover letter is shown in Exhibit 2.4 on page 35.

The following guidelines will help you write good cover letters:

1. Be sure to type your letter neatly; ensure there are no misspellings.
2. Avoid unusual typefaces, such as script.
3. Address the letter to an individual, using the person's name and title. To obtain this information, call the company. If answering a blind newspaper advertisement, address the letter "To Whom It May Concern" or omit the salutation.
4. Be sure your cover letter directly indicates the position you are applying for and tells why you are qualified to fill it.
5. Send the original letter, not a photocopy, with your résumé. Keep a copy for your records.
6. Make your cover letter no more than one page.
7. Include a phone number where you can be reached.
8. Avoid trite language and have someone read the letter over to react to its tone, content, and mechanics.
9. For your own information, record the date you send out each letter and résumé.

Exhibit 2.3
COVER LETTER FORMAT

Your Street Address
Your Town, State, Zip
Phone Number
Fax Number
E-mail

Date

Name
Title
Organization
Address

Dear _____:

First Paragraph. In this paragraph state the reason for the letter, name the specific position or type of work you are applying for, and indicate from which resource (career services office, website, newspaper, contact, employment service) you learned of this opening. The first paragraph can also be used to inquire about future openings.

Second Paragraph. Indicate why you are interested in this position, the company, or its products or services and what you can do for the employer. If you are a recent graduate, explain how your academic background makes you a qualified candidate. Try not to repeat the same information found in the résumé.

Third Paragraph. Refer the reader to the enclosed résumé for more detailed information.

Fourth Paragraph. In this paragraph say what you will do to follow up on your letter. For example, state that you will call by a certain date to set up an interview or to find out if the company will be recruiting in your area. Finish by indicating your willingness to answer any questions the recipient may have. Be sure you have provided your phone number.

Sincerely,

Type your name

Enclosure

Exhibit 2.4
SAMPLE COVER LETTER

5 Rogers Lane
Atlanta, GA 30303
404-555-7676
Fax: 404-555-2222

March 20, 2007   roconnor@xxx.net

Ms. Roberta Green
Director of Human Resources
On Target Supplies
48 State Street
Atlanta, GA 30303

Dear Ms. Green:

In May of 2007, I will graduate from Middlesex Community College with an associate's degree in criminal justice. I read of your sales opening on the Corrections Connection website, and I am very interested in the possibilities that it offers.

The job posting indicates that you are looking for knowledgeable individuals with exceptional communication skills, qualities that I believe I possess. I've worked the past two summers at one of downtown's busiest electronics stores, and that experience has sharpened my communication skills. Providing choices, listening, satisfying customer requests, and resolving problems have demonstrated to me that I have skills in this area. In addition to my criminal justices courses, I also took a basic marketing course and another in public speaking. I think the combination of these experiences and my education should prove valuable in the job you're hoping to fill.

As you can see by the enclosed résumé, I was an admissions representative for two years at college, having been selected for the position by a committee through an interview process. The opportunity to present my school to different groups and prospective students and their families allowed me to practice and refine my presentation skills.

continued

I would like to meet with you to discuss how my strengths and interests would be consistent with your needs. I will contact your office next week to discuss the possibility of an interview. In the meantime, if you have any questions or require additional information, please contact me at 404-555-7676, or by e-mail at roconnor@xxx.net.

Sincerely,

Ryan O'Connor

Enclosure

Researching Careers
and Networking

What do they call the job you want? One reason for confusion is perhaps a mistaken assumption that a college education provides job training. In most cases it does not. Of course, applied fields such as engineering, management, or education provide specific skills for the workplace as well as an education. Regardless, your overall college education exposes you to numerous fields of study and teaches you quantitative reasoning, critical thinking, writing, and speaking, all of which can be successfully applied to a number of different job fields. But it still remains up to you to choose a job field and to learn how to articulate the benefits of your education in a way the employer will appreciate.

Collect Job Titles

The world of employment is a complex place, so you need to become a bit of an explorer and adventurer and be willing to try a variety of techniques to develop a list of possible occupations that might use your talents and

"What can I do with my degree?" is the question frequently asked of career counselors. Criminal justice majors often struggle with the variety of choices they have in a field that continues to grow. Unlike students who may be pursuing well-focused career goals, such as accounting or nursing, the criminal justice major faces many possible career paths. Choices range from a behind-the-scenes legal researcher to the very much front-line role of a victim advocate. An accounting major becomes an accountant. An engineering major becomes an engineer. But how will you use your criminal justice degree?

education. You might find computerized interest inventories, reference books and other sources, and classified ads helpful in this respect. Once you have a list of possibilities that you are interested in and qualified for, you can move on to find out what kinds of organizations have these job titles.

Computerized Interest Inventories

One way to begin collecting job titles is to identify a number of jobs that call for your degree and the particular skills and interests you identified as part of the self-assessment process. There are excellent interactive career-guidance programs on the market to help you produce such selected lists of possible job titles. Most of these are available at colleges and at some larger town and city libraries. Two of the industry leaders are *CHOICES* and *DISCOVER*. Both allow you to enter interests, values, educational back-ground, and other information to produce lists of possible occupations and industries. Each of the resources listed here will produce different job title lists. Some job titles will appear again and again, while others will be unique to a particular source. Investigate all of them!

Reference Sources

Books on the market that may be available through your local library or career counseling office also suggest various occupations related to specific majors. The following are only a few of the many good books on the market: *The College Board Guide to 150 Popular College Majors* and *College Majors and Careers: A Resource Guide for Effective Life Planning* both by Paul Phifer, and *Kaplan's What to Study: 101 Fields in a Flash*. All of these books list possible job titles within the academic major.

Many different organizations have a police force, and it's likely not every one will be equally desirable to you. Some environments may be more attractive to you than others, and some might not appeal to you at all. If you're thinking of using your criminal justice major to pursue a career in a law enforcement, you could work in a small rural village, a midsize town, or a large metropolitan area. And there are plenty more options. There are police jobs within campus police forces, airports, port authorities, railroads, and a host of other jurisdictions. Each of these settings offers a different environment with varying degrees of risk and types of crimes, pace of work, and professionalism of colleagues and supervisors. Although the job title may be the same, not all police jobs may offer you the right fit.

If you majored in criminal justice and enjoyed the investigation classes and lab work and developed good research and reporting skills, you might think that working as a detective is an attainable goal. You may even be considering graduate school and pursuing a law degree. But criminal justice majors with these skills may also become FBI agents, forensic specialists, police chiefs, private investigators, and criminal justice consultants. Each of these job titles can also be found in a variety of different settings.

Each job title deserves your consideration. Like removing the layers of an onion, the search for job titles can go on and on! As you spend time doing this activity, you are actually learning more about the value of your degree. What's important in your search at this point is not to become critical or selective but rather to develop as long a list of possibilities as you can. Every source used will help you add new and potentially exciting jobs to your growing list.

Classified Ads

It has been well publicized that the classified ad section of the newspaper represents only a small fraction of the current job market. Nevertheless, the weekly classified ads can be a great help to you in your search. Although they may not be the best place to look for a job, they can teach you a lot about the job market. Classified ads provide a good education in job descriptions, duties, responsibilities, and qualifications. In addition, they provide insight into which industries are actively recruiting and some indication of the area's employment market. This is particularly helpful when seeking a position in a specific geographic area and/or a specific field. For your purposes, classified ads are a good source for job titles to add to your list.

Read the Sunday classified ads in a major market newspaper for several weeks in a row. Cut and paste all the ads that interest you and seem to call for something close to your education, skills, experience, and interests. Remember that classified ads are written for what an organization *hopes* to find; you don't have to meet absolutely every criterion. However, if certain requirements are stated as absolute minimums and you cannot meet them, it's best not to waste your time and that of the employer.

The weekly classified want ads exercise is important because these jobs are out in the marketplace. They truly exist, and people with your qualifications are being sought to apply. What's more, many of these advertisements describe the duties and responsibilities of the job advertised and give you a beginning sense of the challenges and opportunities such a position presents. Some will indicate salary, and that will be helpful as well. This information will better define the jobs for you and provide some good material for possible interviews in that field.

Explore Job Descriptions

Once you've arrived at a solid list of possible job titles that interest you and for which you believe you are somewhat qualified, it's a good idea to do some research on each of these jobs. The preeminent source for such job information is the *Dictionary of Occupational Titles*, or *DOT* (wave.net/upg/immigration/dot_index.html). This directory lists every conceivable job and provides excellent up-to-date information on duties and responsibilities, interactions with associates, and day-to-day assignments and tasks. These descriptions provide a thorough job analysis, but they do not consider the possible employers or the environments in which a job may be performed. So, although a position as public relations officer may be well defined in terms of duties and responsibilities, it does not explain the differences in doing public relations work in a college or a hospital or a factory or a bank. You will need to look somewhere else for work settings.

Learn More About Possible Work Settings

After reading some job descriptions, you may choose to edit and revise your list of job titles once again, discarding those you feel are not suitable and keeping those that continue to hold your interest. Or you may wish to keep your list intact and see where these jobs may be located. For example, if you are interested in public relations and you appear to have those skills and the requisite education, you'll want to know which organizations do public relations. How can you find that out? How much income does someone in public relations make a year and what is the employment potential for the field of public relations?

To answer these and many other questions about your list of job titles, we recommend you try any of the following resources: *Careers Encyclopedia*, the professional societies and resources found throughout this book, *College to Career: The Guide to Job Opportunities*, and the *Occupational Outlook Handbook* (http://stats.bls.gov/ocohome.htm). Each of these resources, in a different way, will help to put the job titles you have selected into an employer context. Perhaps the most extensive discussion is found in the *Occupational Outlook Handbook*, which gives a thorough presentation of the nature of the work, the working conditions, employment statistics, training, other qualifications, and advancement possibilities as well as job outlook and earnings. Related occupations are also detailed, and a select bibliography is provided to help you find additional information.

Continuing with our public relations example, your search through these reference materials would teach you that the public relations jobs you find attractive are available in larger hospitals, financial institutions, most corporations (both consumer goods and industrial goods), media organizations, and colleges and universities.

Networking

Networking is the process of deliberately establishing relationships to get career-related information or to alert potential employers that you are available for work. Networking is critically important to today's job seeker for two reasons: It will help you get the information you need, and it can help you find out about *all* of the available jobs.

Get the Information You Need

Networkers will review your résumé and give you feedback on its effectiveness. They will talk about the job you are looking for and give you a candid appraisal of how they see your strengths and weaknesses. If they have a good sense of the industry or the employment sector for that job, you'll get their feelings on future trends in the industry as well. Some networkers will be very forthcoming about salaries, job-hunting techniques, and suggestions for your job search strategy. Many have been known to place calls right from the interview desk to friends and associates who might be interested in you. Each networker will make his or her own contribution, and each will be valuable.

Because organizations must evolve to adapt to current global market needs, the information provided by decision makers within various organizations will be critical to your success as a new job market entrant. For example, you might learn about the concept of virtual organizations from a networker. Virtual organizations coordinate economic activity to deliver value to customers by using resources outside the traditional boundaries of the organization. This concept is being discussed and implemented by chief executive officers of many organizations, including Ford Motor, Dell, and IBM. Networking can help you find out about this and other trends currently affecting the industries under your consideration.

Find Out About All of the Available Jobs

Not every job that is available at this very moment is advertised for potential applicants to see. This is called the *hidden job market*. Only 15 to 20 percent of all jobs are formally advertised, which means that 80 to 85 percent of available jobs do not appear in published channels. Networking will help you become more knowledgeable about all the employment opportunities available during your job search period.

Although someone you might talk to today doesn't know of any openings within his or her organization, tomorrow or next week or next month an opening may occur. If you've taken the time to show an interest in and knowledge of his or her organization, if you've shown the company representative how you can help achieve organizational goals and that you can fit into the organization, you'll be one of the first candidates considered for the position.

Networking: A Proactive Approach

Networking is a proactive rather than a reactive approach. You, as a job seeker, are expected to initiate a certain level of activity on your own behalf; you cannot afford to simply respond to jobs listed in the newspaper. Being proactive means building a network of contacts that includes informed and interested decision makers who will provide you with up-to-date knowledge of the current job market and increase your chances of finding out about employment opportunities appropriate for your interests, experience, and level of education. An old axiom of networking says, "You are only two phone calls away from the information you need." In other words, by talking to enough people, you will quickly come across someone who can offer you help.

Preparing to Network

In deliberately establishing relationships, maximize your efforts by organizing your approach. Five specific areas in which you can organize your efforts include reviewing your self-assessment, reviewing your research on job sites and organizations, deciding who you want to talk to, keeping track of all your efforts, and creating your self-promotion tools.

Review Your Self-Assessment

Your self-assessment is as important a tool in preparing to network as it has been in other aspects of your job search. You have carefully evaluated your personal traits, personal values, economic needs, longer-term goals, skill base, preferred skills, and underdeveloped skills. During the networking process you will be called upon to communicate what you know about yourself and relate it to the information or job you seek. Be sure to review the exercises that you completed in the self-assessment section of this book in preparation for networking. We've explained that you need to assess which skills you have acquired from your major that are of general value to an employer; be ready to express those in ways he or she can appreciate as useful in the organizations.

Review Research on Job Sites and Organizations

In addition, individuals assisting you will expect that you'll have at least some background information on the occupation or industry of interest to you. Refer to the appropriate sections of this book and other relevant publications to acquire the background information necessary for effective networking. They'll explain how to identify not only the job titles that might be of interest to you but also which kinds of organizations employ people to do that job. You will develop some sense of working conditions and expectations about duties and responsibilities—all of which will be of help in your networking interviews.

Decide Who You Want to Talk To

Networking cannot begin until you decide who you want to talk to and, in general, what type of information you hope to gain from your contacts. Once you know this, it's time to begin developing a list of contacts. Five useful sources for locating contacts are described here.

College Alumni Network. Most colleges and universities have created a formal network of alumni and friends of the institution who are particularly interested in helping currently enrolled students and graduates of their alma mater gain employment-related information.

It is usually a simple process to make use of an alumni network. Visit your college's website and locate the alumni office and/or your career center. Either or both sites will have information about your school's alumni network. You'll be provided with information on shadowing experiences, geographic information, or those alumni offering job referrals. If you don't find what you're looking for, don't hesitate to phone or e-mail your career center and ask what they can do to help you connect with an alum.

Alumni networkers may provide some combination of the following services: day-long shadowing experiences, telephone interviews, in-person interviews, information on relocating to given geographic areas, internship information, suggestions on graduate school study, and job vacancy notices.

Present and Former Supervisors. If you believe you are on good terms with present or former job supervisors, they may be an excellent resource for providing information or directing you to appropriate resources that would have information related to your current interests and needs. Additionally, these supervisors probably belong to professional organizations that they might be willing to utilize to get information for you.

Employers in Your Area. Although you may be interested in working in a geographic location different from the one where you currently reside, don't overlook the value of the knowledge and contacts those around you are able to provide. Use the local telephone directory and newspaper to identify the types of organizations you are thinking of working for or professionals who have the kinds of jobs you are interested in. Recently, a call made to a local hospital's financial administrator for information on working in health-care financial administration yielded more pertinent information on training seminars, regional professional organizations, and potential employment sites than a national organization was willing to provide.

Employers in Geographic Areas Where You Hope to Work. If you are thinking about relocating, identifying prospective employers or informational contacts in the new location will be critical to your success. Here are some tips for online searching. First, use a "metasearch" engine to get the most out of your search. Metasearch engines combine several engines into one powerful tool. We frequently use dogpile.com and metasearch.com for this purpose. Try using the city and state as your keywords in a search. *New Haven, Connecticut* will bring you to the city's website with links to the chamber of commerce, member businesses, and other valuable resources. By using looksmart.com you can locate newspapers in any area, and they, too, can provide valuable insight before you relocate. Of course, both dogpile and metasearch can lead you to yellow and white page directories in areas you are considering.

Professional Associations and Organizations. Professional associations and organizations can provide valuable information in several areas: career paths that you might not have considered, qualifications relating to those career choices, publications that list current job openings, and workshops or seminars that will enhance your professional knowledge and skills. They can also be excellent sources for background information on given industries: their health, current problems, and future challenges.

There are several excellent resources available to help you locate professional associations and organizations that would have information to meet your needs. Two especially useful publications are the *Encyclopedia of Associations* and *National Trade and Professional Associations of the United States.*

Keep Track of All Your Efforts

It can be difficult, almost impossible, to remember all the details related to each contact you make during the networking process, so you will want to develop a record-keeping system that works for you. Formalize this process by using your computer to keep a record of the people and organizations you want to contact. You can simply record the contact's name, address, and telephone number, and what information you hope to gain.

You could record this as a simple Word document and you could still use the "Find" function if you were trying to locate some data and could only recall the firm's name or the contact's name. If you're comfortable with database management and you have some database software on your computer, then you can put information at your fingertips even if you have only the zip code! The point here is not technological sophistication but good record keeping.

Once you have created this initial list, it will be helpful to keep more detailed information as you begin to actually make the contacts. Those details should include complete contact information, the date and content of each contact, names and information for additional networkers, and required follow-up. Don't forget to send a letter thanking your contact for his or her time! Your contact will appreciate your recall of details of your meetings and conversations, and the information will help you to focus your networking efforts.

Create Your Self-Promotion Tools

There are two types of promotional tools that are used in the networking process. The first is a résumé and cover letter, and the second is a one-minute "infomercial," which may be given over the telephone or in person.

Techniques for writing an effective résumé and cover letter are discussed in Chapter 2. Once you have reviewed that material and prepared these important documents, you will have created one of your self-promotion tools.

The one-minute infomercial will demand that you begin tying your interests, abilities, and skills to the people or organizations you want to network with. Think about your goal for making the contact to help you understand what you should say about yourself. You should be able to express yourself easily and convincingly. If, for example, you are contacting an alumnus of your institution to obtain the names of possible employment sites in a distant city, be prepared to discuss why you are interested in moving to that location, the types of jobs you are interested in, and the skills and abilities you possess that will make you a qualified candidate.

To create a meaningful one-minute infomercial, write it out, practice it as if it will be a spoken presentation, rewrite it, and practice it again if necessary until expressing yourself comes easily and is convincing.

Here's a simplified example of an infomercial for use over the telephone:

Hello, Ms. Bennett. My name is Margaret Parsons. I have recently graduated from Lincoln College and hope to enter the law field as a paralegal. I majored in criminal justice and believe that I have many skills that would be valuable in paralegal work. I enjoy research and have strong computer skills. I'm familiar with two relational database software programs and have a significant amount of experience doing research on the Web. I believe that my degree has given me a thorough background in legal issues and terminology.

Ms. Bennett, I'm calling you because I still need more information about using my criminal justice degree to enter the paralegal field. I'm hoping that you'll be willing to sit down with me for half hour or so to discuss how I might best present myself for employment at a law firm. I would certainly be willing to pursue additional education, but I am eager to begin working and hope to acquire some on-the-job training.

Would you be willing to talk with me about beginning my career? I would greatly appreciate your insight and am available at your convenience.

It very well may happen that your employer contact wishes you to communicate by e-mail. The infomercial quoted above could easily be rewritten for an e-mail message. You should "cut and paste" your résumé right into the e-mail text itself.

Other effective self-promotion tools include portfolios for those in the arts, writing professions, or teaching. Portfolios show examples of work, photographs of projects or classroom activities, or certificates and credentials that are job related. There may not be an opportunity to use the portfolio during an interview, and it is not something that should be left with the organization. It is designed to be explained and displayed by the creator. However, during some networking meetings, there may be an opportunity to illustrate a point or strengthen a qualification by exhibiting the portfolio.

Beginning the Networking Process

Set the Tone for Your Communications

It can be useful to establish "tone words" for any communications you embark upon. Before making your first telephone call or writing your first letter, decide what you want the person to think of you. If you are networking to try to obtain a job, your tone words might include descriptors such as *genuine, informed,* and *self-knowledgeable.* When you're trying to acquire information, your tone words may have a slightly different focus, such as *courteous, organized, focused,* and *well-spoken.* Use the tone words you establish for your contacts to guide you through the networking process.

Honestly Express Your Intentions

When contacting individuals, it is important to be honest about your reasons for making the contact. Establish your purpose in your own mind and be able and ready to articulate it concisely. Determine an initial agenda, whether it be informational questioning or self-promotion, present it to your contact, and be ready to respond immediately. If you don't adequately prepare before initiating your overture, you may find yourself at a disadvantage if you're asked to immediately begin your informational interview or self-promotion during the first phone conversation or visit.

Start Networking within Your Circle of Confidence

Once you have organized your approach—by utilizing specific researching methods, creating a system for keeping track of the people you will contact, and developing effective self-promotion tools—you are ready to begin networking. The best way to begin networking is by talking with a group of people you trust and feel comfortable with. This group is usually made up of your family, friends, and career counselors. No matter who is in this inner circle, they will have a special interest in seeing you succeed in your job search. In addition, because they will be easy to talk to, you should try taking some risks in terms of practicing your information-seeking approach. Gain confidence in talking about the strengths you bring to an organization and the underdeveloped skills you feel hinder your candidacy. Be sure to review the section on self-assessment for tips on approaching each of these areas. Ask for critical but constructive feedback from the people in your circle of confidence on the letters you write and the one-minute infomercial you have developed. Evaluate whether you want to make the changes they suggest, then practice the changes on others within this circle.

Stretch the Boundaries of Your Networking Circle of Confidence

Once you have refined the promotional tools you will use to accomplish your networking goals, you will want to make additional contacts. Because you will not know most of these people, it will be a less comfortable activity to undertake. The practice that you gained with your inner circle of trusted friends should have prepared you to now move outside of that comfort zone.

It is said that any information a person needs is only two phone calls away, but the information cannot be gained until you (1) make a reasonable guess about who might have the information you need and (2) pick up the telephone to make the call. Using your network list that includes alumni, instructors, supervisors, employers, and associations, you can begin preparing your list of questions that will allow you to get the information you need.

Prepare the Questions You Want to Ask

Networkers can provide you with the insider's perspective on any given field and you can ask them questions that you might not want to ask in an interview. For example, you can ask them to describe the more repetitious or mundane parts of the job or ask them for a realistic idea of salary expectations. Be sure to prepare your questions ahead of time so that you are organized and efficient.

Be Prepared to Answer Some Questions

To communicate effectively, you must anticipate questions that will be asked of you by the networkers you contact. Revisit the self-assessment process you undertook and the research you've done so that you can effortlessly respond to questions about your short- and long-term goals and the kinds of jobs you are most interested in pursuing.

General Networking Tips

Make Every Contact Count. Setting the tone for each interaction is critical. Approaches that will help you communicate in an effective way include politeness, being appreciative of time provided to you, and being prepared and thorough. Remember, *everyone* within an organization has a circle of influence, so be prepared to interact effectively with each person you encounter in the networking process, including secretarial and support staff. Many information or job seekers have thwarted their own efforts by being rude to some individuals they encountered as they networked because they made the incorrect assumption that certain persons were unimportant.

Sometimes your contacts may be surprised at their ability to help you. After meeting and talking with you, they might think they have not offered much in the way of help. A day or two later, however, they may make a contact that would be useful to you and refer you to that person.

With Each Contact, Widen Your Circle of Networkers. Always leave an informational interview with the names of at least two more people who can help you get the information or job that you are seeking. Don't be shy about asking for additional contacts; networking is all about increasing the number of people you can interact with to achieve your goals.

Make Your Own Decisions. As you talk with different people and get answers to the questions you pose, you may hear conflicting information or get conflicting suggestions. Your job is to listen to these "experts" and decide what information and which suggestions will help you achieve *your* goals. Only implement those suggestions that you believe will work for you.

Shutting Down Your Network

As you achieve the goals that motivated your networking activity—getting the information you need or the job you want—the time will come to inactivate all or parts of your network. As you do, be sure to tell your primary supporters about your change in status. Call or write to each one of them and give them as many details about your new status as you feel is necessary to maintain a positive relationship.

Because a network takes on a life of its own, activity undertaken on your behalf will continue even after you cease your efforts. As you get calls or are contacted in some fashion, be sure to inform these networkers about your change in status, and thank them for assistance they have provided.

Information on the latest employment trends indicates that workers will change jobs or careers several times in their lifetime. Networking, then, will be a critical aspect in the span of your professional life. If you carefully and thoughtfully conduct your networking activities during your job search, you will have a solid foundation of experience when you need to network the next time around.

Where Are These Jobs, Anyway?

Having a list of job titles that you've designed around your own career interests and skills is an excellent beginning. It means you've really thought about who you are and what you are presenting to the employment market. It has caused you to think seriously about the most appealing environments to work in, and you have identified some employer types that represent these environments.

The research and the thinking that you've done thus far will be used again and again. They will be helpful in writing your résumé and cover letters, in talking about yourself on the telephone to prospective employers, and in answering interview questions.

Now is a good time to begin to narrow the field of job titles and employment sites down to some specific employers to initiate the employment contact.

Find Out Which Employers Hire People Like You

This section will provide tips, techniques, and specific resources for developing an actual list of specific employers that can be used to make contacts. It is only an outline that you must be prepared to tailor to your own particular needs and according to what you bring to the job search. Once again, it is important to communicate with others along the way exactly what you're looking for and what your goals are for the research you're doing. Librarians, employers, career counselors, friends, friends of friends, business contacts, and bookstore staff will all have helpful information on geographically specific and new resources to aid you in locating employers who'll hire you.

Identify Information Resources

Your interview wardrobe and your new résumé might have put a dent in your wallet, but the resources you'll need to pursue your job search are available for free. The categories of information detailed here are not hard to find and are yours for the browsing.

Numerous resources described in this section will help you identify actual employers. Use all of them or any others that you identify as available in your geographic area. As you become experienced in this process, you'll quickly figure out which information sources are helpful and which are not. If you live in a rural area, a well-planned day trip to a major city that includes a college career office, a large college or city library, state and federal employment centers, a chamber of commerce office, and a well-stocked bookstore can produce valuable results.

There are many excellent resources available to help you identify actual job sites. They are categorized into employer directories (usually indexed by product lines and geographic location), geographically based directories (designed to highlight particular cities, regions, or states), career-specific directories (e.g., *Sports MarketPlace*, which lists tens of thousands of firms involved with sports), periodicals and newspapers, targeted job posting publications, and videos. This is by no means meant to be a complete treatment of resources but rather a starting point for identifying useful resources.

Working from the more general references to highly specific resources, we provide a basic list to help you begin your search. Many of these you'll find easily available. In some cases reference librarians and others will suggest even better materials for your particular situation. Start to create your own customized bibliography of job search references.

Geographically Based Directories. The Job Bank series published by Bob Adams, Inc. (aip.com) contains detailed entries on each area's major employers, including business activity, address, phone number, and hiring contact name. Many listings specify educational backgrounds being sought in potential employees. Each volume contains a solid discussion of each city's or state's major employment sectors. Organizations are also indexed by industry. Job Bank volumes are available for the following places: Atlanta, Boston, Chicago, Dallas–Ft. Worth, Denver, Detroit, Florida, Houston, Los Angeles, Minneapolis, New York, Ohio, Philadelphia, San Francisco, Seattle, St. Louis, Washington, D.C., and other cities throughout the Northwest.

National Job Bank (careercity.com) lists employers in every state, along with contact names and commonly hired job categories. Included are many small companies often overlooked by other directories. Companies are also indexed by industry. This publication provides information on educational backgrounds sought and lists company benefits.

Periodicals and Newspapers. Several sources are available to help you locate which journals or magazines carry job advertisements in your field. Other resources help you identify opportunities in other parts of the country.

- *Where the Jobs Are: A Comprehensive Directory of 1,200 Journals Listing Career Opportunities*
- *Corptech Fast 5,000 Company Locator*
- *National Ad Search* (nationaladsearch.com)
- *The Federal Jobs Digest* (jobsfed.com) and *Federal Career Opportunities*
- *World Chamber of Commerce Directory* (chamberofcommerce.org)

This list is certainly not exhaustive; use it to begin your job search work.

Targeted Job Posting Publications. Although the resources that follow are national in scope, they are either targeted to one medium of contact (telephone), focused on specific types of jobs, or less comprehensive than the sources previously listed.

- Careers.org (careers.org/index.html)
- *The Job Hunter* (jobhunter.com)
- *Current Jobs for Graduates* (graduatejobs.com)

- *Environmental Opportunities* (ecojobs.com)
- *Y National Vacancy List* (ymca.net/employment/ymca_recruiting/jobright.htm)
- *ArtSEARCH*
- *Community Jobs*
- *National Association of Colleges and Employers: Job Choices series*
- *National Association of Colleges and Employers* (jobweb.com)

Videos. You may be one of the many job seekers who likes to get information via a medium other than paper. Many career libraries, public libraries, and career centers in libraries carry an assortment of videos that will help you learn new techniques and get information helpful in the job search.

Locate Information Resources

Throughout these introductory chapters, we have continually referred you to various websites for information on everything from job listings to career information. Using the Web gives you a mobility at your computer that you don't enjoy if you rely solely on books or newspapers or printed journals. Moreover, material on the Web, if the site is maintained, can be the most up-to-date information available.

You'll eventually identify the information resources that work best for you, but make certain you've covered the full range of resources before you begin to rely on a smaller list. Here's a short list of informational sites that many job seekers find helpful:

- Public and college libraries
- College career centers
- Bookstores
- The Internet
- Local and state government personnel offices
- Career/job fairs

Each one of these sites offers a collection of resources that will help you get the information you need.

As you meet and talk with service professionals at all these sites, be sure to let them know what you're doing. Inform them of your job search, what you've already accomplished, and what you're looking for. The more people who know you're job seeking, the greater the possibility that someone will have information or know someone who can help you along your way.

Interviewing and
Job Offer Considerations

Certainly, there can be no one part of the job search process more fraught with anxiety and worry than the interview. Yet seasoned job seekers welcome the interview and will often say, "Just get me an interview and I'm on my way!" They understand that the interview is crucial to the hiring process and equally crucial for them, as job candidates, to have the opportunity of a personal dialogue to add to what the employer may already have learned from the résumé, cover letter, and telephone conversations.

Believe it or not, the interview is to be welcomed, and even enjoyed! It is a perfect opportunity for you, the candidate, to sit down with an employer and express yourself and display who you are and what you want. Of course, it takes thought and planning and a little strategy; after all, it *is* a job interview! But it can be a positive, if not pleasant, experience and one you can look back on and feel confident about your performance and effort.

For many new job seekers, a job, any job, seems a wonderful thing. But seasoned interview veterans know that the job interview is an important step for both sides—the employer and the candidate—to see what each has to offer and whether there is going to be a "fit" of personalities, work styles, and attitudes. And it is this concept of balance in the interview, that both sides have important parts to play, that holds the key to success in mastering this aspect of the job search strategy.

Try to think of the interview as a conversation between two interested and equal partners. You both have important, even vital, information to deliver and to learn. Of course, there's no denying the employer has some leverage, especially in the initial interview for recruitment or any interview scheduled by the candidate and not the recruiter. That should not prevent the interviewee from seeking to play an equal part in what should be a fair exchange of information. Too often the untutored candidate allows the interview to become one-sided. The employer asks all the questions and the candidate simply responds. The ideal would be for two mutually interested parties to sit down and discuss possibilities for each. This is a conversation of significance, and it requires preparation, thought about the tone of the interview, and planning of the nature and details of the information to be exchanged.

Preparing for the Interview

The length of most initial interviews is about thirty minutes. Given the brevity, the information that is exchanged ought to be important. The candidate should be delivering material that the employer cannot discover on the résumé, and in turn, the candidate should be learning things about the employer that he or she could not otherwise find out. After all, if you have only thirty minutes, why waste time on information that is already published? The information exchanged is more than just factual, and both sides will learn much from what they see of each other, as well. How the candidate looks, speaks, and acts are important to the employer. The employer's attention to the interview and awareness of the candidate's résumé, the setting, and the quality of information presented are important to the candidate.

Just as the employer has every right to be disappointed when a prospect is late for the interview, looks unkempt, and seems ill-prepared to answer fairly standard questions, the candidate may be disappointed with an interviewer who isn't ready for the meeting, hasn't learned the basic résumé facts, and is constantly interrupted by telephone calls. In either situation there's good reason to feel let down.

There are many elements to a successful interview, and some of them are not easy to describe or prepare for. Sometimes there is just a chemistry between interviewer and interviewee that brings out the best in both, and a good exchange takes place. But there is much the candidate can do to pave the way for success in terms of his or her résumé, personal appearance, goals, and interview strategy—each of which we will discuss. However, none of this preparation is as important as the time and thought the candidate gives to personal self-assessment.

Self-Assessment
Neither a stunning résumé nor an expensive, well-tailored suit can compensate for candidates who do not know what they want, where they are going, or why they are interviewing with a particular employer. Self-assessment, the

process by which we begin to know and acknowledge our own particular blend of education, experiences, needs, and goals, is not something that can be sorted out the weekend before a major interview. Of all the elements of interview preparation, this one requires the longest lead time and cannot be faked.

Because the time allotted for most interviews is brief, it is all the more important for job candidates to understand and express succinctly why they are there and what they have to offer. This is not a time for undue modesty (or for braggadocio either); it is a time for a compelling, reasoned statement of why you feel that you and this employer might make a good match. It means you have to have thought about your skills, interests, and attributes; related those to your life experiences and your own history of challenges and opportunities; and determined what that indicates about your strengths, preferences, values, and areas needing further development.

If you need some assistance with self-assessment issues, refer to Chapter 1. Included are suggested exercises that can be done as needed, such as making up an experiential diary and extracting obvious strengths and weaknesses from past experiences. These simple assignments will help you look at past activities as collections of tasks with accompanying skills and responsibilities. Don't overlook your high school or college career office. Many offer personal counseling on self-assessment issues and may provide testing instruments such as the *Myers-Briggs Type Indicator (MBTI)*, the *Harrington-O'Shea Career Decision-Making System (CDM)*, the *Strong Interest Inventory (SII)*, or any other of a wide selection of assessment tools that can help you clarify some of these issues prior to the interview stage of your job search.

The Résumé

Résumé preparation has been discussed in detail, and some basic examples were provided. In this section we want to concentrate on how best to use your résumé in the interview. In most cases the employer will have seen the résumé prior to the interview, and, in fact, it may well have been the quality of that résumé that secured the interview opportunity.

An interview is a conversation, however, and not an exercise in reading. So, if the employer hasn't seen your résumé and you have brought it along to the interview, wait until asked or until the end of the interview to offer it. Otherwise, you may find yourself staring at the back of your résumé and simply answering "yes" and "no" to a series of questions drawn from that document.

Sometimes an interviewer is not prepared and does not know or recall the contents of the résumé and may use the résumé to a greater or lesser degree as a "prompt" during the interview. It is for you to judge what that may indicate about the individual performing the interview or the employer. If your interviewer seems surprised by the scheduled meeting, relies on the résumé to an inordinate degree, and seems otherwise unfamiliar with your background, this lack of preparation for the hiring process could well be a symptom of general management disorganization or may simply be the result of poor planning on the part of one individual. It is your responsibility as a potential employee to be aware of these signals and make your decisions accordingly.

If you find the interviewer is reading from your résumé, it is perfectly acceptable for you to get the interview back to a more interpersonal level by saying something like, "Mr. Connelly, you may be interested in some research experience I recently gained in a volunteer position at a county court that isn't detailed on my résumé. May I tell you about it?" This can return the interview to two people talking, rather than one reading and the other responding.

By all means, bring at least one copy of your résumé to the interview. Occasionally, at the close of an interview, an interviewer will express an interest in circulating a résumé to several departments, and you could then offer the copy you brought. Sometimes, an interview appointment provides an opportunity to meet others in the organization who may express an interest in you and your background, and it may be helpful to follow up with a copy of your résumé. Our best advice, however, is to keep it out of sight until needed or requested.

Employer Information

Whether your interview is for graduate school admission, an overseas corporate position, or a position with a local company, it is important to know something about the employer or the organization. Keeping in mind that the interview is relatively brief and that you will hopefully have other interviews with other organizations, it is important to keep your research in proportion. If secondary interviews are called for, you will have additional time to do further research. For the first interview, it is helpful to know the organization's mission, goals, size, scope of operations, and so forth. Your research may uncover recent areas of challenge or particular successes that may help to fuel the interview. Use the "What Do They Call the Job You Want?" section of Chapter 3, your library, and your career or guidance office to help you locate this information in the most efficient way possible. Don't be shy in asking advice of these counseling and guidance professionals on how best to spend your preparation time. With some practice, you'll soon learn how much information is enough and which kinds of information are most useful to you.

Interview Content

We've already discussed how it can help to think of the interview as an important conversation—one that, as with any conversation, you want to find pleasant and interesting and to leave you with a good feeling. But because this conversation is especially important, the information that's exchanged is critical to its success. What do you want them to know about you? What do you need to know about them? What interview technique do you need to particularly pay attention to? How do you want to manage the close of the interview? What steps will follow in the hiring process?

Except for the professional interviewer, most of us find interviewing stressful and anxiety provoking. Developing a strategy before you begin interviewing will help you relieve some stress and anxiety. One particular strategy that has worked for many and may work for you is interviewing by objective. Before you interview, write down three to five goals you would like to achieve for that interview. They may be technique goals: smile a little more, have a firmer handshake, be sure to ask about the next stage in the interview process before leaving. They may be content-oriented goals: Find out about the company's current challenges and opportunities; be sure to speak of your recent research, writing experiences, or foreign travel. Whatever your goals, jot down a few of them as goals for each interview.

Most people find that in trying to achieve these few goals, their interviewing technique becomes more organized and focused. After the interview, the most common question friends and family ask is "How did it go?" With this technique, you have an indication of whether you met *your* goals for the meeting, not just some vague idea of how it went. Chances are, if you accomplished what you wanted to, it improved the quality of the entire interview. As you continue to interview, you will want to revise your goals to continue improving your interview skills.

Now, add to the concept of the significant conversation the idea of a beginning, a middle, and a closing and you will have two thoughts that will give your interview a distinctive character. Be sure to make your introduction warm and cordial. Say your full name (and if it's a difficult-to-pronounce name, help the interviewer to pronounce it) and make certain you know your interviewer's name and how to pronounce it. Most interviews begin with some "soft talk" about the weather, chat about the candidate's trip to the interview site, or national events. This is done as a courtesy to relax both you and the interviewer, to get you talking, and to generally try to defuse the atmosphere of excessive tension. Try to be yourself, engage in the conversation, and don't try to second-guess the interviewer. This is simply what it appears to be—casual conversation.

Once you and the interviewer move on to exchange more serious information in the middle part of the interview, the two most important concerns become your ability to handle challenging questions and your success at asking meaningful ones. Interviewer questions will probably fall into one of three categories: personal assessment and career direction, academic assessment, and knowledge of the employer. Here are a few examples of questions in each category:

Personal Assessment and Career Direction
1. What motivates you to put forth your best effort?
2. What do you consider to be your greatest strengths and weaknesses?
3. What qualifications do you have that make you think you will be successful in this career?

Academic Assessment
1. What led you to choose your major?
2. What subjects did you like best and least? Why?
3. How has your college experience prepared you for this career?

Knowledge of the Employer
1. What do you think it takes to be successful in an organization like ours?
2. In what ways do you think you can make a contribution to our organization?
3. Why did you choose to seek a position with this organization?

The interviewer wants a response to each question but is also gauging your enthusiasm, preparedness, and willingness to communicate. In each response you should provide some information about yourself that can be related to the employer's needs. A common mistake is to give too much information. Answer each question completely, but be careful not to run on too long with extensive details or examples.

Questions About Underdeveloped Skills
Most employers interview people who have met some minimum criteria of education and experience. They interview candidates to see who they are, to

learn what kind of personality they exhibit, and to get some sense of how they might fit into the existing organization. It may be that you are asked about skills the employer hopes to find and that you have not documented. Maybe it's grant-writing experience, knowledge of the European political system, or a knowledge of the film world.

To questions about skills and experiences you don't have, answer honestly and forthrightly and try to offer some additional information about skills you do have. For example, perhaps the employer is disappointed you have no grant-writing experience. An honest answer may be as follows:

No, unfortunately, I was never in a position to acquire those skills. I do understand something of the complexities of the grant-writing process and feel confident that my attention to detail, careful reading skills, and strong writing would make grants a wonderful challenge in a new job. I think I could get up on the learning curve quickly.

The employer hears an honest admission of lack of experience but is reassured by some specific skill details that do relate to grant writing and a confident manner that suggests enthusiasm and interest in a challenge.

For many students, questions about their possible contribution to an employer's organization can prove challenging. Because your education has probably not included specific training for a job, you need to review your academic record and select capabilities you have developed in your major that an employer can appreciate. For example, perhaps you read well and can analyze and condense what you've read into smaller, more focused pieces. That could be valuable. Or maybe you did some serious research and you know you have valuable investigative skills. Your public speaking might be highly developed and you might use visual aids appropriately and effectively. Or maybe your skill at correspondence, memos, and messages is effective. Whatever it is, you must take it out of the academic context and put it into a new, employer-friendly context so your interviewer can best judge how you could help the organization.

Exhibiting knowledge of the organization will, without a doubt, show the interviewer that you are interested enough in the available position to have done some legwork in preparation for the interview. Remember, it is not necessary to know every detail of the organization's history but rather to have a general knowledge about why it is in business and how the industry is faring.

Sometime during the interview, generally after the midway point, you'll be asked if you have any questions for the interviewer. Your questions will tell the employer much about your attitude and your desire to understand the organization's expectations so you can compare them to your own strengths. The following are just a few questions you might want to ask:

1. What is the communication style of the organization? (meetings, memos, and so forth)
2. What would a typical day in this position be like for me?
3. What have been some of the interesting challenges and opportunities your organization has recently faced?

Most interviews draw to a natural closing point, so be careful not to prolong the discussion. At a signal from the interviewer, wind up your presentation, express your appreciation for the opportunity, and be sure to ask what the next stage in the process will be. When can you expect to hear from them? Will they be conducting second-tier interviews? If you are interested and haven't heard, would they mind a phone call? Be sure to collect a business card with the name and phone number of your interviewer. On your way out, you might have an opportunity to pick up organizational literature you haven't seen before.

With the right preparation—a thorough self-assessment, professional clothing, and employer information—you'll be able to set and achieve the goals you have established for the interview process.

Interview Follow-Up

Quite often there is a considerable time lag between interviewing for a position and being hired or, in the case of the networker, between your phone call or letter to a possible contact and the opportunity of a meeting. This can be frustrating. "Why aren't they contacting me?" "I thought I'd get another interview, but no one has telephoned." "Am I out of the running?" You don't know what is happening.

Consider the Differing Perspectives

Of course, there is another perspective—that of the networker or hiring organization. Organizations are complex, with multiple tasks that need to be accomplished each day. Hiring is a discrete activity that does not occur as frequently as other job assignments. The hiring process might have to take second place to other, more immediate organizational needs. Although it may be very important to you, and it is certainly ultimately significant to the employer, other issues such as fiscal management, planning and product development, employer vacation periods, or financial constraints may prevent an organization or individual within that organization from acting on your employment or your request for information as quickly as you or they would prefer.

Use Your Communications Skills

Good communication is essential here to resolve any anxieties, and the responsibility is on you, the job or information seeker. Too many job seekers and networkers offer as an excuse that they don't want to "bother" the organization by writing letters or calling. Let us assure you here and now, once and for all, that if you are troubling an organization by overcommunicating, someone will indicate that situation to you quite clearly. If not, you can only assume you are a worthwhile prospect and the employer appreciates being reminded of your availability and interest. Let's look at follow-up practices in the job interview process and the networking situation separately.

Following Up on the Employment Interview

A brief thank-you note following an interview is an excellent and polite way to begin a series of follow-up communications with a potential employer with whom you have interviewed and want to remain in touch. It should be just that—a thank-you for a good meeting. If you failed to mention some fact or experience during your interview that you think might add to your candidacy, you may use this note to do that. However, this should be essentially a note whose overall tone is appreciative and, if appropriate, indicative of a continuing interest in pursuing any opportunity that may exist with that organization. It is one of the few pieces of business correspondence that may be handwritten, but always use plain, good-quality, standard-size paper.

If, however, at this point you are no longer interested in the employer, the thank-you note is an appropriate time to indicate that. You are under no obligation to identify any reason for not continuing to pursue employment with that organization, but if you are so inclined to indicate your professional reasons (pursuing other employers more akin to your interests, looking for greater income production than this employer can provide, a different geographic location), you certainly may. It should not be written with an eye to negotiation, for it will not be interpreted as such.

As part of your interview closing, you should have taken the initiative to establish lines of communication for continuing information about your candidacy. If you asked permission to telephone, wait a week following your thank-you note, then telephone your contact simply to inquire how things are progressing on your employment status. The feedback you receive here should be taken at face value. If your interviewer simply has no information, he or she will tell you so and indicate whether you should call again and when. Don't be discouraged if this should continue over some period of time.

If during this time something occurs that you think improves or changes your candidacy (some new qualification or experience you may have had), including any offers from other organizations, by all means telephone or write to inform the employer about this. In the case of an offer from a competing but less desirable or equally desirable organization, telephone your contact, explain what has happened, express your real interest in the organization, and inquire whether some determination on your employment might be made before you must respond to this other offer. An organization that is truly interested in you may be moved to make a decision about your candidacy. Equally possible is the scenario in which they are not yet ready to make a decision and so advise you to take the offer that has been presented. Again, you have no ethical alternative but to deal with the information presented in a straightforward manner.

When accepting other employment, be sure to contact any employers still actively considering you and inform them of your new job. Thank them graciously for their consideration. There are many other job seekers out there just like you who will benefit from having their candidacy improved when others bow out of the race. Who knows, you might at some future time have occasion to interact professionally with one of the organizations with which you sought employment. How embarrassing it would be to have someone remember you as the candidate who failed to notify them that you were taking a job elsewhere!

In all of your follow-up communications, keep good notes of whom you spoke with, when you called, and any instructions that were given about return communications. This will prevent any misunderstandings and provide you with good records of what has transpired.

Job Offer Considerations

For many recent college graduates, the thrill of their first job and, for some, the most substantial regular income they have ever earned seems an excess of good fortune coming at once. To question that first income or to be critical in any way of the conditions of employment at the time of the initial offer seems like looking a gift horse in the mouth. It doesn't seem to occur to many new hires even to attempt to negotiate any aspect of their first job. And, as many employers who deal with entry-level jobs for recent college graduates will readily confirm, the reality is that there simply isn't much movement in salary available to these new college recruits. The entry-level hire generally does not have an employment track record on a professional level to provide any leverage for negotiation. Real negotiations on salary, benefits, retirement provisions, and so forth come to those with significant employment records at higher income levels.

Of course, the job offer is more than just money. It can be composed of geographic assignment, duties and responsibilities, training, benefits, health and medical insurance, educational assistance, car allowance or company vehicle, and a host of other items. All of this is generally detailed in the formal letter that presents the final job offer. In most cases this is a follow-up to a personal phone call from the employer representative who has been principally responsible for your hiring process.

That initial telephone offer is certainly binding as a verbal agreement, but most firms follow up with a detailed letter outlining the most significant parts of your employment contract. You may, of course, choose to respond immediately at the time of the telephone offer (which would be considered a binding oral contract), but you will also be required to formally answer the letter of offer with a letter of acceptance, restating the salient elements of the employer's description of your position, salary, and benefits. This ensures that both parties are clear on the terms and conditions of employment and remuneration and any other outstanding aspects of the job offer.

Is This the Job You Want?

Most new employees will respond affirmatively in writing, glad to be in the position to accept employment. If you've worked hard to get the offer and the job market is tight, other offers may not be in sight, so you will say, "Yes, I accept!" What is important here is that the job offer you accept be one that does fit your particular needs, values, and interests as you've outlined them in your self-assessment process. Moreover, it should be a job that will not only use your skills and education but also challenge you to develop new skills and talents.

Jobs are sometimes accepted too hastily, for the wrong reasons, and without proper scrutiny by the applicant. For example, an individual might readily accept a sales job only to find the continual rejection by potential clients unendurable. An office worker might realize within weeks the constraints of a desk job and yearn for more activity. Employment is an important part of our lives. It is, for most of our adult lives, our most continuous productive activity. We want to make good choices based on the right criteria.

If you have a low tolerance for risk, a job based on commission will certainly be very anxiety provoking. If being near your family is important, issues of relocation could present a decision crisis for you. If you're an adventurous person, a job with frequent travel would provide needed excitement and be very desirable. The importance of income, the need to continue your education, your personal health situation—all of these have an impact on whether the job you are considering will ultimately meet your needs. Unless you've spent some time understanding and thinking about these issues, it will be difficult to evaluate offers you do receive.

More important, if you make a decision that you cannot tolerate and feel you must leave that job, you will then have both unemployment and self-esteem issues to contend with. These will combine to make the next job search tough going, indeed. So make your acceptance a carefully considered decision.

Negotiate Your Offer

It may be that there is some aspect of your job offer that is not particularly attractive to you. Perhaps there is no relocation allotment to help you move your possessions, and this presents some financial hardship for you. It may be that the health insurance is less than you had hoped. Your initial assignment may be different from what you expected, either in its location or in the duties and responsibilities that comprise it. Or it may simply be that the salary is less than you anticipated. Other considerations may be your official starting date of employment, vacation time, evening hours, dates of training programs or schools, and other concerns.

If you are considering not accepting the job because of some item or items in the job offer "package" that do not meet your needs, you should know that most employers emphatically wish that you would bring that issue to their attention. It may be that the employer can alter it to make the offer more agreeable for you. In some cases it cannot be changed. In any event the employer would generally like to have the opportunity to try to remedy a difficulty rather than risk losing a good potential employee over an issue that might have been resolved. After all, they have spent time and funds in securing your services, and they certainly deserve an opportunity to resolve any possible differences.

Honesty is the best approach in discussing any objections or uneasiness you might have over the employer's offer. Having received your formal offer in writing, contact your employer representative and indicate your particular dissatisfaction in a straightforward manner. For example, you might explain that while you are very interested in being employed by this organization, the salary (or any other benefit) is less than you have determined you require. State the terms you need, and listen to the response. You may be asked to put this in writing, or you may be asked to hold off until the firm can decide on a response. If you are dealing with a senior representative of the organization, one who has been involved in hiring for some time, you may get an immediate response or a solid indication of possible outcomes.

Perhaps the issue is one of relocation. Your initial assignment is in the Midwest, and because you had indicated a strong West Coast preference, you are surprised at the actual assignment. You might simply indicate that while you understand the need for the company to assign you based on its needs, you are disappointed and had hoped to be placed on the West Coast. You could inquire if that were still possible and, if not, would it be reasonable to expect a West Coast relocation in the future.

If your request is presented in a reasonable way, most employers will not see this as jeopardizing your offer. If they can agree to your proposal, they will. If not, they will simply tell you so, and you may choose to continue your candidacy with them or remove yourself from consideration. The choice will be up to you.

Some firms will adjust benefits within their parameters to meet the candidate's need if at all possible. If a candidate requires a relocation cost allowance, he or she may be asked to forgo tuition benefits for the first year to accomplish this adjustment. An increase in life insurance may be adjusted by some other benefit trade-off; perhaps a family dental plan is not needed. In these decisions you are called upon, sometimes under time pressure, to know how you value these issues and how important each is to you.

Many employers find they are more comfortable negotiating for candidates who have unique qualifications or who bring especially needed expertise to the organization. Employers hiring large numbers of entry-level college graduates may be far more reluctant to accommodate any changes in offer conditions. They are well supplied with candidates with similar education and experience so that if rejected by one candidate, they can draw new candidates from an ample labor pool.

Compare Offers

The condition of the economy, the job seeker's academic major and particular geographic job market, and individual needs and demands for certain employment conditions may not provide more than one job offer at a time. Some job seekers may feel that no reasonable offer should go unaccepted for the simple fear there won't be another.

In a tough job market, or if the job you seek is not widely available, or when your job search goes on too long and becomes difficult to sustain financially and emotionally, it may be necessary to accept an inferior offer. The alternative is continued unemployment. Even here, when you feel you don't have a choice, you can at least understand that in accepting this particular offer, there may be limitations and conditions you don't appreciate. At the time of acceptance, there were no other alternatives, but you can begin to use that position to gain the experience and talent to move toward a more attractive position.

Sometimes, however, more than one offer is received, and the candidate has the luxury of choice. If the job seeker knows what he or she wants and has done the necessary self-assessment honestly and thoroughly, it may be clear that one of the offers conforms more closely to those expressed wants and needs.

However, if, as so often happens, the offers are similar in terms of conditions and salary, the question then becomes which organization might provide the necessary climate, opportunities, and advantages for your professional development and growth. This is the time when solid employer research and astute questioning during the interviews really pay off. How much did you learn about the employer through your own research and skillful questioning? When the interviewer asked during the interview "Do you have any questions?" did you ask the kinds of questions that would help resolve a choice between one organization and another? Just as an employer must decide among numerous applicants, so must the applicant learn to assess the potential employer. Both are partners in the job search.

Reneging on an Offer

An especially disturbing occurrence for employers and career counseling professionals is when a job seeker formally (either orally or by written contract) accepts employment with one organization and later reneges on the agreement and goes with another employer.

There are all kinds of rationalizations offered for this unethical behavior. None of them satisfies. The sad irony is that what the job seeker is willing to do to the employer—make a promise and then break it—he or she would be outraged to have done to him- or herself: have the job offer pulled. It is a very bad way to begin a career. It suggests the individual has not taken the time to do the necessary self-assessment and self-awareness exercises to think and judge critically. The new offer taken may, in fact, be no better or worse than the one refused. You should be aware that there have been incidents of legal action following job candidates' reneging on an offer. This adds a very sour note to what should be a harmonious beginning of a lifelong adventure.

PART TWO

THE CAREER PATHS

Criminal Justice:
A Degree in Demand

So many opportunities abound for people with formal education in criminal justice that the list of possible jobs is nearly endless. More jobs are becoming available each year, with new positions being created in public safety, private protective services, and the growing field of Internet security. Though you'll see statistics quoted, it is impossible to delineate all the available positions and vacancies in criminal justice that exist on the federal, state, and local levels.

Along with strong employment prospects overall and in the variety of job titles, *Great Jobs for Criminal Justice Majors* highlights the dramatic shift in criminal justice–related jobs from semiprofessional to professional status. In both the fieldwork and research involved in producing this career guide, we saw an increasing emphasis on the educational preparation of job applicants and a growing number of advanced degrees among established criminal justice workers. As the supply of more highly educated workers has increased, the education standards for entry-level jobs have correspondingly been raised. The job market begins to demand what the market can deliver!

Criminal justice jobs cannot be encompassed in one prototypical job or assignment. The occupations in this field span a broad spectrum of responsibilities, functions, and stressors. Higher entry-level education requirements, training, professional development, and additional postsecondary education are molding the modern criminal justice professional. This second half of the book gives you a close-up look at five career categories, or paths, that are open to you.

The safety and well-being of our nation's citizens greatly depend on the police officers, sheriffs, state troopers, highway patrol officers, federal agents, and others in law enforcement responsible for enforcing statutes, laws, and regulations. Those in the field of corrections are responsible for overseeing individuals who have been arrested, are awaiting trial or some other hearing, or who have been convicted of a crime and sentenced to serve time in jail, prison, or community service. Juvenile justice professionals work with the courts, social service agencies, caregivers, and the community to provide, where possible, alternatives to the criminal court system as they attempt to rehabilitate young people who have broken the law. The courts offer positions in security, administration, research, and legal affairs that can provide a stimulating and engrossing viewpoint on the criminal justice system as it is played out in the courtroom. The business sector was once chiefly the alternative for retired criminal justice professionals, who would go on to serve as consultants on criminal proceedings, security, and the prevention of theft, fire, vandalism, and illegal entry. Now, with the growth, complexity, emphasis on professionalism and training, and technological sophistication of the criminal justice field, business opportunities have expanded beyond those bounds. Claims investigation, property loss management, private security, and protection specialists are now all viable career areas.

Each of these exciting areas is surveyed in the chapters that follow. As you read about the five career paths, you'll probably be pleased to see how often employers ask specifically for your major. In writing this book, we drew upon job ads we see every day in our work as career counselors. Employers want criminal justice majors for these jobs in law enforcement, juvenile justice, court-related occupations, and corrections. They may go on to list other acceptable educational backgrounds in the social sciences, but the criminal justice major involves a distinctly different academic preparation.

For employers, the important difference in the background of criminal justice majors is the combination of a liberal arts education with the specialized knowledge of policing, the courts, corrections, and the justice system. Most criminal justice curricula provide students with a theoretical foundation of the discipline along with a solid grounding in the social science methodologies as they apply to criminal justice. Criminal justice majors have had special work in social interactions and the related forces that contribute to social order, conflict, and societal change. Employers realize that other curricula in the social sciences offer some of the same background but that it is not targeted as in the criminal justice curriculum and does not include the practical applications.

Perhaps you have added to your college preparation with an internship or practicum experience, either as part of your formal studies or on your own during summer or winter breaks. If you are reading this book *before* you graduate, maximize the value of an internship or other hands-on experience in criminal justice. The opportunity to work alongside seasoned professionals, to observe the pace and nature of their day-to-day activities and routines, brings a new awareness and reality to your appreciation of law enforcement work. If your experience is a formal internship, you'll have an opportunity to make your own contribution to the efforts of your employer, and that experience is likely to be a deeply satisfying one. You'll begin to see that others treat you as a colleague and that you are able to do the work, and then you can assess whether you like the work or not and whether the job holds promise for you as a career field. That's the whole point of internships. Even if they end up teaching you that a particular field is not the right one for you, they are immensely valuable because they give you the insight that helps you make better choices after you graduate—whatever those choices are.

Because criminal justice confronts societal issues as they are happening right now, the people who work in criminal justice comprise a microcosm of society. Being able to choose from inner-city, rural, or urban settings for a variety of career interests, including police work; juvenile probation; correctional security; counseling; arson investigation; and local, state, and federal law enforcement means that you can aim for the type of criminal justice career and the particular environment that best fits your needs. Criminal justice is so dynamic and is growing so rapidly that it's difficult to confidently predict what the future holds for the field. For instance, as we will discuss in Chapter 10, the current issues surrounding the Internet—including concerns about privacy, security of information (especially credit card data), and the legitimacy of electronic signatures—all concern law enforcement.

You'll be working with people from a wide variety of cultural, religious, socioeconomic, racial, ethnic, and gender orientations. This diversity is important to conscientious criminal justice majors because, as a group, they are inquisitive about people and what makes them tick. Police on the street need this curiosity and so do correctional officers and counseling professionals. Sensitivity to diversity, strong interpersonal skills, and healthy attitudes combined with solid critical thinking skills and high ethical standards are the prerequisites across the board in all the jobs described in Part Two. Another common denominator underlying all the career paths presented is the need to be proactive in crime prevention.

However, the appreciation of diversity that is a strength in the workforce of criminal justice is not without some attendant problems. It would be naive to ignore the challenges that race, ethnicity, and gender bring to the workplace. Not a week goes by that the popular press does not carry a story reflecting one of these themes. It may be contested opportunities for women in law enforcement management, inadequate promotional rates for African Americans in the FBI, or any of numerous possible accusations of discriminatory practices by the public against the police. But, as you read and examine these stories, you'll frequently find corresponding "sidebar" articles detailing improved opportunities, less discrimination, and more equity in hiring and promotion. Because of the strong public scrutiny, employment areas in criminal justice come in for some significant attention by various interested publics, and because of that attention, employment practices just get better and better.

A Full Plate of Choices

This is an exciting professional field to be considering for your life's work, and this book presents many wonderful career options. Because of that, in reading these chapters you may become overwhelmed by the number and variety of jobs and by your own enthusiasm and interest in every one of them! It's kind of like moving your tray along the line of a particularly wonderful buffet. It gets increasingly frustrating as you proceed because the choices get tougher. You want a bit of everything.

Well, here's the good news! Most of the jobs profiled here are entry-level positions; in the first few years of your career, you'll still be exploring your options, and nothing you do now will cast your future in stone. Your employers know that as well. Sometimes they know better than you do that after a year or two, you may decide to try your hand in some other aspect of the profession. And that's OK! In the criminal justice field, your degree gives you wonderful flexibility, and most of these entry-level jobs are highly appropriate stepping stones in many paths, not just the one you originally chose.

So, enjoy the variety presented in this book, and don't get frustrated over "the decision." You can make changes as your career develops. One thing you must do: listen to yourself; listen to your heart. You know who you are, and you know the decisions you've made in the past and what's worked and what hasn't. Even the self-assessment exercises in Chapter 1 are more about confirming what you already knew intuitively about yourself. After all, given your twenty years or so of experience, you should be an expert on *you*! So, as you learn about the possibilities for the beginning of your career in criminal justice, hold each job up to what you know about yourself and your interests and enthusiasms, and go with your personal preferences and your strong intuition about who you are and what you want. You won't go wrong!

Path 1: Law Enforcement

Patrol Your Possibilities

Policing is the front line of law enforcement. In the United States, more than three-quarters of a million men and women serve in police positions. It's a big job, and it's an important one. Police work has a long and proud tradition; police officers are part of our social and cultural landscape and have been ever since we were old enough to answer the question "What do you want to be when you grow up?" Like doctor, firefighter, and teacher, "policeman" was a common childhood aspiration. These were the idealized jobs of our youth because they were important, they were helpful, and—although maybe we couldn't articulate it—they were noble, too.

While we hope this book will serve to strengthen your belief in and esteem for the policing profession, along with that respect you should have a realistic and grounded view of the career path as it stands today. In general, policing and law enforcement are changing and evolving. It's an exciting field that's responding positively and with dramatic new initiatives to a dynamic society. How exciting to be part of that! But with those changes and new initiatives come new demands on anyone who wants to work in law enforcement at the local, state, or federal level.

In our field research for this volume of the Great Jobs series, we frequently came away from an interview with law enforcement officials feeling grateful that these high-quality people had elected to devote their lives to law enforcement. But our gratitude was almost overtaken by our surprise at the range of concerns and demands placed on those whose job it is to enforce the law. In this chapter, we hope to give you an accurate picture of what you need to succeed as a law enforcement officer today.

First and foremost, the new mandate for recent graduates thinking about careers in law enforcement is a need to be intelligent, open, and curious. You must have a positive outlook about people and a sincere appreciation that your role in law enforcement is most successfully fulfilled if it is preventive and anticipatory, not reactive and punitive. At one meeting we had in a mid-size city police department, the captain told us that he wants his officers to be in the community "like a fish among the reeds." He wants them and the public to be comfortable with police mixing into the community—causing few, if any, ripples in the social fabric. While sensitively and poetically expressed, this officer's view of policing today is not unusual. As the pool of qualified applicants has become increasingly talented, educated, and prepared for the larger scope of law enforcement today, the individuals doing the hiring have raised the hurdles accordingly.

For all the policing jobs described in this path, a group interview is almost always part of the final stages of the job search. Even for small city police departments, it is not uncommon for the candidate to appear before an interview "board" made up of police representatives, city officials, and other interested parties. Some variation on the question "Why did you decide to enter law enforcement?" is sure to be asked. Before facing that question, you need to ask yourself if you are ready for the law enforcement jobs of today. You'll need to sort through your motives, thinking clearly about your role as a law enforcement official. These examining and interviewing boards are not interested in swagger or bullying. They want sensitive, intelligent, thoughtful police officers who can react first with their minds and resolve problems to avoid having situations escalate into trouble. It's clear, then, that law enforcement today is a more demanding and challenging job than ever before. It also follows that the interviewing and screening processes to enter the field have become correspondingly sophisticated.

Definition of the Career Path

Most people think they have a pretty good idea of what police officers do on the job. What they may discover is that the common view of law enforcement jobs has been distorted by images from television, movies, and the press. These portrayals don't always provide an accurate and complete depiction of a police officer's job. There are many varieties of police work, and each has its own demands and rewards. State troopers, detectives, police officers on the "beat," and many other types of law enforcement officials (sheriffs, animal control officers, liquor commission officials, and so forth) keep public order and protect lives and property by enforcing the ordinances, statutes, laws, and regulations decided upon by local, regional, state, and federal legislatures and other governing bodies. The functions of each of these officers and officials can vary widely. Differences occur because of the size and type of the organization, the specific job description, and sometimes the impact of being "on" or "off" duty. Generally, however, these officials are required to exercise the authority they have been given whenever that action is necessary.

Exhibit 10.1 shows the possible positions and their missions in local and county, state, and federal law enforcement jobs:

Exhibit 10.1
POSSIBLE POSITIONS AND THEIR MISSIONS

Local and County Law Enforcement

Position	Basic Mission
Police officer	On patrol. A "generalist" who maintains law and order and arrests violators.
Sheriff	Similar to police officer, with the added responsibility of maintaining the county jail.
Animal control officer	Patrols and takes complaints regarding violations of laws regarding domestic animals, pertaining to both animal cruelty and public health and safety.

State Law Enforcement

Position	Basic Mission
State trooper	Statewide patrol; maintains law and order
Highway patrol officer	Patrols state highways, conducts traffic, and performs general law enforcement duties
University police officer/college public safety officer	Maintains law and order on state university or college campuses or properties
Conservation and wildlife officer	Patrols the outdoors for violations of laws regarding wildlife and natural resources
Park police	Patrols state parks and reservations
Corrections officer	Maintains the custody, security, and well-being of inmates in a state correctional facility
Parole officer	Provides supervision and guidance to an assigned caseload of releasees from state and local correctional facilities

---

continued

Federal Law Enforcement

Position	Basic Mission
Border patrol agent	Protects U.S. borders from illegal entry
Federal police officer	Maintains protection of employees and property of designated federal agencies
Federal corrections officer	Maintains safekeeping, care, and protection of federal inmates
Federal parole officer	Maintains supervision and guidance of federal releasees
Federal protection officer	Maintains protection of federal buildings nationwide
Postal inspector	Conducts investigations of postal crimes
DEA special agent	Enforces laws and regulations involving narcotics and controlled substances
Deputy U.S. marshal	Provides protection for U.S. courts and judges; apprehends federal fugitives; transports federal prisoners
IRS agent	Conducts criminal investigations involving tax laws
Customs inspector	Enforces laws governing the importation of merchandise, including the inspection of persons and carriers
Immigration inspector	Prevents ineligible people from entering the United States
FBI agent	Investigates violations of federal criminal law; protects the United States from foreign intelligence activities
Secret service agent	Protects the president and other dignitaries and investigates threats against them; investigates counterfeiting crimes
U.S. park ranger	Patrols and protects United States parks and reservations
ATF special agent	Investigates criminal use of firearms and explosives; enforces federal alcohol and tobacco regulations
Transportation security officer	Screens passengers and bags boarding commercial aircraft
Federal air marshal	Travels incognito to insure security and law enforcement on commercial aircraft

These lists do not enumerate all the possible law enforcement positions available. Not included here, for example, are the many law enforcement agencies found in the military, nor all the "special" police forces formed to protect airports, harbors, transit systems, railroads, and other authorities.

Police Officers

Some new entrants into local law enforcement will start as police officers and begin their careers as patrol officers (discussed at length in the following section, "Working Conditions"). Other police officers specialize and become proficient in a variety of law enforcement areas, such as chemical and microscopic analysis, firearms identification, or handwriting and/or fingerprint analysis. Others want to work with specialized units, such as K-9, horse-mounted, or motorcycle patrol units. You could also pursue work, depending on your location, with harbor patrols or with special weapon or emergency response teams, including bomb detection and disposal units. Beyond these assignments, many specific units are assembled to combat certain types of crime, including Internet crimes.

You may be interested in the work of detectives or special agents. These are plainclothes positions involving collecting and assembling evidence for criminal cases. Detectives and special agents do a lot of interviewing, researching records, observing suspects, and participating in raids or arrests. Curiosity, patience, judgment, discernment, and good research skills, including Web search skills, are essential.

Entry-level positions in law enforcement vary with the hiring agency. For example, most police officers begin with basic patrol duties for a specific area. As you rise in the ranks, duties become more specific, and you become eligible for candidacy in other types of police work. Federal positions, such as those in the Federal Bureau of Investigation (FBI), usually pair new entrants into the force with a more experienced agent and rotate the new entrants through a variety of cases so that they receive a solid grounding in surveillance, report writing, and investigative procedures. While not very glamorous, perhaps, this type of work is important for gaining competence to achieve more sophisticated assignments.

State Troopers and Sheriffs

Some graduates will be attracted to jobs as state troopers or with sheriff's departments. Sheriffs and state troopers maintain order in bigger areas than those of local police—large, thinly populated areas and, of course, our nation's highways.

The roles of sheriffs can vary greatly in scope and variety from one end of the country to the other. Think of sheriffs' duties as those of local or county police chiefs with far smaller departments, and you'll have a sense of the role.

Generally, the position is analogous to the commanding officer of a county's law enforcement provider. In states where counties play a larger part in state governance, sheriffs' roles tend to be larger. In some states, regular police fulfill the county law enforcement job, while in other states, both sheriffs and regular police provide services for the county. In larger cities, the sheriff's department may maintain the jail or serve legal papers. In many counties, sheriffs are assigned principally to court and prison tasks. In most situations in the United States, sheriffs are elected and have significant administrative workloads, so computer skills, writing, management, and some accounting background are useful.

State police officers (which you may know as state troopers or the highway patrol, depending on where you live) patrol our nation's highways and enforce motor vehicle laws and regulations. If an accident occurs, they reroute traffic, give first aid, summon appropriate emergency equipment and personnel, and, most important, write up the report of the accident to determine cause. State police have another role as well, and that is to assist officers of other law enforcement agencies in enforcing criminal laws. In some very rural or underpopulated areas with poor local police coverage, the state police may take over even some of the routine primary law enforcement activities, such as the investigation of burglaries and assaults.

Federal Law Enforcers

College graduates can find a host of law enforcement employment opportunities with the federal government. While many of them are addressed in this chapter, for a fine guide to accessing federal law enforcement jobs and how to apply, you should visit the website of Dr. Tom O'Connor of North Carolina Wesleyan College, Department of Justice Studies, where he has assembled a federal jobs "employment mega-site" at http://faculty.ncwc.edu/toconnor/employ.htm.

The Department of Justice is the umbrella under which many federal law enforcement agencies operate. Within the department, the FBI remains the principal federal agency charged with investigating violations of most federal statutes. Agents of the FBI use surveillance techniques (observation as well as sophisticated electronic surveillance, including court-ordered wiretaps, and powerful distance microphones), examine records (a large area of FBI investigative effort is "white-collar crime"), participate in undercover activities involving sensitivity and high risk, and track the interstate movement of property and individuals for criminal purposes.

Other special agents employed by the Department of Justice work for the Bureau of Alcohol, Tobacco, Firearms, and Explosives (ATF) investigating violations of federal firearms and explosives laws.

The Drug Enforcement Administration (DEA) is also well known for its work in enforcing our federal drug laws. The investigations carried out by this agency can be intensive and complex, as drug activity is highly secretive and drug rings can involve numerous people and business entities to disguise their illegal activities.

Jobs with the Department of Homeland Security include working with Customs and Border Protection (protecting our land and water boundaries), and Immigration and Customs Enforcement (identifying and shutting down vulnerabilities in the nation's border, economic, transportation and infrastructure security). The U.S. Secret Service protects our president and vice president and their families and investigates counterfeiting and fraudulent check and credit card use. The mission of the Transportation Security Administration (TSA) is to prevent terrorist attacks and to protect the U.S. transportation network. The most highly visible TSA employees are security officers who screen all passengers and baggage prior to boarding commercial flights. Federal air marshals travel undercover to protect commercial aircraft and passengers from terrorist attacks and other security breaches.

Within the Department of the Treasury, special agents with the Internal Revenue Service (IRS) collect evidence against those defrauding the federal government by nonpayment or underpayment of taxes.

The U.S. Marshals Service is responsible for transporting prisoners, witnesses, juries, and judges and providing court security. Federal air marshals, working for the Federal Aviation Administration (FAA), ensure the safety of passengers and crews on commercial airliners.

In Canada, the Royal Canadian Mounted Police (RCMP) is the Canadian national police service. The RCMP acts as a national, federal, provincial, and municipal police force, providing a total federal police service to all Canadians.

The Canadian Security Intelligence Service (CSIS) is a federal agency dedicated to protecting the national security interests of Canada. The agency is the government's principal advisor on matters of national security, working with the objective of investigating and reporting on threats to the nation's security. Intelligence Officers with CSIS conduct investigations, perform research, analyze information, and prepare reports on national security-related matters.

Canada's Border Services Agency employs people at hundreds of locations across the country. These professionals work to keep restricted goods and people from entering the country, help locate missing children, and protect Canada from illegal drugs and weapons.

Working Conditions

One of the marvelous things about a career in law enforcement is that unlike some other professions, police officers are located everywhere, from the smallest, most rural areas to the great cities of our country and everywhere in between. Because of that flexibility, we encourage you to spend some time in your self-assessment work in Chapter 1 thinking about the advantages and disadvantages of various locales and how you'd fit into various environments. For example, you may prefer a very rural area that in addition to its natural beauty might also provide lower housing costs and even the future opportunity to own a home on a sizeable piece of land. Thinking further ahead, however, you may also plan to raise a family and may find that having proximity to good schools, neighbors and friends for the children, services, and medical care makes a more populous area attractive.

Police Officers

Your classroom work, your textbooks, law enforcement guests on campus, job fairs, and other activities, including your own work and internship experience, have probably given you some sense of the reality of the police officer's job—especially at the entry level. General law enforcement duties and responsibilities are the name of the game in your first job as a police officer. Directing traffic, frequently at the scene of a fire or accident (or parade!), is a common activity. Investigating a burglary or even administering first aid likewise are parts of a "normal" day's activity, if there is such a thing for a police officer.

If you work in a larger police department, your duties will be less generalized. In larger departments, new recruits are often assigned to a specific type of duty, such as patrolling a designated business district or residential community to prevent crime. Patrol work can be immensely satisfying on many counts. You may be working with a regular partner—or a series of regular partners—and often strong friendships develop as you learn to appreciate each other's special skills and talents and realize the synergy that can occur in a team situation. Best of all, you become deeply acquainted with an area and its residents and realize that your active presence is a deterrent to criminal activities. Even in larger cities, you will know your patrol area well and be able to recognize suspicious circumstances easily as the rhythm of your "beat" becomes familiar to you. Even such mundane events as an open door, unusual activity in a building, or a missing manhole cover will be readily noted and corrected.

Training and Qualifications

To join a police force, whether for a small community or a state and federal criminal justice position, applicants must typically meet strict criteria to be considered competitive. While it may seem that it's easier to secure a local police position than a state trooper or federal law enforcement job, the reality is a bit more complicated. Although standards do become increasingly tougher for state and federal positions, you may be unprepared for the scrutiny given candidates for local police jobs. Successful completion of a formal police academy program; extensive interviewing, both one on one and before commissions or panels; physical and psychological testing; fitness evaluations; and subjection to a wide variety of evaluative tools mean that anyone entering policing today is going to have his or her candidacy scrutinized for fitness, suitability, motive, and potential to succeed.

Civil service regulations govern police and other criminal justice positions in almost every state. Candidates must be U.S. citizens, be at least twenty years of age, and meet rigorous personal and physical qualifications. There will be written examinations and physical tests that include vision, hearing, strength, and agility. You will also undergo a formal personal interview, frequently before a board made up of police and other interested parties.

A word about education: criminal justice programs abound in both two- and four-year colleges. It has been and is, without doubt, a popular major. While the major is increasingly available at four-year colleges and universities, we found many honest hiring officials who were not clear on the advantages of a bachelor's degree over an associate's degree. Some went so far as to say that law enforcement on the local level has yet to convincingly validate the importance of any formal criminal justice education per se. What officials did agree on is that there is an ample supply of applicants with bachelor's degrees. The result is that most hiring officials, regardless of their view of the value of the degree, interview only bachelor-degreed graduates because the market has abundantly supplied them. Their philosophy can be summarized as "While we don't necessarily agree that a bachelor's degree means a better law enforcement officer than an associate's degree, if there are plenty of four-year applicants, wouldn't we want those candidates with more education?"

The implications of this are clear: students with associate's degrees may find that their opportunities are better in areas that are less well supplied with candidates, and they should consider enrolling in some courses toward a bachelor's degree to better qualify for promotions. In fact, many observers predict that because of the growing number of graduates with bachelor's degrees in criminal justice, in five years' time a bachelor's degree will become the standard educational requirement for most police positions.

When your candidacy advances and you become a finalist for the position you seek, most employers (even in small towns) will institute a background check. Because these background checks are expensive, they are often reserved for finalists or even selected candidates for whom the job offer is pending on the results of the background examination. Because your ethics, honesty, judgment, and sense of maturity bear directly on your profession, it's important that hiring officials have detailed knowledge of how others perceive you and of your personal record.

Local and State Police

During an interview with a police chief in a small rural town, we asked who got patrol officer jobs in his department. He said, "People I know. I only hire people I know." When we asked why they would opt to work in his town when only thirty minutes away law enforcement salaries average $8,000 to $9,000 more, he said, "The people who apply here might have worked in other towns and not been rehired or even been fired. I'm their last chance to stay in law enforcement." But even in making such an honest statement about the employee pool, the chief maintained that in a small town such as his, he wouldn't hire anyone he didn't know. So, if you live in a small town and think you want to someday police in that town, make yourself known to the police department. Volunteer your time, do an internship, or make an appointment for an informational interview. Let them know who you are and what your career goals are.

Twelve to fourteen weeks of training at the state police academy is standard for all new recruits before they receive any assignments and frequently even before the hiring process is complete. The program includes intensive training in legal issues, civil rights, constitutional law, and state laws and ordinances, as well as technique training in reporting accidents, directing traffic, use of weapons, self-defense, first aid, and how to respond to a variety of emergency situations. While police academy standards of education vary from state to state, the Texas Commission on Law Enforcement 560-Hour Basic Peace Officer Course can be used as a guide. It can be found on the Web at http://interoz.com/spag/lawenf1.htm. The general subject areas include:

Introduction and Orientation
Texas and U.S. Constitutions and Bill of Rights
Penal Code
Use of Force—Law
Use of Force—Concepts
Strategies of Defense—Mechanics of Arrest
Strategies of Defense—Firearms
Traffic Law
Code of Criminal Procedure

Emergency Medical Assistance
Professionalism and Ethics
Juvenile Issues—Family Code
Arrest Search and Seizure
Patrol Procedures
Civil Process and Liability
Interpersonal Communications/Report Writing
Field Notetaking
Texas Alcoholic Beverage Code
Emergency Communications
Family Violence and Related Assaultive Offenses
Recognizing and Interacting with Persons with
Mental Illness and Mental Retardation
Illegal Drugs
Multiculturalism and Human Relations
Victims of Crime
Crowd Management
Hazardous Materials Awareness
Fitness and Wellness
Criminal Investigations
Professional Police Driving
History of Policing
Criminal Justice System
Stress Management for Peace Officers
Problem Solving and Critical Thinking
Professional Police Approaches

Requirements for employment in Canadian provincial police forces are similar to those of American local and state departments. While specific criteria differ among the provinces, in general, applicants must be eighteen or nineteen years of age and a Canadian citizen or legal resident. Most departments require two years of post-secondary education, or a combination of education and work experience. Additionally, a valid driver's license and First Aid Certificate with CPR are also necessary. Applicants must be in excellent physical health and must pass extensive security and background checks.

In general, successful candidates are hired as probationary constables and attend eleven to fourteen weeks of training at the provincial police academy, studying police skills, legal studies, physical fitness, foot drill (dress and deportment), and an introduction to the social sciences. Following this, the recruit constable may return to their home police department for a period of thirteen to seventeen weeks of field training, working under the guidance of an experienced, specially trained constable (known as a *field trainer*). In some provinces, the recruit constable returns to the academy for additional training and then spends a probationary period working in the home department.

Federal Police Work

You need to be between twenty-three and thirty-seven years of age to be an FBI agent. That restriction may present some problems for students graduating at age twenty-two or even twenty-one, and it may be best for those candidates to consider entering the police academy and pursuing a job at the local or state level—or to be prepared to enter the FBI in a nonagent position—until they qualify in age to be an FBI agent.

Beyond physical requirements, which are strict, a bachelor's degree is the minimum required educational attainment, and candidates with master's or law degrees are not uncommon. The FBI has five entry programs: Accounting/Finance, Computer Science/Information Technology, Language, Law, and Diversified. Each of these programs has its own specific academic requirements.

The application process is legendary for its thoroughness. Screening includes background checks on character and history; credit checks; criminal checks; and interviews with neighbors, friends, and roommates. Drug tests, a physical exam, and often a polygraph test are also part of the qualifying process. If you make it through this intensive selection procedure, you will spend four months at the FBI Academy in Virginia studying investigative techniques, personal defense, and a variety of firearms. Even during this training, you are under scrutiny, and candidates are disqualified if they display any physical, emotional, or mental handicaps that would impair their performance of the potentially dangerous duties of the FBI agent.

Applicants to the Royal Canadian Mounted Police must meet the following requirements: be a Canadian citizen; be of good character; be proficient in either of Canada's official languages; have a Canadian secondary school diploma or its equivalent; possess a valid, unrestricted Canadian driver's license; be nineteen years of age at the time of acceptance; be able to pass a written aptitude test; meet rigorous physical and medical requirements; and be willing to relocate anywhere within Canada. In addition, prior to enrollment in cadet training candidates must obtain certificates in keyboarding or typing and first aid.

In addition to the position of customs inspector and other professional titles, the Canada Border Services Agency also offers employment opportunities for students. As a Student Border Services Officer, you can earn an hourly wage working part-time during the school year or full-time in the summer. The Federal Student Work Experience Program employs seven thousand students annually in temporary jobs among various federal agencies; co-op and internship programs are also available.

More on the Background Investigation

The subject of background investigations raises a very serious point. Though you may be well along in your degree program or even have already graduated, it may not be too late to benefit from a strict admonishment heard frequently in criminal justice circles: if you want to be selected for a law enforcement position, keep your record clean! In addition to frequently required drug testing or lie detector tests, applicants' criminal records (if any) will be researched, and candidates with no record or minimal violations stand a much stronger chance of being hired. During our research for this book, we heard stories of arrests made during college dorm parties that resulted in an applicant's disqualification from candidacy for a law enforcement position. While that is not always the case with an arrest, a felony conviction would, in almost every instance, prevent you from being considered for a law enforcement job.

Job candidates must also have a responsible financial history and a pattern of respect and honesty in dealings with individuals and organizations. Improper conduct, a poor employment and/or military record, and a poor driving history record can all affect a candidate's suitability for consideration in law enforcement work.

Requirements for Promotion

Advancement opportunities carry different requirements at the various levels of law enforcement.

Local and State Police

Promotions allow people to move into specialized fields. Line promotion (going up in rank within a police force) requires a high passing score on a written exam and favorable performance evaluations. Your seniority and place on the list of those eligible for promotion are equally significant determinants.

Generally speaking, you must serve on the force for five years before you are eligible to sit for the lieutenant's exam, and after two years as a lieutenant, you can take the captain's test. Each advancement also requires additional education, and as degree levels in the profession continue to rise, it is expected that these requirements for additional educational attainment will become correspondingly more demanding.

After starting your law enforcement job, in most cases, you'll be eligible for promotion after these periods, which may vary depending on the size and complexity of your employer. Almost all police begin with a period of six months' probation. Generally these probationary periods have a great deal to do with the kind of training and grooming you are receiving as a new officer. Organizations whose probationary periods are longer than six months do more training and cross training, more professional development, and more mentoring of new officers, so your career is hardly on hold during that time.

Federal

Again using the example of the FBI, agents begin their careers paired with more experienced agents in a specific division. They learn the tools of their trade (report writing, surveillance, investigation, etc.) and rotate through assignments over the first few years to gain exposure to a range of divisions.

After about five years, agents can apply for a variety of other positions, including senior status in the field as well as more deskbound administrative positions. Continued promotion to managerial level and assistant directorship (and higher) positions occur at about ten years and beyond into your career. These promotions go to those agents who continue to develop their skills, build a track record of performance, participate in lifelong learning, and stay motivated and energized about their jobs. Often at this point in their careers, successful FBI agents return to the training school at Quantico, Virginia, to serve as instructors, trainers, and educators for new recruits.

Stories from the Field: So Near and Yet So Far

Two accounts we heard as we researched this book demonstrate that no matter how successful someone is in all the testing, training, and pre-employment screening, employment is never guaranteed. In the first instance, a candidate was hired by a midsize city police force after graduating from the state's police academy, passing all the physical and psychological exams, successfully completing his board interview, and passing his background investigation. During the background investigation, several former employers and contacts commented on the candidate's pronounced ability to follow orders. According to the detective recounting this story, those comments proved to be prophetic. Once hired, the young patrolman did nothing without being told. "Get out of the car!" or "Finish your paperwork before you sign off." It didn't matter what the task, this young man had to be directed. As you can imagine, it became a burden to his colleagues and he was fired.

In another instance, a candidate who also had passed all prerequisites with flying colors caused his prospective employer concern when he continually called the station to double-check his next scheduled meeting (he had forgotten the time and date) or to confirm information that he had already received. This behavior led them to question how organized and mature he was, and he was not hired.

Law enforcement continues to raise the hurdles in the employment race. Most hiring officials want only the very best, and this chapter should give you a sense of the many dimensions on which you'll be evaluated. The following list highlights some of the skills and aptitudes that employers consider desirable in this career path.

Computer skills   Teamwork
Interpersonal communication   Written communication
Presentation skills   Initiative
Critical thinking   Listening
Problem solving   Investigative skills
Sensitivity to issues and culture   Foreign language

Any related training or certifications you can pick up along the way such as CPR, first aid, EMT, disaster response, lifesaving, mediation skills, and/or grant writing will further enhance your value as a job candidate.

Earnings

Salaries can be very different, depending on what part of the country you are considering. Even at the local level of law enforcement, you will find varying salary ranges within each state and even between communities that border one another. We found a good example right in our local area. The entry-level salary for a police officer in a small rural community was $20,800, while literally down the road in a small city the starting salary for a police officer was $29,000.

Local Law Enforcement

According to the latest data provided by the U.S. Bureau of Labor Statistics, the median salary for police patrol officers in 2004 was $45,310. Most earned between $34,410 and $56,360. Keep in mind that these figures represent the base salary, which does not include a uniform allowance provided by most departments, holiday pay, hazard pay, overtime, educational incentives, shift differential, or special-detail assignments. Such additional payments can be significant and can, in some cases, nearly double your salary. The size of the department and the community help determine how much additional income you can anticipate. It stands to reason that in a small town with a correspondingly small police force, the opportunity for special-detail assignments, such as directing traffic around road construction crews, will be more limited than those you would find in a large metropolitan area.

In many communities, a college degree automatically qualifies you for a higher salary. Then, as you continue to move up the ladder to sergeant, captain, and so on, you will garner a steady increase. Police chiefs may earn a base salary of between $72,924 and $92,983. The median salary for detectives and criminal investigators is $53,990, with most earning between $40,690 and $72,280.

In other law enforcement positions at the local level, such as health and building code inspector, you can expect to earn, on average, $31,800. Once again, this will vary with geographic location, size, and even the community's budget.

Constables in Canadian police departments had an average starting salary of $43,379 in 2005; following incremental increases, the annual salary for fifth-level constables was $66,738.

County and State Law Enforcement

According to the most recently released data from the Department of Justice Bureau of Justice Statistics, in a study of state police agencies employing 100 officers or more, base salaries for entry-level officers ranged from $21,063 in Florida to $45,696 in Alaska. As you can see, geographic location can make quite a difference!

Law enforcement officials employed by state governments outside of the state police, such as state park rangers and tax examiners, earned a median salary of $43,490 according to the *Occupational Outlook Handbook*.

At the county level, most recent available data, from 2004, show that the majority of sheriffs and deputy sheriffs earned a median salary of $45,011 per year.

Federal Law Enforcement

All federal employees are paid according to a government pay scale, and a special salary rate table applies for federal employees working in law enforcement. For example, in 2005 FBI agents entered as GS-10 employees on the pay scale at a base salary of $42,548, yet they earned about $53,185 a year with availability pay. They could advance to the GS-13 grade level in field non-supervisory assignments at a base salary of $64,478, which was worth $80,597 with availability pay. FBI supervisory, management, and executive positions in grades GS-14 and GS-15 paid a base salary of about $76,193 and $89,625 a year, respectively, which amounted to $95,241 or $112,031 per year including availability pay. Salaries were slightly higher in selected areas where the prevailing local pay level was higher. Because federal agents may be eligible for a special law enforcement benefits package, applicants should ask their recruiter for more information.

Most entry-level professional positions in federal law enforcement start at the GS-5 through GS-7 level, which generally translates to an annual salary of $25,195 to $31,209. For complete salary rate information, visit the website of the U.S. Office of Personnel Management at opm.gov/oca/ 06tables/ html/gs.asp.

The salary for a constable with the Royal Canadian Mounted Police consists of four levels, and the increments are not granted automatically. Officers must complete certain duties and achieve specific experience before receiving salary increases. The starting salary for a cadet in 2006 was $43,438; after thirty-six months of employment and incremental increases, it was $70,366.

Intelligence Officers with the Canadian Security Intelligence Service serve an initial probationary period of five years. The starting salary in 2006 was $41,520, progressing to $66,810 during the probationary period, based on successful completion of training, attaining the required experience and on job performance.

Canada's Border Services Agency employs people in a variety of positions. Salaries are dependent upon the job description, education, and experience.

For those who choose to work in government law enforcement, be it local, state, or federal, most agencies offer liberal pension plans that include early retirement benefits. Often you are eligible to retire after twenty to twenty-five years of service. This means that if you enter the field in your early twenties, you may be eligible to retire in your forties. At that point, you could receive a pension (and benefits) and still work full- or part-time in another career!

Career Outlook

Security is a major concern to all citizens today. As a result, employment of police officers, detectives, and criminal investigators is expected to grow about as fast as the average for all occupations through 2014, with an expected increase of 9 to 17 percent in employment. A more security-conscious society and concern about drug-related crimes should contribute to the increasing demand for police services. However, employment growth may be hindered by reductions in federal hiring grants to local police departments and by expectations of low crime rates by the general public.

Most of the projected increase is expected to be at the local and state levels. Since the level of government spending determines the level of employment for police and detectives, the number of job opportunities can vary from year to year and from place to place. On the other hand, layoffs are rare because retirements enable most staffing cuts to be handled through attrition. Trained law enforcement officers who lose their jobs because of budget cuts usually have little difficulty finding jobs with other agencies. The need to replace workers who retire, transfer to other occupations, or stop working for other reasons will be the source of many job openings.

Although the career outlook for law enforcement jobs is promising, keep in mind that the competition is keen. The jobs are appealing for many reasons: they are challenging and sometimes exciting, they satisfy one's desire to serve and protect other members of society, and they enjoy the public's respect and admiration. Salaries and benefit packages are attractive, and opportunities for advancement are widely available. Also, job security is considerable, and layoffs are rare. Therefore, the number of qualified candidates exceeds the number of openings not only in federal agencies but also in most local and state departments. However, applicants with college training in police science, military police experience, or both should have the best opportunities.

Strategy for Finding the Jobs

As you probably know by now, virtually all law enforcement positions are with local, county, state, or federal government agencies, which will enable you to focus or target your job search more narrowly. The application process can be more challenging than the private-sector equivalent, as it may include detailed application forms, extensive job announcements, and specific hiring rules. Try to remember that the government at all levels is made up of people just like you. They are interested in your application and are looking for you to be a good fit for the position. So, if the going gets tough, and it may, ask for help.

General Words of Advice

Now that you have specific information about careers in law enforcement, you also need to keep some general pointers in mind as you search for a job.

Personalize Your Search. Successful government job seekers say that one way to break through the bureaucracy is to personalize your efforts. Call the agencies and departments with which you are seeking employment, and speak to a representative. Tell him or her what you're doing, and ask for assistance and guidance. This will put a voice and a name to the employer, and he or she will likely have valuable advice about the job specifications and application and hiring procedures.

Follow Up as You Would with Any Other Employer. Following up on your federal, state, or local government application is just as important as it is in the private sector. You can verify that your materials were received and that your application is complete. You'll show the hiring official that you are committed to your job search and remind him or her that you are qualified and available for employment.

Because of the highly structured classification of employees in these sectors, most applicants believe that once you submit your application, there is little you can do but wait out the process. However, in many important ways government employers are no different from any other employers. When faced with a hiring decision, they want to employ the best person for the job and one who will be a good fit with the existing organization. So, while the application processes and hiring conditions are definitely more codified than in the private sector, it does not mean you cannot put a face to your application or a voice to your name with a visit or a phone call. If you are near enough to visit a potential employment site, by all means do so. You may get a tour and an opportunity to meet some staff. Remember to be on your best behavior and respectful to every person you meet. Don't believe that your professional behavior and attitude are to be saved for the hiring officer. Everyone with whom you interact has the potential to influence the decision to hire you.

Before trying to find where the jobs are, you have to decide in which level of government or area of law enforcement you are most interested. Once that has been determined, you can take advantage of some specific tips for finding jobs in each category.

Local and State

Civil service exams, which are administered by individual states, are required of almost all police and detectives at this level. You can find out about upcoming test dates through your local civil service commission, which is usually located in your town or city hall personnel office. You can also visit your state's website, where you should find civil service exam information listed on the human resources or personnel page. To prepare for this exam, it's a good idea to study and take practice exams so that you're familiar with the subject matter and types of questions that will be asked. While exams will vary by state, you can expect questions about judgment, memory, picture identification, face matches, grammar, reading comprehension, and mathematics. Don't worry, there are guides that can help you, such as Barron's *How to Prepare for the Police Officer Examination*. In addition, some states have produced guides to help you prepare for their specific exams. You can purchase many of these at your local bookstore or at online bookstores such as amazon.com or barnesandnoble.com.

When it comes to locating law enforcement jobs in your city or town, here is one place where the Internet may not be of much help since many smaller communities do not have extensive websites, if they have one at all. Once again, visit your town or city hall personnel office for information on available openings. Don't just visit once; establish a routine in which you visit every couple of weeks, depending on when the job boards are updated. While you're there, you may want to request an informational meeting with the chief of police or a representative. Introduce yourself, and let these people get to know you and witness your motivation, enthusiasm, knowledge, and commitment to the field of local law enforcement. Find out about upcoming opportunities that may not be posted yet, and learn what you can do to position yourself as a top candidate.

Job openings at the state level are usually advertised on each state's human resources page on the Internet, or you can visit the office in person. Lots of good websites provide job vacancy announcements in state law enforcement (see Chapter 3). A particularly good one is The Official Directory of State Patrol and State Police Sites at statetroopersdirectory.com. This site links you to individual state police/highway patrol Web pages as well as to each state's overall website. In many cases, you will also find specific recruiting information for state police and links to special police units such as forensics, K-9, and criminal investigation.

Most local and state openings will also be posted in your local newspaper, so get into the habit of checking these once a week, preferably on Sundays, when the classified section is largest. If you're interested in working in local or state law enforcement outside of where you're living now, you may want to visit careerbuilder.com, where you will be connected to newspaper classifieds from around the country.

Federal

Within the federal government there are approximately sixty police agencies, and each is responsible for enforcing different kinds of laws. So, your first step is to investigate the various individual agencies, the area of enforcement for which they are responsible, and the types of employment they have to offer. Most of the agencies with which you are likely to be familiar fall under either the Department of Justice, which includes the FBI, or the Department of the Treasury, which includes the Secret Service. These agencies have created their own websites at which you will discover comprehensive information on the mission of the agency, types of employment, qualifications, and application procedures. Here's a list of some in which you may be interested:

Popular Federal Agencies
Department of Justice (usdoj.gov)
Drug Enforcement Administration (dea.gov)
FBI (fbi.gov)
U.S. Marshals Service (usmarshalls.gov)
Department of the Treasury (treasury.gov)
Alcohol and Tobacco Tax and Trade Bureau (ttb.gov)
Internal Revenue Service (irs.gov)
Financial Crimes Enforcement Network (fincen.gov)
Department of Homeland Security (dhs.gov)
Customs and Border Protection (cbp.gov)
U.S. Secret Service (secretservice.gov)
Citizenship and Immigration Services (uscis.gov)

Other Federal Agencies and Departments
Central Intelligence Agency (cia.gov)
Department of State (state.gov)
Bureau of Diplomatic Security (state.gov/m/ds)
Federal Aviation Administration (faa.gov)
Federal Trade Commission (ftc.gov)
National Park Service (nps.gov)
U.S. Park Police (nps.gov/uspp)
National Security Agency (nsa.gov)
Securities and Exchange Commission (sec.gov)
U.S. Environmental Protection Agency (epa.gov)
U.S. Fish and Wildlife Service (fws.gov)
U.S. Postal Inspection Service (usps.com/postalinspectors)

Canadian Federal Agencies
Canadian Security Intelligence Service (csis-scrs.gc.ca)
Canada Revenue Agency (cra-arc.gc.ca)
Canada Border Services Agency (cbsa-asfc.gc.ca)
Royal Canadian Mounted Police (rcmp-grc.gc.ca)

You will also find a listing of U.S. military police departments at militarypolice.com.

The federal government lists its current openings on its website at usajobs.com. In Canada, visit jobs-emplois.gc.ca for federal job postings. These sites are valuable because they centrally locate job listings available at all of the government agencies. It may be worth reviewing some of these job vacancy announcements to get a sense of the variety and scope of opportunities available. The announcements are somewhat lengthy, but they contain a wealth of information and are all presented in the following format, which makes them easier to track:

- Salary range and promotion potential
- Specific duties (Carefully review this section to see if you would like this particular kind of work.)
- Qualifications (If you find that you're not qualified for a position in which you're interested, how can you become qualified? Do you need a year of graduate course work? A year of law enforcement experience? It may at first seem frustrating to be unqualified, but at least you'll have a plan of action if you want to pursue this option.)
- Knowledge, skills, and abilities required (Pay particular attention to this section, and match the requirements against the results of your self-assessment from Chapter 1.)
- Conditions of employment (This section tells you whether drug testing or a physical examination is required, whether you will be expected to qualify for and carry firearms, how much overtime can be anticipated, if a uniform is required, and so forth.)
- Application procedures

Applying used to be a much more difficult—and dreaded—process than it is now. The preferred method for most federal jobs is online application. For most federal positions, you can apply with either a résumé or the Optional Application for Federal Employment (OF 612). A word of caution here: as you will see, the job descriptions are quite detailed and specific. When you apply, be sure to indicate all of the experience and skills you have that qualify you for the job. In most cases, your résumé does not reflect everything you've done or are capable of doing. Therefore, it may behoove you to fill out the more detailed application form instead of, or in addition to, using your résumé. It is often worth checking with the agency to see which format is preferred. The USAJobs website (usajobs.com) provides convenient online and downloadable application formats. If you decide to use one of the applications, be sure to complete it carefully and with no errors.

Possible Employers

As noted previously, virtually all law enforcement jobs are in local, state, and federal government agencies. At the local level, the town or city police department is the primary employer, accounting for approximately 82 percent of police patrol officers in the country and 64 percent of detectives and criminal investigators. Local county sheriff's departments employ more than 99 percent of all sheriffs and deputy sheriffs.

Among the fifty states, there are twenty-six highway patrol agencies, twenty-three state police agencies, and one department of public safety (in Hawaii). These account for approximately 15 percent of the police officers hired in this country and more than 11 percent of detectives and criminal investigators. In addition to police, other state agencies that employ law enforcement personnel include:

College and university campuses
Department of Agriculture
Department of Alcohol Beverage Control
Department of Environmental Resources
Department of Finance
Department of Industrial Relations, including:
   Division of Labor Law Enforcement and Fair Employment
   Practices
   Department of Insurance
   Department of Investments
Department of Justice, including:
   Bureau of Criminal Investigation
   Bureau of Narcotics
   Department of Motor Vehicles
   Department of Parks and Recreation
Department of Public Health, including:
   Bureau of Food and Drug Inspection
   Department of Social Services
   Port Authority

According to the most recent report from the Bureau of Justice Statistics, as of 2000, federal agencies employed 93,446 full-time federal officers. The majority of those, 37,208, were employed in investigation/enforcement, followed by police response and patrol with 20,955. The largest employers of federal officers, in order, were the Immigration and Naturalization Service, Federal Bureau of Prisons, U.S. Customs Service, and FBI. Geographic location is a significant factor in these numbers. About half of these officers were employed in Texas, California, the District of Columbia, New York, and Florida.

Possible Job Titles

The list that follows is purposely extensive to demonstrate the variety and scope of positions available to you in using your education and interest in criminal justice within the specific path of law enforcement.

Local and State

As you can see, the possibilities extend well beyond "police officer" and "special agent."

Public Safety

Airport security officer
Animal control officer
Booking officer
Communications specialist
Community policing officer
Community service officer
Constable
Crossing guard
Deputy sheriff
Emergency dispatcher/911 call taker
K-9 officer
Law enforcement officer
Mounted police officer
Park ranger
Park security officer

Patrol cadet
Peace officer
Police cadet
Police dispatcher
Police inspector
Police manager
Police officer
Public safety officer
School resource officer
Sheriff
State trooper
Traffic safety officer
University/campus police officer
Water patrol officer

Investigative

Animal treatment investigator
Arson investigator
Detective

Investigator
Narcotics investigator
Police detective

Compliance

Bank examiner
Compliance manager
Discrimination investigator
Environmental conservation officer

Fish and game warden
Gaming enforcement officer
Safety inspector

Specialist

Ballistics expert
Crime intelligence analyst

Forensic chemist
Forensic pathologist

Criminalist
Criminologist
Document examiner
Fingerprint examiner

Polygraph examiner
Serology specialist
Toolmark specialist

Technical
Crime lab analyst
Crime lab technician

Crime scene investigator
Technician

Federal
Federal Agents
Air Force special agent
Alcohol, Tobacco, and Firearms agent
Army special agent
Border patrol agent
CIA agent
Customs agent

Drug Enforcement agent
FBI agent
Foreign Service officer
Fish and Wildlife Service
Special agent
Secret Service agent

Compliance
Adjudication officer
Bank examiner
Compliance manager
Consumer safety inspector
Consumer safety officer
Customs canine enforcement officer
Customs inspector
Deportation officer

Discrimination investigator
Environmental health inspector
FAA aviation safety inspector
Fish and game warden
Food inspector
Immigration and naturalization
  inspector

Investigative
Federal investigations investigator
Inspector general investigator
Internal revenue internal security
Internet crime investigator
Narcotics investigator

Naval investigator
Postal service investigator
Revenue officer investigator
Securities investigator

Protective
Capitol police officer
Federal protective service officer
Military officer
National park ranger

Secret service uniformed
  officer
U.S. marshal

Related Occupations

Still other occupations could tap into your interest in the enforcement of laws and regulations in settings within and outside of the government. They include:

Contracts administrator
Employment agency recruiter
Housing/tenant representative
Photographer
Public relations officer

Real estate portfolio manager
Records manager
Research analyst/statistician
Sanitation officer
Sexual assault prevention educator

Professional Associations

Listed in this section are some of the associations that relate to careers in law enforcement. For more information about these professional associations, either visit the websites listed or consult the *Encyclopedia of Associations*, published by Thomson Gale. Review the Members/Purpose notes for each organization to determine if it pertains to your interests. Membership in one or more of these organizations may gain you access to job listings, networking opportunities, and employment search services. Some provide information at no charge, but if you want to receive specific publications that list job opportunities, you may need to join. If you're still in college, check for student member rates.

American Academy of Forensic Sciences
410 North 21st St.
Colorado Springs, CO 80904-2798
http://aafs.org
Members/Purpose: A professional society dedicated to the application of science to the law. Membership includes physicians, criminalists, toxicologists, attorneys, dentists, physical anthropologists, document examiners, engineers, psychiatrists, educators, and others who practice and perform research in the many diverse fields relating to forensic science. Members reside in all fifty states, Canada, and fifty-six other countries throughout the world.
Publications: *Journal of Forensic Sciences*; job postings
Training: AAFS annual meeting, held every February, at which time more than 500 scientific papers, breakfast seminars, workshops, and other special events are presented

American Association of State Troopers
1949 Raymond Diehl Rd.
Tallahassee, FL 32308
statetroopers.org
Members/Purpose: To improve conditions of law enforcement officers by solidifying their strength and promoting their mutual welfare.
Publication: *Trooper Connection*
Training: Scholarships available for qualified dependents of members

American Federation of Police and Concerned Citizens
6350 Horizon Dr.
Titusville, FL 32790
aphf.org/afp_cc.html
Members/Purpose: Governmental and private law enforcement officers united for the prevention of crime and the apprehension of criminals.
Publication: *Police Times* magazine
Training: Biennial conference

Association of National Park Rangers
P.O. Box 108
Larned, KS 67550-0108
anpr.org
Members/Purpose: An organization created to communicate for, about, and with park rangers and to promote and enhance the park ranger profession and its spirit.
Publications: *Ranger* magazine; job postings
Training: Facilitated mentoring program; annual meeting

Association of Public-Safety Communications Officials International, Inc.
351 North Williamson Blvd.
Daytona Beach, FL 32114-1112
apcointl.org
Members/Purpose: Dedicated to the enhancement of public safety communications. Membership comprises employees of public safety organizations, including 911 emergency call centers; municipal, state, county, and federal public safety agencies; emergency medical services; emergency management centers; transportation agencies and facilities; highway maintenance; forestry services; and manufacturers of public safety communication products.
Publications: *Public Safety Communications* magazine; job postings

Training: Annual international conference and exposition, plus three regional conferences in the United States and one in Canada; APCO Institute provides customized education and training programs, technical and operations publications, and information services for members

Canadian Association of Violent Crime Analysts
cavca.net

Members/Purpose: To encourage and develop cooperation among police organizations in the professional and ethical use of criminal investigative analysis and related techniques; to promote and maintain high standards of ethics, integrity, honor and conduct; to provide a clearing house for ideas and experience, as well as promoting and participating in research and discussion on all aspects of violent crime analysis.

Publications: None

Training: None offered

Canadian Professional Police Association
WaterPark Place
20 Bay St., Suite 1500
Toronto, ON M5J 2N8
cppa-acpp.ca

Members/Purpose: The national voice for police across Canada, the association provides a collective support network, advocates for equitable distribution of resources, and serves as liaison with the international police community.

Publications: *Express* magazine

Training: Conferences and meetings

Federal Criminal Investigators Association
P.O. Box 23400
Washington, DC 20026
fedcia.org

Members/Purpose: Dedicated to promoting professional excellence through training and communication, enhancing the image of federal law enforcement officers, fostering cooperation among all law enforcement professionals, and providing a fraternal environment for the advancement of the membership and the community.

Publications: *The Federal Investigator*, job postings

Training: National conference; training seminars

Federal Law Enforcement Officers Association
P.O. Box 236
Lewisberry, PA 17339
fleoa.org
Members/Purpose: Provides access to legal advice and representation and gives voice to the concerns of more than 600,000 enforcement officers on matters critical to working federal agents.
Publication: Newsletter
Training: Scholarships are available to high school graduates who are children of current, retired, or deceased federal law enforcement officers.

High Technology Crime Investigation Association
4021 Woodcreek Oaks Blvd., Suite 156, #209
Roseville, CA 95749
htcia.org
Members/Purpose: Designed to encourage, promote, aid, and affect the voluntary interchange of data, information, experience, ideas, and knowledge about methods, processes, and techniques relating to investigations and security in advanced technologies among members.
Publications: Job postings
Training: International conference; regional seminars

International Association of Campus Law Enforcement Administrators (IACLEA)
342 North Main St.
West Hartford, CT 06117-2507
iaclea.org
Members/Purpose: Advances public safety for educational institutions by providing educational resources, advocacy, and professional development to its members.
Publications: *Campus Law Enforcement* journal; job postings
Training: Annual conferences and meetings. Professional training and development is a high priority for IACLEA. The annual conference, regional meetings, and state workshops provide a variety of training opportunities in all phases of campus security, public safety, and law enforcement administration.

International Association of Crime Analysts
9218 Metcalf Ave., #364
Overland Park, KS 66212
iaca.net

Members/Purpose: Organized to enhance effectiveness and consistency in the fields of crime and intelligence analysis.
Publications: Articles; job postings
Training: Certification program; annual conference

International Association of Financial Crimes Investigators
1020 Suncast Ln., Suite 102
El Dorado Hills, CA 95762
iafci.org
Members/Purpose: This nonprofit international organization provides services and an environment within which information about financial fraud, fraud investigation, and fraud prevention methods can be collected, exchanged, and taught for the common good of the financial payment industry and our global society.
Publication: Newsletter
Training: Annual training seminar

International Association of Women Police
P.O. Box 184
Marble Hill, GA 30148
iawp.org
Members/Purpose: Strives to ensure equity for women in the criminal justice field by using, investing, and celebrating the individual strengths, talents, and skills of its members.
Publications: *Women Police* magazine; job postings
Training: Annual conference; regional training events

International Crime Scene Investigators Association
PMB 385
15774 S. LaGrange Rd.
Orland Park, IL 60462
icsia.org
Members/Purpose: To encourage the exchange of information useful in crime-scene-related matters, and to improve the level of expertise in the field by providing timely answers through membership participation.
Publications: *The Examiner* newsletter; job postings
Training: Training classes through a host agency; Web-based online training courses

International Footprint Association
P.O. Box 1652
Walnut, CA 91788-1652
thomsonwebdesign.com/footprinterorg/index
Members/Purpose: Promotes and encourages fellowship, respect, cooperation, and helpfulness between all arms of law enforcement (local, county, state, and federal) and all others (individuals, business persons, and professionals) who are sympathetic with and understanding toward law enforcement and all its agencies.
Publications: None
Training: None available

National Animal Control Association
P. O. Box 480851
Kansas City, MO 64148
nacanet.org
Members/Purpose: Members include animal control officers, animal control directors, and shelter directors. NACA's purpose is to support the public health and safety mandate of animal control departments nationwide while also providing leadership on issues surrounding responsible pet ownership. The organization was formed in 1978 to provide training for all those involved with animal regulatory agencies and to provide a means for communication between those agencies.
Publication: Bimonthly magazine *NACA News*
Training: Annual national training conference; three-level animal control academy offered at locations all around the country; also, specialized courses on topics such as bite stick use, chemical immobilization, and humane euthanasia

National Association of Blacks in Criminal Justice
1801 Fayetville St.
Durham, NC 27707-3129
nabcj.org
Members/Purpose: Established to examine and act upon the needs, concerns, and contributions of African Americans and other minorities as they relate to the administration of equal justice. The NABCJ seeks to focus attention on relevant legislation, law enforcement, prosecution, and defense-related needs and practices, with emphasis on the courts, corrections, and the prevention of crime. Among its chief concerns are the general welfare and increased influence of African Americans in and

on the administration of justice. It also coordinates the efforts of any and all organizations that are concerned with the elimination of injustice within the justice system.

Publications: Newsletters

Training: Annual conference and training institute

National Association of Police Organizations Inc.

750 First St. NE, Suite 920

Washington, DC 20002

napo.org

Members/Purpose: A coalition of police unions and associations from across the United States that serves to advance the interests of America's law enforcement officers through legislative and legal advocacy, political action, and education.

Publications: *The Washington Report*, newsletter

Training: Seminars throughout the year; annual convention

National Association of School Resource Officers

1951 Woodlane Dr.

St. Paul, MN 55125

nasro.org

Members/Purpose: NASRO is dedicated to the children of America; its mission is to break down the barriers between law enforcement and youth by establishing better communication about the legal system.

Publications: *Resourcer* magazine; lesson plans for members to use in classrooms

Training: School resource training classes; annual conference

National Black Police Association

3251 Mt. Pleasant St. NW, 2nd Floor

Washington, DC 20010-2103

blackpolice.org

Members/Purpose: A nationwide organization of African American police associations dedicated to the promotion of justice, fairness, and effectiveness in law enforcement.

Publications: *What to Do When Stopped by the Police; Sergeant Assessment Center, Volumes I and II; Police Brutality, A Strategy to Stop the Violence*

Training: An annual education and training conference for its members and others interested in law enforcement, as well as regional training conferences

National Constables Association
16 Stonybrookr Dr.
Levittown, PA 19055
angelfire.com/la/nationalconstable/
Members/Purpose: To unite the constables of America; to help preserve
and clearly define the role of the constable in the delivery of the justice
system; and to train, educate, and upgrade the quality of performance.
Publication: Newsletter
Training: National convention

National Criminal Justice Association
720 7th St. NW, 3rd Floor
Washington, DC 20001-3706
ncja.org
Members/Purpose: A special-interest group that represents states on crime
control and public safety matters. The NCJA's work focuses primarily on
helping develop and implement national policy in the criminal justice
field and on helping states address related problems.
Publications: *NCJA InfoLetter; Justice Bulletin; The Beacon*
Training: National forum; internships available; regional training seminars

National Drug Enforcement Officers Association
Drug Enforcement Administration
Office of Training/TRDS
FBI Academy, P.O. Box 1475
Quantico, VA 22134-1475
ndeoa.org
Members/Purpose: To promote cooperation, education, and exchange of
information among all law enforcement agencies involved in the
enforcement of controlled substance laws.
Publications: None
Training: Annual training conference; numerous training sessions
throughout the year on a variety of topics, including surveillance, gangs,
investigations, computers and the Internet, and more

National Police Canine Association
P.O. Box 264
Robert, LA 70455
npca.net
Members/Purpose: Established to promote and assist in the utilization of
police service dogs in prevention and detection of crime; promote

educational programs in the use of police service dogs in law enforcement; provide assistance to law enforcement agencies in the implementation of police service dogs; and promote a task-related, minimum standard of certification of police service dogs.

Publications: Training articles

Training: National training seminar

National Sheriffs' Association

1450 Duke St.

Alexandria, VA 22314-3490

sheriffs.org

Members/Purpose: A nonprofit organization dedicated to raising the level of professionalism in the criminal justice field. Through the years, the NSA has been involved in numerous programs to enable sheriffs, their deputies, chiefs of police, and others in the field of criminal justice to perform their jobs in the best possible manner and to better serve the people of their cities/counties or jurisdictions.

Publications: *Sheriff* magazine; *Sheriff Directory* book or CD-ROM

Training: Seminars and training on topics such as school violence and jail privatization; annual conference and exhibition

North American Police Work Dog Association

4222 Manchester Ave.

Perry, OH 44081

napwda.com

Members/Purpose: The NAPWDA is composed of law enforcement officers throughout the United States and several other countries who are dedicated to assisting police work dog teams throughout the world.

Publications: None

Training: National and state workshops

Path 2: The Courts

The Case for Great Careers

Criminal justice is such an exciting college major and a rewarding career field because of the diversity of occupational areas that it offers. This chapter highlights a large number of jobs surrounding the legal system and court proceedings, including probation and parole officers, attorneys, victim advocates, bailiffs, court reporters, paralegals, and legal researchers. Juvenile justice occupations are covered separately in Chapter 9.

Of the five career paths presented in Chapters 6 through 10, the courts present the greatest number of open and varied occupations. Students exploring careers in the court system will find that all of these occupations are strongly interpersonal. In addition to working with people, you'll be helping to ensure that our court system functions the way it was meant to: people are presumed innocent, the trial process is fair and orderly, and sanctions meted out to those convicted are appropriate within the law. Criminal justice majors working in the court system help in the same way that law enforcement officials do: by preventing crime and protecting the public. Their part in the effective operation of our court system can serve not only as a corrective but also as a deterrent to criminal activity.

Something else the court system shares with law enforcement careers is that the area of work has been glamorized by the media. The courtroom is almost always depicted as "high drama," fast-paced, and full of action. The truth is that working in the court system is demanding, and there is often an expectation to produce high-quality work under pressure of time. The real excitement of working in the courts comes from skillful teamwork, daily exercise of your growing interpersonal skills, and opportunities to employ your analytical mind and to make decisions. But as with most other jobs, the court system is not nonstop excitement. It is a blend of tasks including desk duty and paperwork that provide variety, stimulation, and a never-ending stream of new situations for those committed to the job.

As with any of the criminal justice career paths, if you are interested in working in the courts, plan ahead. Talk to your professors and your career counselor in college about connecting with a local judge, bailiff, or parole officer. Meet with these professionals for an informational interview. Prepare some good questions (see Chapter 3 on networking), and begin to build your understanding of court-related criminal justice occupations. Courts vary from state to state, between state and federal levels, and sometimes even from community to community. Talking to people who work in the courts and perhaps volunteering or doing a recognized internship will give you the insight you need to make a good decision about your future in this important area of criminal justice.

How Courts Work

All courts are part of the judicial branch of government and are authorized to decide the cases brought before them. Courts (and those who administer them) decide cases based on laws of the state and the U.S. Constitution. They try to be fair, consistent, and efficient in administering justice to all. In thinking about employment in the court system, it's important to remember there are more than sixteen thousand federal and state courts in the United States. Each has its own jurisdiction—the limited area in which it can make decisions. When this authority to make decisions is challenged by participants in the legal process, we have trial courts, appellate courts, and courts of last resort at both the state and federal levels, including the U.S. Supreme Court.

An individual's arrest is generally the first step in a case moving into the court system. Trial courts rule based on the verbal testimony and physical evidence presented, and they can hear both civil and criminal cases. Civil cases have to do with injustices of one person against another, while criminal cases are about injustices that affect the rights of all of us.

Above trial courts in the hierarchy of the court system are the appellate courts. *Appellate* means just what it sounds and looks like—"appeal." These courts review the decisions of trial courts and how the law was interpreted and determine whether the decision was well founded in the law.

Supreme courts (both state and federal) handle appeals from courts under them, and their decisions are binding on all lower courts.

The U.S. Information Agency publishes an electronic journal entitled *Issues of Democracy*. An entire issue devoted to "How U.S. Courts Work" includes noted articles on the functions of the court system, key players in the judicial process, and common law and civil law systems. You can find all this at http://usinfo.state.gov/journals/itdhr/0999/ijde/ijde0999.htm.

The Courtroom Process

The court process begins with a preliminary hearing. During this initial court appearance, police often turn over their evidence to a prosecutor because they believe the evidence justifies arrest. A judge or magistrate then decides if the case warrants the court's attention.

If the case is deemed sufficiently sound for the suspect's arrest, then the suspect is arraigned. If a judge or magistrate does not feel the evidence is sufficient, then the suspect is released. Arraignment is the formal charge of the crime. This is the point at which the person charged pleads guilty or not guilty. Once the plea is entered, the court must decide how to handle the person charged. Some people are released to their homes and families on their own recognizance because the court feels they pose no threat to society and they are considered good risks for future court appearances. If, however, the judge or magistrate believes there is a possibility of nonappearance or any risk associated with releasing the suspect back into society, the judge may ask for bail to be posted. The amount of bail is related to the seriousness of the offense and the risk posed by not incarcerating the suspect. For danger-ous crimes or highly suspect individuals, bail is not allowed, and the indi-vidual is jailed until the date of the court case.

Sometimes, when the suspect pleads guilty, the court (the judge, the sus-pect and his or her attorneys, and the prosecutor) will work out a plea bar-gain, which generally results in a less severe sentence than could have been imposed had the case gone to trial. The plea bargain decides the sentence and ends the trial process. The reduction in the severity of punishment is a recognition of saving the court's time and money in bringing the judicial pro-cess to a quicker, yet still judicially sound, close. Of course, if the suspect does not plead guilty, then the case must go to court trial.

Not very many cases actually reach the trial stage, and not all trials involve a jury. Some cases are conducted as "bench trials" in front of the judge, who decides the sentence after hearing all the evidence and arguments. In either type of trial, if the decision is not guilty, the defendant is released.

Of course, if the defendant is found guilty, by either the judge or the jury, a sentencing follows. The sentence could be a fine, probation, or jail time. Conditions of the sentence include stipulations of time and/or money or pro-bation. Once sentenced, the defendant and his or her lawyers may appeal the conviction to a higher court.

Once part of a sentence has been served, the individual serving the sen-tence may become eligible for revocation of the sentence or some form of conditional release (probation or parole). Probation and parole involve strict conditions that are designed to help the convicted individual safely transition back into mainstream society. Violation of these conditions can result in further punishment. Once the probation or parole period is successfully completed, the parolee is discharged, and the case is closed.

Probation and Parole Officers

Probation and Parole Officers have direct contact with criminals prior to sentencing and after release from incarceration.

Definition of the Career Path

The probation officer enters the court process before a criminal is sentenced. The officer writes a report recommending the types and conditions of sentencing, which may include probation. If that is the case, then the probation officer will supervise that offender, or probationer. The officer often works with the offender's family and even the person's employer to help everyone understand the conditions surrounding the probation. The probation officer enforces the conditions of probation and helps to guide and encourage the offender in making the necessary social adjustments. The probationer and the probation officer meet regularly to record and discuss the offender's progress.

The parole officer's job is remarkably similar except that the client has been jailed and his or her release is conditional. The parole officer helps the client to readjust to life in the community and observe the parole conditions to avoid returning to jail.

This is a great field with fair employment prospects because we, as a nation, are concerned about the overcrowding of our prisons. These positions are part of the solution of avoiding prison and also reducing prison populations. Both positions serve to enhance the efficiency of the criminal justice system. With experience on the job and continued education, including a master's degree, you can be eligible for promotion to a district or regional administrator.

Working Conditions

You'll walk a delicate line between social worker and rules enforcer. It's a constant balancing act between caring and discipline—firm yet fair. This is definitely challenging work, but it can be deeply rewarding, as you may be a catalyst in turning someone's life around.

While although you may be confronted with some of the starkest realities of negative human behavior, your job is to provide stability and structure to allow people to regain their freedom and dignity. You will find the frustrations and challenges of this job very difficult to handle unless you come to your own personal philosophy of what your role should be vis-à-vis your clients. Parole and probation officers develop their own individual styles for working with their clientele, and most of these ways of doing business are a combination of that individual's personality and understanding of the job.

Personal counseling, referrals to community resources, home visits, interviews and briefings of families, extensive telephone work, and detailed record keeping are the day-to-day activities that will occupy most of your time.

Training and Qualifications

Probation and parole officers are required to have a bachelor's degree. Frequently the degree is in criminal justice or other social sciences such as human behavior, psychology, anthropology, or sociology. Probation and parole jobs are often filled on the basis of the results of civil service testing. Talk to your college career office or local civil service office for specific eligibility requirements and test dates.

Most probation officers must complete a training program sponsored by the state or federal government, after which a certification test may be required. Applicants are generally required to be at least twenty-one years of age. Strong writing skills are useful because probation and parole officers must prepare reports. Computer skills are also important, since technology plays an increasing role in this type of work.

Probation officers generally work as trainees or serve a probationary period for up to a year before being offered permanent positions. A typical agency has several levels of probation and parole officers and supervisors. To advance through the ranks, a graduate degree may be helpful, particularly a master's degree in criminal justice, social work, or psychology.

Victim Advocate

Victim services, or victim advocacy, represents an exciting development in the court system and a job field that is still defining itself, still setting professional standards, and growing by leaps and bounds. You can enter this field on the ground floor and become part of its history.

Definition of the Career Path

Victim advocacy provides an opportunity to serve crime victims by performing the important job of sending notification of a perpetrator's probation or parole and offering a unique and important overview of our legal system from the standpoint not of the offender but of the victim.

To receive services from a victim advocate, crime victims must register with the state office of victim advocacy (which may be called victim services or a similar name). In most situations, they are alerted to their rights as victims by the state's attorney general prior to sentencing of the offender. Following this registration, the office of victim services provides the victim with notifications of probation or parole of the offender as well as of the right to comment to the parole or probation board on these decisions. Victims also are afforded the right to be notified if an offender has escaped or been transferred to another facility.

Advocates represent victims' interests in other ways as well. During the trial, they provide victims with information and support that may affect their decision to testify. Advocates know full well that a victim may suffer, rather than benefit, from the prosecutorial process. For example, in a domestic violence case, the offender could be the sole financial support of the family. The victim advocate may reluctantly support intensive mediation and supervision rather than incarceration, as incarceration may mean that the victim and any children become penniless and further victimized.

Working Conditions

This is obviously a job with considerable pressure. Serious crimes and social problems, including rape and domestic violence, drug and alcohol abuse, incest, child abuse, and a host of other heinous offenses, are the daily work of victim advocates. You will be exposed frequently to disturbing crisis situations. It takes strength and moral courage to be able to support and inform victims day after day in the face of such egregious events.

As with any other direct service dealing with human problems, building trust, being empathetic, reducing client stress, supporting your client, and presenting options without making decisions for your client are essential skills. In addition to your personal skills as a counselor and advocate, you will need to have in-depth knowledge of legal policy as it relates to victim services in your state and to develop a network of community resources that can provide support.

Training and Qualifications

Because the field of victim advocacy is relatively new, there are many ways to access these jobs. First, you may simply use your desire to work for victims' rights and your criminal justice degree to enter the field. Many victims' rights offices will provide extensive in-service training in specific issues and techniques. To stay competitive as an employee, you'll want to continue your self-development with additional course work on your own time.

Job seekers with either an associate's or a bachelor's degree in criminal justice may want to consider one of the new certificate programs in victim services offered by some two- and four-year colleges. These certificate programs (often an offshoot of a fully developed two-year degree program) offer courses in victimology, social problems, psychology, diversity issues, the grieving process, and criminal law. Many include fieldwork or a practicum that you can accomplish on the job. A good example of the variety of programs offered can be seen at the website of the Kansas City Kansas Community College Victim Services Program at kckcc.cc.ks.us/ss/sspvicti.htm. This program, the first in the Midwest, is one of the more extensive programs offered and a good benchmark for your consideration.

Bailiff

Bailiff is a position you might not have thought of during your criminal justice studies. It's worth your consideration, especially as an entry-level position, if you're eager to start your career in criminal justice and are interested in the courts as your arena of work. Remember that the United States has more than sixteen thousand courts of various types, and more than a quarter of them utilize the position of bailiff. There may be an opening for you!

Definition of the Career Path

The bailiff is an interesting position from a historical perspective. It dates from the thirteenth century in England, where bailiffs were used as night watchmen to patrol the streets and protect against fire. "Nine o'clock and all's well" was the bailiff's cry, and the populace could then sleep worry-free. In the event of a crime, a fire, or some other incident, the bailiff would rouse the public with his alarm.

The bailiff in today's courtroom still serves as an alert watchman over the proceedings, charged with keeping order. Bailiffs accompany defendants into and out of the courtroom and serve to prevent their escape. Likewise, they are responsible for the safety of juries; they escort jurors into and out of the courtroom and remain while the jury is sequestered. They also protect jurors from the public and the media, if need be. It is the bailiff who announces the entry of the judge into the courtroom and calls each witness to the stand. The opening words "Oyez, oyez" are Middle English and are a living reminder of the heritage of our legal system.

Working Conditions

While most bailiffs would say that day to day they are comfortable and relaxed in their jobs, new entrants to the field must weigh the realities and possible worst-case scenarios of any prospective career. You do carry a gun in this position, and that weapon is not just an ornament. Courtrooms are places of extremely heightened emotions, and outbursts often occur. That's why physical fitness and alertness are stressed. Although you hope nothing happens, you need to be ready and have a plan if something does. In this job, standard procedures and a fairly orderly and static workplace always contain the threat of some untoward action or event for which you must be ready. Anticipation is everything!

Training and Qualifications

In many instances, you will find that the qualifications for this position are similar to those of an entry-level law enforcement officer, including graduation from a police academy and passing physical and written examinations. In fact, bailiffs serving in federal courtrooms are U.S. marshals; they have the same jobs as bailiffs in other courts but their prisoners, juries, and judges are all federal.

Bailiffs must remain alert and must be well schooled in the use of a handgun. At one time a high school degree was sufficient, but competition and increasingly higher educational attainment among law enforcement professionals have raised the hurdle on minimum qualifications.

Court Reporter

Definition of the Career Path

You've seen court reporters, often located between the attorneys' tables and the judge's bench, using a stenotype machine to record court proceedings. The stenotype machine is an unusual typewriter that allows court reporters to press multiple keys at a time to record combinations of letters that represent sounds, words, or phrases. These symbols are recorded on computer discs or CD-ROMs, which are then translated and displayed as text using computer-aided transcription. Sometimes the stenotype machine is linked directly to a computer for real-time transcription so that the text being recorded is instantly available to closed-circuit television viewers, hearing-impaired audiences, courts, classrooms, or meetings. Of course, accuracy is imperative, as one person is responsible for the official transcript. You have to be good at what you do when what you do is court reporting!

Because the accuracy of your transcription is the measure of your competence as a reporter, it takes only one or two incidents of carelessness to lose any possibility of future job referrals. The best court reporters speak of attaining an almost trancelike state, in which words enter their ears and move through their fingers onto the keyboard effortlessly. Most say that this sense of "flow" is one of the most attractive parts of their job.

Electronic reporting refers to the use of audio equipment to record court proceedings. The court reporter monitors the process, takes notes to identify speakers, and listens to the recording to ensure clarity and quality. The equipment used may include analog tape recorders or digital equipment. Electronic reporters and transcribers often are responsible for producing a subsequent written transcript of the recorded proceeding.

Another method of court reporting is called voice writing. Using this method, a court reporter speaks directly into a voice silencer, which is a handheld mask containing a microphone. The mask prevents the reporter from being heard while repeating the testimony into the recorder. Voice writers record everything that is said by judges, witnesses, attorneys, and other parties to a proceeding, including gestures and emotional reactions.

Although it's common to see the court reporter on television and in the movies as well as in television news of actual trials, we seldom see the majority of court reporters who work outside the court. Many work as freelancers, taking depositions in attorneys' offices and recording meetings and procedures from government agencies. Some specialists in the field, called stenocaptioners, work for television and caption live sporting events, news broadcasts, or emergency newscasts.

Working Conditions

This is indoor work in nice surroundings—generally climate controlled. One concern worth noting is that the job requires you to maintain a certain body position for long periods. Strains to the back, neck, or eyes may result, and there is always the possibility of some repetitive-motion syndrome (such as carpal tunnel syndrome). This can be a serious hazard because your entire career depends on your ability to type. Whereas most of us who type as part of our jobs could compensate and work around a repetitive-motion injury, for a court reporter, such an injury means no work. On the positive side, the workplace is becoming more ergonomically astute, and furniture and computer placement design are increasingly able to minimize these risks.

The workweek is a standard forty hours, with frequent possibilities for overtime, especially during busy court periods. Approximately one in four court reporters works part-time, and many are self-employed, which may result in irregular but self-determined hours.

Because your work involves no emotional commitment (in fact, objectivity is a requirement), most court reporters find their lives sharply divided between work and nonwork activities. Likewise, since there is no promotional ladder (other than professional certifications), you'll note an absence of politics.

Training and Qualifications

More than 300 postsecondary vocational and technical colleges offer the court reporter training program. Approximately 110 of these are approved by the National Court Reporters Association (NCRA), and those programs offer training in computer-aided transcription and real-time reporting. NCRA-sanctioned programs require students to be able to capture at least 225 words per minute; court reporters in the federal government employment system must be able to capture a minimum of 205 words a minute.

You'll need at least an associate's degree, and more commonly a bachelor's degree, to enter the field. Some states require that a court reporter be a notary public or a certified court reporter (CCR). To earn the CCR designation, you must pass a state certification test administered by a board of examiners. The NCRA also offers other professional certifications such as registered professional reporter (RPR) and certified real-time reporter (CRR). The American Association of Electronic Reporters and Transcribers offers voluntary certification of electronic court reporters.

Learning the skill of court reporting requires lots of study and practice, practice, practice. You need superb grammatical skills and lots of patience. The work, in addition to its physical demands, requires intense concentration because your performance directly influences the decision rendered and you must certify that your transcript is an accurate and faithful copy of what took place in the proceedings you transcribed.

Clerk of the Court

Sometimes called the court clerk, this position is frequently an elected or appointed court officer. Clerks of court are visible during a trial, but much of their real work occurs before and after.

Definition of the Career Path

Tasks performed by the clerk of court include summoning potential jurors and subpoenaing witnesses for both the prosecution and the defense. In some larger courts, the clerk's office is a full department with assistants. In certain jurisdictions, clerks of court have the power to issue warrants. In smaller courts, clerk of court positions wield considerable influence, as magistrates may be itinerant and part-time and the clerk's position may be the only constant. When there is no contest involved, the clerk of court can exercise all of the power and authority of a probate judge.

During the trial, the clerk of court swears in witnesses and identifies and marks physical evidence as it is entered into the record of the court proceedings. The clerk of court is also responsible for the physical storage and security of evidence during a trial. Some clerks collect fees, fines, costs, and bail payments. In some states they issue marriage licenses, administer oaths, take depositions, and act as county recorders.

Working Conditions

This is a busy and responsible job that requires you to be in constant contact with other court personnel as you coordinate courtroom activity and judges' schedules. You'll have an office, but your work is varied; you appear in the courtroom when you are not behind the scenes managing the operations of the court. Telephone work, much one-on-one contact, and writing memos and many internal communications, including some protocol and procedural documents, mean a busy and varied day.

As in any other management-type position that is salaried, your day may not have a crisp definition as to its beginning or end. Each day will be different, and you'll need to remain poised and ready to handle a variety of situations. For people who enjoy change, a varied work setting, and constant challenges, this is an exciting opportunity.

Training and Qualifications

A bachelor's degree in criminal justice is a strong qualification, although you may still find smaller court jurisdictions that will accept less than a bachelor's degree. In some larger courts, you may find the position of clerk of court restricted to individuals with a law degree.

Court Administrator

You've discussed the overcrowding of courts in your criminal justice classes, and you've probably become more sensitized to hearing news and television reports about time-to-trial lags, case backlogs, and delays for sentencing. Up until now, courts have managed with judges and clerks of court handling the increasingly demanding administrative workload. But as our criminal justice system grows and changes, the courts have had to change as well. To alleviate the backlog and bottlenecks in the judicial process, a new level of administration has been added, and that is represented by the job of court administrator.

Definition of the Career Path

The court administrator works closely with the judge or magistrate to create the court's docket, or calendar. Since the object of the court administrator is to streamline operations, the position places strong emphasis on the budget—monitoring existing budget allocations and planning for future fiscal years.

All of the court administrator's functions may be reduced to analysis and problem solving. With a systems approach, the court administrator seeks to refine and improve the court system to reduce backlogs, speed the process, and eliminate inefficiencies and redundancies in procedures.

Working Conditions

Of the many jobs detailed in this chapter, it would be easy to make the case that court administrators have the most demanding and most detailed job description. Because this position was created to alleviate bottlenecks, you will find it in the larger court systems. Consequently, the conditions of the job are multidimensional, ranging from complex scheduling issues to personnel and staffing concerns. Court administrators are involved in every aspect of the court's functioning, from cleaning services to climate control.

This is a hands-on management position that requires you to be "out and about," anticipating problems before they occur and quickly deciding on solutions for a wide range of situations. Working conditions vary in proportion to the size of the court that employs you. You will need energy, patience, creativity, and good judgment to meet the surprises that will, without fail, arise.

Training and Qualifications

Organizational skills are paramount in this job. Managing court dockets, personnel schedules, staff supervision, case monitoring, and a host of other duties and responsibilities calls for someone who is truly comfortable with multitasking and who can develop viable systems to manage time and work flow.

Because efficiency is also a prime responsibility of this position and the impact it should have on the court's proceedings, you need to be a decision maker, comfortable with bringing closure to a situation.

It's not surprising, then, that an increasing number of court administrators have master's degrees in business administration; likewise, many applicants have law degrees. However, if you can present solid administrative experience and documented skills along with your bachelor's degree in criminal justice, you may be in a good competitive position. Nevertheless, even with your strong background, it's advisable to seek additional training in accounting practices and the various software programs available for calendar and budget management.

Paralegal

Paralegals are employed in all areas of the law, assisting attorneys with an increasing number of duties.

Definition of the Career Path

Paralegals are part of a growing trend of professionals (including nurse practitioners and religious lay leaders) who are assuming a larger range of tasks in their professions. While lawyers assume responsibility for their legal work, they often assign many of their tasks to paralegals. Paralegals thus perform many of the same tasks as lawyers, but they cannot perform any duties that could be perceived as the practice of law, such as setting fees, representing clients in legal proceedings, rendering legal advice, or presenting cases in court. Paralegals are crucial to lawyering today, and the numbers entering the profession and the numbers being hired prove it!

Paralegals are found in law firms, corporate legal departments, and various levels of government. They work in all areas of the law, including litigation, personal injury, corporate law, criminal law, employee benefits, intellectual property, labor law, and real estate. Within specialties, functions may be broken down so that paralegals deal with a specific area. For example, a paralegal specializing in labor law may deal only with employee benefits.

If work in the courts is not immediately available to you or you desire a change, it should be encouraging to know that paralegals are found in corporate work settings as well, where they often assist attorneys with employee contracts, shareholder agreements, stock option plans, and employee benefit plans. They may help prepare and file annual financial reports, maintain minutes of corporate meetings and resolutions, and help with the paperwork to secure loans for the corporation. They may be asked to review government regulations to ensure that the corporation is in compliance.

If you choose to work in the public sector, your job will be determined largely by the kind of agency that employs you. Researching for attorneys and collecting and analyzing evidence for agency hearings will be important tasks. You may prepare material for agency staff on relevant laws and regulations or policy for use by the agency itself or by the general public. Your constituency may include poor people, senior citizens, or other disadvantaged groups in need of legal assistance. You may help these individuals file forms, conduct research, or prepare documents, and, where authorized, you may even represent these clients at administrative (nonlegal) hearings.

If you work in a small or midsize law firm, you may research judicial opinions or help prepare contracts. Your work will probably range over a variety of tasks demanding a comprehensive general knowledge of the law. In the largest firms, you will most likely specialize in one aspect of the law.

Working Conditions

Generally, the workweek is a standard forty hours, although that depends on your employer. Some law firms may require significant overtime during big cases or busy seasons. Rewards include overtime pay or additional vacation and/or end-of-year bonuses. Initial assignments usually are routine and repetitive until you gain content knowledge and begin to demonstrate your experience. Although some paralegals have jobs that involve travel or time out of the office, most have jobs that keep them close to their desks and computers or law libraries.

Training and Qualifications

For job seekers who have either an associate's or a bachelor's degree in criminal justice, the best route to a paralegal career is to add a certification program in paralegal training. The combination of your criminal justice academic training and paralegal certification will make you a viable candidate. Many firms still prefer to train their paralegals themselves, hiring college graduates whose academic backgrounds (such as criminal justice or other social science degrees) are complementary.

Approximately 1,000 colleges, universities, law schools, and proprietary schools offer formal paralegal training programs; about 260 of these are approved by the American Bar Association (ABA). Although many programs don't require such approval, graduation from an ABA-approved program can enhance your employment opportunities. Admission requirements vary; some programs require certain college courses or a bachelor's degree, others accept high school graduates or those with legal experience, and a few require standardized tests and personal interviews.

Computer use, especially of specific software packages, has become commonplace, and you will use a variety of CD-ROM research databases in your work as well. Database management, software familiarity, imaging technology (many documents will be scanned into computer files), and billing programs all require a high level of computer literacy.

In addition to being computer literate, paralegals need to be good readers because reading the law is a major activity in the profession. Writing is another required skill, as you distill the results of your research and present your findings to attorneys; a sizable portion of your work will be writing reports and drafting documents for litigation. Solid research skills are also paramount.

Although professional certification is not a requirement of most employers, gaining some credentials may not only help your job search but also prolong your career. The National Association of Legal Assistants offers a certified legal assistant (CLA) certification. Also, the National Federation of Paralegal Associations offers the paralegal competency exam; passing the exam allows you to use the designation "registered paralegal" (RP).

Legal Researcher

Perhaps your criminal justice degree program left you with a real interest in the law and how it works. Maybe you found that you enjoyed your reading assignments about case law, the courts, and the history of jurisprudence in the United States. Completing the self-assessment exercises in Chapter 1 may confirm that your preference is to work with data rather than people and you enjoy wrestling with and solving problems. If this description applies, a legal research position in the court system may be for you!

Definition of the Career Path
Legal precedence for a particular argument, contract research, case histories, average times to trial, analyses of sentences handed down, demographics of crime statistics—your days will be filled with fascinating assignments, and many people will come to depend on you as "the person with all the answers." Your corresponding responsibility for all that praise is to be consistent, accurate, and thorough in all of your research and to present that information (which may involve considerable editing on your part) in a manner that is clear and concise and yet faithful to the facts.

Working Conditions
The working conditions are those of professional offices. Your workweek in most cases will be a standard forty hours. Some circumstances may require extra hours, and those would be compensated by overtime pay (if you are hourly) or compensatory time off (for salaried positions). Because the bulk of your work will be on the computer, you'll want to ensure that you have an ergonomically appropriate workstation to minimize body stress.

Some legal researchers occasionally travel to specialized law libraries and other research facilities. Others work independently, frequently from home, on a part-time or case-by-case basis. Of course, independent freelancers must support their own benefits package and must invest in sometimes costly CD-ROM packages of legal research databases. Given the high demands in this position for access to information, good advice for entry-level people is to first take a staff position with ample support services and gain some expertise before assuming the risk of becoming an independent contractor.

Training and Qualifications

Legal research is a support position in the court system, and your criminal justice degree is a strong qualifier. However, your degree isn't training enough. Because much of your work will be computer-based and in libraries (although even those resources are increasingly available on database search engines), you need to be a skilled researcher.

In addition to strong research skills, you'll need a working familiarity with computers. Good legal researchers don't waste time doing the same search more than once. To avoid that, they frequently build their own databases to help them find materials they've used before. Strong word-processing skills, database management skills, and knowledge of relational databases will be especially helpful in securing and staying competitive in your job.

If your position also includes managing statistics for the court, you must have the appropriate quantitative background. It is not unusual for job descriptions for research analyst/statistician positions to cite a bachelor's degree as a minimum requirement, with a preference for a master's degree and demonstrated familiarity with descriptive and qualitative statistics.

Many of your assignments will present investigative challenges. You need to be a person who enjoys the challenge of a problem and figuring out all the possible ways to solve it. Especially in legal research, patience is a virtue! If you are easily frustrated or need a high level of variety and change in a working day, legal research may prove to be too static for you. It is largely a mental process, requiring persistence, logic, a good memory, and creativity.

Interpersonal skills are also important in these positions. Yes, you'll have many hours of uninterrupted work (although you need to be comfortable with last-minute emergency requests for data), but you'll be interacting with attorneys, magistrates, judges, court administrators, and a host of other judicial workers. Your interpersonal skills help you clarify what people need. You must master questioning and probing skills so that you have a firm grasp of the research assignment ahead of you, and you must be willing to approach colleagues and receive feedback along the way so that you don't get too far into an assignment and discover you're barking up the wrong tree!

Lawyer

Lawyers are officers of the court who require intense training and must adhere to strict requirements and codes of ethics.

Definition of the Career Path

Obviously, the job of attorney requires additional education: specifically, a degree from a law school. Notwithstanding, we feature attorneys as one of the jobs in our career path on the courts for three reasons. First, many criminal justice majors go on to complete a law degree at some point in their careers. It's a logical extension of their undergraduate studies and can be a smart and satisfying career move. In fact, many law enforcement officers have or are working on a J.D. (Juris Doctor, doctor of jurisprudence) degree to advance up the career ladder.

Second, positions in this career path are often supervised by lawyers. Paralegals and legal researchers, for instance, get most of their direction and work at the behest of lawyers. Many naturally begin to think about the advantages of having a law degree themselves. If you are entering the courts as a career path, you may come to this decision at some point on your own.

Third, and most pertinent to this chapter, lawyers are principal operatives of the court system. They are the active agents of the courtroom process and are often seen as the ones who "get things done" and can effect real change as they seek to either prosecute or exonerate in their pursuit of justice. The media have also done their part to glamorize the profession, and although it is true that there are many wealthy lawyers, a very small percentage accounts for the highest income strata, and that income is achieved after years and years of professional experience. Perhaps a more instructive statistic is the $55,000 average median salary of lawyers nine months into their profession (reported by the U.S. Bureau of Labor Statistics). Bear in mind also that the J.D. is a graduate degree that can mean another $80,000 of debt; in comparison, undergraduate professional and technical majors may well have starting salaries that exceed the $55,000 median salary for lawyers in their first year. So, if guaranteed huge income production is your primary aim, you may want to do more investigation.

Keep in mind, too, that many men and women entering the legal profession have been disappointed with the career. More than 30 percent of people with law degrees are not practicing law. Maybe those people not practicing the profession for which they prepared were disappointed in the long hours, or perhaps law school corridor gossip had inflated income projections. Or maybe they did realize some good income potential, but it took a toll on their personal lives that they weren't willing to sustain. Speculations aside, you, at least, can enter this profession with your eyes wide open to both its potential rewards and its great demands and can weigh those against your personal needs.

Working Conditions

Working conditions for lawyers depend on the setting. If you go into public-interest law, you won't earn much money and you'll work long hours, but you'll also gain valuable experience and the knowledge that you have made a significant contribution to the welfare of people less fortunate. Many lawyers who choose to pursue private work after a time in public service find the contacts they made over that period to be valuable during the transition. If you work in a busy private law firm, you may also find your hours long, of course, but your paycheck may be compensation enough for the job demands.

Most lawyers work hard, despite the public's often jaded perception. Eighteen-hour days are not uncommon, so it's important that you like what you do. In the first few years, you may begin to clarify your preferences. Maybe you like the crisp definition of transactional law (contracts and real estate, for example), or you may be drawn to litigation (criminal or civil work). It is an intellectually challenging job that puts equal emphasis on the details and the "big picture."

Training and Qualifications

To qualify for the bar exam in most states, you must have a law degree from a law school accredited by the American Bar Association (ABA). In addition to criminal justice majors moving on to earn law degrees, many other people come to law school with backgrounds in the liberal arts. Everyone must take the Law School Admission Test (LSAT). Currently there are only 191 accredited law schools in the United States, so competition for entrance is stiff.

Most law students work in one or more legal settings during their law school days (usually during the summer) as they explore what area of law they want to practice. Even law schools themselves focus on specific areas. For example, Franklin Pierce Law School in Concord, New Hampshire, is known for its expertise in intellectual property, while Vermont Law School in Royalton, Vermont, attracts students interested in environmental law.

To practice law in a particular state, you must pass that state's bar exam, which is a two-day written test of the specific laws of that state. Some states have formed reciprocity pacts that admit you to practice in several states by passing one exam. Once you have passed that examination, some states require an oral examination to determine your character and fitness to practice in that state.

Although there is no nationwide bar exam, forty-eight states, the District of Columbia, Guam, the Northern Mariana Islands, Puerto Rico, and the Virgin Islands require the six-hour Multistate Bar Examination (MBE) as part of the overall bar exam (the MBE is not required in Louisiana or Washington). The exam covers a broad range of issues, and sometimes a locally prepared state bar examination is given in addition to it. The three-hour Multistate Essay Examination (MEE) is used as part of the bar examination in several states. States vary in their use of MBE and MEE scores.

Many states also require Multistate Performance Testing (MPT) to test the practical skills of beginning lawyers. Requirements vary by state, although the test usually is taken at the same time as the bar exam and is a one-time requirement.

Simply put, the best qualifications for anyone considering becoming a lawyer are strong work habits (the job can be demanding, requiring long hours), excellent oral and written skills, curiosity, and a pronounced ability to work with, and for, others.

Canadian Requirements

In Canada, the legal profession is a self-governing body, regulated in each province by a Law Society. The Law Society determines whether an applicant may be licensed to practice law. The basic procedure for a prospective lawyer is to graduate from an approved law school and complete the bar admission course in the province in which you want to practice.

The academic prerequisite for taking the bar admission course is either graduation from a common law program approved by the Law Society, in a university in Canada, or a certificate of qualification issued by the National Committee on Accreditation. There are sixteen universities in Canada that offer law courses approved by the Law Society. A student must meet the requirements of the university in order to study law. An approved law course takes three years to complete and leads to a bachelor of laws (LL.B.) or doctor of jurisprudence (J.D.) degree.

The specific requirements for the bar admission course differ among the provinces, but in general, the course is comprised of three phases: a skills phase, a substantive/procedural phase, and an articling phase. The skills and substantive/procedural phases usually run from eight to ten weeks each. The articling phase (the development of practical legal skills under the supervision of a lawyer) can last ten to twelve months. The bar examination is taken upon successful completion of the bar admission course. All lawyers must join the Law Society in the province where they practice.

Earnings

Jobs in the court system are available at local, county, state, and federal levels. As is true of other career fields that fit these criteria, salaries vary, sometimes significantly, from one level of government to the next and from one part of the country to another. Generally, the higher the level of government, the greater the salary. Also keep in mind that the same job title can sometimes carry very different responsibilities (and salary levels). For example, the position of court clerk in some courts is an administrative or managerial position charged with overseeing all of the court's operations. Such a position commands a relatively high salary. In other courts, a court clerk is an office-support position focused on providing mostly clerical services and, as you would guess, earning a relatively low salary. Always read job descriptions carefully to be certain the job is the type and level of sophistication you seek.

Probation and Parole Officers

According to the U.S. Bureau of Labor Statistics, the median salary of probation officers in 2004 was $39,600. Most earned between $31,500 and $52,100. For those employed by state governments, median earnings were $39,810; for those in local government, $40,560. Salaries tend to be higher in urban areas. The average salary for the position of combined probation/parole officer is generally slightly lower than that of probation officer.

With significantly increased experience and a master's degree or, for some, a law degree (J.D.), you can advance to chief probation officer and into district or regional administration. The average probation administrator earned $79,293, the average parole administrator earned $71,810, and the average combined probation/parole administrator earned $68,504. Salaries may increase with the level of government. One recent vacancy announcement for a deputy chief probation officer at a U.S. district court stated a salary range of $70,007 to $113,822.

Victim Advocate

Victim advocates are often viewed as human service workers and not as criminal justice team members, and this status is reflected in a reduced earning potential as well. A recent sampling of actual job openings around the country turned up salaries ranging from the low $20,000s for entry-level positions to as high as $40,000 for more experienced staff positions or for those requiring additional education or training, such as licensed social workers. The majority of the salaries fell within the upper $20,000 range. As you gain experience in victim advocacy services, and perhaps complete an advanced degree in either a human service field or business if your ultimate goal is administration or management, you will find salaries in the $40,000-to-$50,000 range.

Bailiff

Bailiffs earned an average annual salary of $33,870 in 2004, with half earning $24,710 to $44,240. Those employed in local government earned a median salary of $30,410.

As mentioned previously, bailiffs in U.S. federal courts are U.S. marshals. All positions are filled at the GS-5 or GS-7 levels. If you are appointed at the GS-5 grade level, your annual salary will be between $27,000 and $34,000. If appointed at the GS-7 grade level, your annual salary will be between $31,000 and $39,000. Your actual salary would be determined by the geographic location in which you are employed. Unlike some other federal employees, marshals are not eligible for additional law enforcement availability pay (LEAP).

Court Reporter

In court reporting, income depends on the type of reporting jobs, the experience of the reporter, certification, and how much time the reporter is willing to devote to the job, as many court reporters choose to work on a part-time basis. Many also work as independent contractors, and some even own their own agencies and hire other court reporters.

Official court reporters earn a salary and a per-page fee for transcripts. Many salaried court reporters supplement their income by doing freelance work. Freelance court reporters are paid per job and receive a per-page fee for transcripts. Providers of communications access realtime translation (CART), who supply communication access services for deaf and hard-of-hearing people, are paid by the hour. Stenocaptioners receive a salary and benefits if they work as employees of a captioning company; those working as independent contractors are paid by the hour.

Court reporters earned an average annual salary of $42,920 in 2004, with half earning between $30,680 and $60,760. The lowest paid 10 percent earned less than $23,690, and the highest paid 10 percent earned more than $80,300. Median annual earnings in 2004 were $41,070 for court reporters working in local government. For court reporters working part-time, hourly wages for entry-level transcriptionists ranged from $10 to $16 per hour.

Overall, salaries for court reporters are considered relatively high and, in view of the number of hours worked, may in fact be some of the highest within the legal field.

Clerk of the Court

Clerks of court oversee much of the court process aside from trials: they call cases, maintain the records, formulate policies and administrative procedures, supervise office personnel, and often even hear traffic ticket cases (a "clerk's hearing"). These positions can range from high-level managerial posts with salary levels of $90,000 to $100,000 to lower-level, more supervisory or clerical functions with salaries ranging from $30,000 to $40,000. Positions on the higher end often require advanced degrees, including a J.D., and years of administrative and court experience, while positions at the lower end may require some college course work and a minimal number of years of court experience. Here's an example of what you're more likely to encounter when researching clerk of court jobs:

> **Clerk of the Court:** The Clerk of the Chief Administrator of the General District Court, which serves an urban population of 330,000 with four judges hearing traffic, civil, and criminal matters with a caseload in excess of 100,000 per year. The clerk is responsible for all management and administrative responsibilities, and maintains authority over financial performance, staffing, budgets, and efficient caseload processing; monitors and performs procedures to ensure compliance with statutory requirements, the needs of the Court, other criminal justice agencies, and the public, consistent with sound management principles. Twenty-seven full-time staff positions, including four managers, report directly to the clerk. In addition to management responsibilities, the clerk is expected to assist with direct customer service tasks as needed to provide timely public service. Qualifications: High school diploma or equivalent required; college degree preferred. Substantial experience, or combination of education and experience in court, business, or office that provides knowledge, skills, abilities in public relations, recruitment/personnel management and evaluation, individual and group training expertise, and advanced ability in word processing software, especially Microsoft Office. Knowledge of judicial or regulatory requirements that affect court operations desirable. Salary: $88,425.

In some courts the clerk of court is the chief administrative officer. In others the clerk of court may report to the court administrator.

Court Administrator

These positions are considered upper level, require some experience, and often pay quite well. A typical example from the Job Description Databank of the National Center for State Courts is on the next page.

Court administrator positions in larger courts or those overseeing court systems, such as a state court administrator, will pay more. A study by the

Court Administrator. Superior Court. Applicants must have experience in managing an operational or administrative support function in a court system, law office, or criminal justice setting. They must have experience in interpreting and applying federal and/or state statutes, court rules, policies, and procedures related to the jurisdiction of a court or criminal justice agency. Experience in staff supervision and management. Knowledge of the principles and practices of budget preparation, analysis, and administration. Ability to communicate effectively. Salary Range: $73,459–$88,151

National Center for State Courts found that as of 2005, salaries for state court administrators ranged from $62,772 to $147,600, with an average salary of $96,454. These positions will also probably require or, at the very least, prefer additional experience and an advanced degree, either a master's or a law degree.

Paralegal

Salary levels of paralegals vary greatly and depend on geographic location, educational background, work experience, and type and size of employer. Salaries tend to be greater for people with a bachelor's or more advanced degree, and on the West Coast, in larger firms, and in metropolitan areas. The National Association of Legal Assistants (NALA) in its 2004 National Utilization and Compensation Survey Report cites an average salary for legal assistants of $44,373 plus average yearly bonuses of $3,393, making for a total compensation of $46,862. This is an increase of approximately $800 since 2002, the last time the survey was conducted. However, since the 2000 survey, the increase is more than $6,800. According to the National Association of Legal Assistants, employees with less experience (one to five years) averaged lower salaries and bonuses, earning $35,434.

According to the latest available figures from the Bureau of Labor Statistics, as of 2004, the federal government paid the highest salaries to paralegals, with a median of $59,370, while those working in local government earned around $38,260.

As you can see, paralegals earn relatively good salaries. This may be a reflection of the increased emphasis on responsibilities or tasks that previously belonged to attorneys and the correspondingly higher education and professional standards.

Legal Researcher

A sampling of job openings for legal researchers indicated an average salary range of $30,000 to $45,000. Senior and more experienced researchers could earn $55,000 to $80,000 or even more. Here's an example of an ad from a court in New York:

Assistant Court Analyst, Drug Court. Minimum requirements: Bachelor's degree or high school diploma and four years relevant experience or one year as Junior Court Analyst. Assistant Court Analysts provide professional level assistance to Court Analysts and higher level personnel in projects involving personnel, administration, resource allocation, budget development and court finance, administration, and policy formation. They may perform as part of a project team where they may be assigned entry-level professional tasks under the supervision of a Court Analyst. Experience with chemical dependency assessment, together with a working knowledge of the treatment community, and a general understanding of the criminal justice system, and work experience and/or knowledge of drug treatment court is desirable. Base Salary: $38,360 plus $1,302 locality pay.

Lawyer

The National Association for Law Placement reports that in 2004, the median salaries of lawyers nine months after graduation from law school were $55,000, but overall salaries varied depending on the type of work. Those employed in private practice had median earnings of $80,000; those in business and industry earned $60,000. Lawyers working in judicial clerkships and government positions averaged $44,700; and those in academics earned $40,000.

For all lawyers, both new and seasoned, the median salary for 2004 was $94,930, with most earning between $64,620 and $143,620. Trial lawyers, those involved in actual litigation, tend to earn more, particularly if they work in private practice as opposed to the district attorney's office. While lawyers employed by the federal government earned an average of $108,090, those working for local government (such as the city or town attorney) or state government (such as public defenders) make less, usually around $73,410 and $70,280, respectively.

Career Outlook

Generally speaking, employment in the court system is expected to grow about as fast as the average for all occupations, which translates to an increase of 10 to 20 percent between now and 2014. Despite the increased numbers of cases before the court, budget constraints continue to limit the growth of local, state, and federal courts. So, most of the employment opportunities will come from replacing workers who are promoted, retire, or move on to other positions. To a lesser extent, jobs will become available as a result of the limited growth within the court system. Couple this limited growth with, for many people, the appeal of working in the court system, and you will find keen competition for the jobs that do exist. For the most part, court-related jobs pay relatively well, offer job security, and provide a working environment that's interesting and sometimes even exciting.

Being aware of the supply-and-demand constraints in court-related careers should motivate you now to develop skills that are desired in the field in which you're interested. You can serve an internship in which you can gain real-world experience and get to know people who can help you in your job search. Join associations to increase your knowledge of the field as well as your network of contacts, and start early to learn where the jobs are and how to put yourself in the best position to get them.

Keep in mind that we've been talking about the career outlook in general terms. There are some exceptions to the foregoing projections, most notably among paralegals, as you will see.

Probation and Parole Officers

While the population of probationers continues to grow, funding for probation does not always follow. According to the Bureau of Labor Statistics, only about one-tenth of the national corrections budget goes to probation and parole administration. Certainly based on need, employment of probation and parole officers is not expected to decline. It will most likely experience an average growth rate.

Mandatory sentencing guidelines calling for longer sentences and reduced parole for inmates have resulted in a large increase in the prison population. However, many states are reconsidering mandatory sentencing guidelines because of budgetary constraints, court decisions, and doubts about the effectiveness of the guidelines. Instead, states may place more emphasis on rehabilitation and alternate forms of punishment, such as probation, spurring demand for probation and parole officers. However, the job outlook depends primarily on the amount of government funding that is allocated to corrections, and especially to probation systems. Although community supervision is far less expensive than keeping offenders in prison, a change in political trends toward more imprisonment and away from community supervision could result in reduced employment opportunities.

Probation has long been an attractive career field for many students of criminal justice and other social sciences, so expect healthy competition for jobs. Try to gain some on-the-job experience to put you ahead of other new graduates. This is an ideal area in which to pursue an internship. Not only will you gain the relative work experience you need, but you'll meet (and get to know) the important hiring officials as well.

Another tip for positioning yourself in the market is to investigate civil service exam requirements in the state in which you'd like to work. Some states require an exam for probation and parole officers, while others don't. Exams are usually scheduled on specific dates; if you need to take the test, arrange to do so at the earliest possible time. And don't forget to prepare for it!

Victim Advocate

The employment outlook for victim advocates is strong, as the government continues to sponsor grants and fund programs to aid victims of crime. In this new and growing field, opportunities are abundant. Sadly, there are thousands and thousands of victims of crime each year, from abducted children to bomb victims and their families, who are in need of assistance and services. Within the first twelve years of the passage of the Victims of Crime Act of 1984, $2.2 billion in federal criminal fines were transferred to states to fund local victim assistance programs. Today, approximately ten thousand programs exist.

Getting in on the ground floor of a new career field means that opportunities for advancement will be great as well. As you develop experience, to qualify for promotions, in most cases you'll also need to continue your education through professional development activities such as seminars and workshops (often offered through or sponsored by your employer) and through more formalized education leading to a master's degree.

Bailiff

Bailiff jobs are expected to grow more slowly than the average for all occupations nationwide. Only an 8 percent growth rate is predicted through 2014, which means that each year, on average, 1,130 bailiffs will be hired in the country. This will vary from state to state, however, and for some states, such as Florida, the growth rate is expected to be around 23 percent. The number of bailiffs hired in each state varies considerably as well. California employs approximately 5,700 bailiffs, while North Dakota employs only 50! If you're willing to relocate, you can use the online America's Career Infonet, (acinet.org) to explore trends for various states. The variance in numbers reflects the fact that the field itself is relatively narrow. Approximately 44,000 bailiffs are employed nationwide. Compare that with the close to 700,000 lawyers in this country.

Court Reporter

Job opportunities for court reporters are expected to be excellent as job openings continue to outnumber job seekers. Prospects should be best for those with certification. Employment of court reporters is projected to grow between 9 and 17 percent for all occupations through 2014. Demand for court reporter services will be spurred by the continuing need for accurate transcription of proceedings in courts and in pretrial depositions, and by the growing need to create captions for live or prerecorded television and to provide other real-time translating services for the deaf and hard-of-hearing community. Although voice writers have become more widely accepted because of the improved accuracy of speech recognition technology, many courts still allow only stenotypists to perform court reporting duties; as a result, demand for these highly skilled reporters will remain high.

Despite increasing numbers of civil and criminal cases, budget constraints are expected to limit the ability of federal, state, and local courts to expand. This will also limit the demand for traditional court reporting services in courtrooms and other legal venues. In an effort to control costs, many courtrooms have installed tape recorders that are maintained by electronic court reporters and transcribers to record court proceedings. These electronic reporters and transcribers are only used in a limited capacity, however, and court reporters will continue to be used in felony trials and other proceedings. Despite the use of audiotape and videotape technology, court reporters can quickly turn spoken words into readable, searchable, permanent text, and they will continue to be needed to produce written legal transcripts and proceedings for publication.

Clerk of Court

All courts by design include enormous administrative responsibilities, and with the continued increase in cases coming before the courts, these administrative needs will also continue to grow. Thus, you can see why, in order for the court system to run smoothly and efficiently, there will always be a demand for clerks of court and other personnel to work in these offices. Within a clerk's office, you will often find assistant clerks, court clerks, associate clerks, deputy clerks, and so on. If becoming a clerk of court is your career goal, you will likely need to enter the field in one of these support positions. From there, you can gain the experience necessary for promotion. Ultimately, you may advance to a court administrator's position.

Court Administrator

In all likelihood, you will not be qualified for this job at this stage in your career. It's included here because the position is integral to the functioning of the court system and can provide you with a vision of a career path down the road. Not all courts have a court administrator; usually only the bigger and/or busier ones do. In less busy courthouses, you will often see someone with the title "clerk of the court" performing the duties of the court administrator. Where there is a court administrator, the clerk of the court reports to that person. All states have a court administrator, or an equivalent, who oversees the court system in that state. These are appointed positions with high visibility and high salaries. They require years of experience and very often advanced degrees. If you aspire to this position, you will probably start in the clerk's office, where you will gain valuable experience as you continue your education. Opportunities are limited, though, and you will need to be a shining star among the ranks of court clerks to rise to this level.

Paralegal

Paralegals represent the most notable exception to court-related positions in terms of job outlook. The Bureau of Labor Statistics projects that employment of paralegals will grow 27 percent or more by 2014. This expansion is not new. It has been a steady trend in recent years and is probably best explained by the expanded role that paralegals have assumed in law offices and departments and in government agencies. More experienced paralegals are intensively involved in trial preparation and may be called on to produce interrogatories for an attorney's review, assist in trial-related motions, and even meet with clients. Also, senior-level paralegals sometimes supervise lower-level paralegals. The increasing reliance on paralegals to perform such higher-level duties is easy to explain. Paralegals help to reduce costs for law firms and agencies and promote efficiency by freeing up lawyers to concentrate on direct legal services.

Although private law firms should continue to be the largest employers of paralegals, opportunities will also be found with corporate legal departments, insurance companies, real estate and title insurance firms, and banks. Corporations in particular are boosting their in-house legal departments to cut costs. The job outlook should be very good for paralegals who specialize in areas such as real estate, bankruptcy, medical malpractice, and product liability. A growing number of experienced paralegals are expected to establish their own businesses.

The public sector will also provide employment opportunities for paralegals. Community legal-service programs that provide assistance to the poor, elderly, minorities, and middle-income families will employ additional paralegals to minimize expenses and serve the most people. Federal, state, and local government agencies, consumer organizations, and the courts also should continue to hire paralegals in increasing numbers.

Despite the tremendously positive outlook for paralegals, take note that although the field is growing, so is the competition. Paralegal programs have become so popular in U.S. colleges and universities that the number of graduates, combined with others who may be looking to enter the field and are learning on the job, is outpacing job growth. To be competitive for entry-level positions, you need to be an expert in computer software packages and the Internet, possess strong researching skills, and demonstrate a willingness to work extended hours as part of the legal team.

In all probability, you will need to continue your education to be considered qualified for this position. Your criminal justice curriculum may have covered some of the same areas that you find in a paralegal studies curriculum, but it would not include all of the specialty course work. Therefore, although it's possible that a law firm or department will hire and train you, it's more likely that you will have to complete a certificate in paralegal studies. Most certificate programs can be completed in one year if you are attending full-time. Plenty of part-time programs are also available for those who choose to continue to work while taking classes.

Legal Researcher

Similar to paralegals but much smaller in scope, the employment outlook for legal researchers is strong, and for many of the same reasons. Law firms and departments and other employers can decrease their costs and increase their efficiency by hiring researchers to do much of the background function or "legwork" previously done by lawyers. This is especially true in larger organizations. Some employers require legal researchers to have paralegal experience, and you may even encounter some who hire entry-level attorneys to do the job.

Lawyer

Competition is the name of the game for lawyers. It starts right from the beginning with your application to law school, where competition is fierce. If you're lucky enough to get in (and if you successfully complete the program), you're then faced with the fact that the number of law school graduates continues to outpace the growth of jobs and creates a strain on the economy to absorb them, a trend for much of the past thirty years. Employment for lawyers is expected to grow between 9 and 17 percent over the next decade. Most of the gain will be due to population growth, growth in business activities in general, and increased legal action involving health care, intellectual property, the environment, international law, and sexual harassment.

Competition for job openings should continue to be keen because of the large number of students graduating from law school each year. Graduates with superior academic records from highly regarded law schools will have the best job opportunities. Perhaps as a result of this competition for jobs, lawyers are increasingly finding work in nontraditional areas for which legal training is an asset, but not normally a requirement—for example, administrative, managerial, and business positions in banks, insurance firms, real estate companies, government agencies, and other organizations. Employment opportunities are expected to continue to arise in these organizations at a growing rate.

You may have to start out in a position that's outside your field of interest or for which you feel overqualified. Some recent law school graduates who have been unable to find permanent positions are turning to the growing number of temporary staffing firms that place attorneys in short-term jobs until they can secure full-time positions. This service allows companies to hire lawyers on an "as-needed" basis and permits beginning lawyers to develop practical skills while looking for permanent positions.

Strategy for Finding the Jobs

You're in luck! Courts aren't hard to locate. A smart strategy is to first identify all the court settings (local, county, state, and federal) in the geographic area you have under consideration. It's not a bad idea to research these sites on the Internet, where you can gather information about drive time, road conditions, and so forth. Make up a chart, listing each court along with its type and location. You may note, depending on where you live, that some larger cities have more than one court. Following are some techniques for locating all the court possibilities in your area:

- **Local courts:** To determine local court jurisdictions, you can simply call the local police department, which deals with the lower-level court every day. Another alternative is to consult the white pages under the business listing section; look up the towns in your area of interest, and you will find any courts located there. Then, contact them to find where they post their job openings. Once you know that, check on a regular basis so that you don't miss any new opportunities. You'll usually find that in addition to postings on their job bulletin boards, announcements will be placed in the local newspaper. Many towns maintain websites where you can locate the courts and possibly find job postings as well.
- **State courts:** Once again, the Internet has made life easier for you. Visit your state's home page to find a listing for state courts (statelocalgov.net is a great online resource, as it connects you to every state in the country). Once you find your state's judiciary page, you will most likely see not only the locations of courts within the state system but also directions and contact information. You will also learn about the different courts that make up the state system and their areas of responsibility. Any

employment opportunities are usually made available as well. Another good place to look on the Internet is the National Center for State Courts, which publishes job vacancy announcements for all state courts in the country. They can be found at ncsonline.org.

• **Federal courts:** Each federal court does its own advertising and hiring for job positions, so it's important to find out where these courts are located. The Federal Judicial Center at fjc.gov provides links to the home pages of all federal courts when you click on "Courts of the Federal Judiciary." You'll also find a link to uscourts.gov, which provides at least a partial listing of job opportunities at the federal level.

Within each court setting that you identify, you will come across most of the jobs outlined in this chapter, with some exceptions. For instance, although victim advocacy may take place as a "process" within all of these courts, in your search for a position in the field, you may also want to look in the local newspaper, where local social service agencies often advertise, or visit your town hall.

Lawyers and paralegals, on the other hand, will likely be associated with either private law firms or the state district attorney or prosecutor's office. Legal researchers may be employed there as well. Where do these employers advertise? State positions are advertised on the state's website. Private firms and other organizations with law departments are most apt to advertise in local and regional newspapers, on their own websites, or on law employment–related websites such as the Legal Employment Search Site (legalemploy.com). In addition, you can always find listings of local law firms in the yellow pages in the phone book and on the Web. In both paralegal and law careers, your job search should also take into account any specialty of law you have in mind. Some firms specialize in litigation, for example, while others may handle real estate transactions exclusively.

Don't forget to visit your career services office, which will have information on how to find opportunities for your specific career.

Possible Employers

For many of the positions presented in this chapter, local, state, and federal governments are the only employers. This is true for probation and parole officers, bailiffs, court administrators, and most court reporters. It also applies for some lawyers, paralegals, legal researchers, and victim advocates. There are different kinds of courts—municipal, U.S. district, superior, trial, or appeals—for matters as diverse as juvenile justice and bankruptcy, but in each of these courts you are ultimately employed by a government agency. For certain positions, however, there are some further alternatives.

Victim Advocate

Victim advocates often work in partnership with the court system, but they may or may not be direct employees of the court. Grants for victim assistance and services may be awarded to local law enforcement agencies, district attorney's offices, independent state agencies, or any other organizations that may contract with local, state, or federal authorities to provide services to victims. The types of agencies that provide the services vary according to the nature of the crime that's been committed. Victims can include those of child abuse, domestic violence, rape or sexual abuse, stalking, fraud, workplace violence, juvenile crime, hate crime, elder abuse, and discrimination. Agencies that offer such outreach are just as diverse.

Court Reporter

In addition to being employees of the court, court reporters can be independent contractors or can work for a court reporting firm. Many do choose to work outside of the courtroom. In fact, in 2004, about 13 percent of the eighteen thousand working court reporters was self-employed. Given the large number of conventions, conferences, seminars, and meetings, both in the private sector and in government agencies, that take place each year in which the proceedings need to be accurately recorded, court reporters can find ample work outside the court system.

In addition, federal legislation mandates that all new television programming must be captioned for the deaf and hard-of-hearing, as of 2006. The Americans with Disabilities Act gives deaf and hard-of-hearing students in colleges and universities the right to request access to real-time translation in their classes. Both of these factors are expected to increase demand for court reporters to provide real-time captioning and CART services. Although these services forgo transcripts and differ from traditional court reporting, which uses computer-aided transcription to turn spoken words into permanent text, they require the same skills that court reporters learn in their training.

Paralegal, Legal Researcher, and Lawyer

Private law firms employ the vast majority of paralegals, legal researchers, and lawyers. Most of the remainder work in corporate legal departments or various levels of government. At the local level, they may work for the city law department. At the state level, you may find them working in the offices of the attorney general, district attorney, public defender, prosecutor, or individual state departments such as the department of social services or the office of the treasurer. Most employed by the federal government are hired by the Department of Justice, followed by the Departments of the Treasury and Defense, and the Federal Deposit Insurance Corporation. Other paralegals, legal researchers, and lawyers may work for publicly funded legal services centers.

Within organizations, you may deal in all areas of law, or you may want to work within a particular area of specialization, including personal injury, litigation, intellectual property, labor law, family law, criminal law, discrimination, employee benefits, real estate, estate planning, and technology-related concerns.

Possible Job Titles

As you launch your search for an entry-level position in the courts, you're likely to turn up many different jobs with a variety of titles. Are these for you? Do you meet the qualifications? Some of these job titles were introduced in this chapter. Some are simply variations of these titles. Some may be new to you. Begin to build a collection or portfolio of job postings by job title; after you have collected three to five ads in each category, many of your questions will be resolved.

Here are some job titles you are likely to come across. Although the list is long, it in no way encompasses all the jobs in all the courts (or related to the courts) across the country.

Probation and Parole

Aftercare coordinator
Chief probation officer
Community service coordinator
Director of probation
Family service officer
Juvenile probation counselor
Parole officer

Pretrial services officer
Probation and parole officer
Probation counselor
Probation officer
Release-on-own-recognizance
   (ROR) interviewer

Victim Services

Animal treatment investigator
Caseworker
Child and youth counselor
Child support agency worker

Gender issues specialist
Housing/tenant representative
Nonprofit organization advocate
Support services coordinator

Counselor
Crisis counselor
Domestic violence counselor
Family service clinician
Victim advocate

Victim restitution coordinator
Victim services specialist
Victim-witness coordinator
Witness protection worker

Law Enforcers

Bailiff
Bondsman
Constable
Court officer

Court security officer
Process server
U.S. marshal

Court Reporting

Court reporter
Diplomat reporter
Legal video specialist
Manager of reporting services
Merit reporter

Real-time reporter
Registered professional reporter
Reporting instructor
Stenocaptioner
Stenographer

Court Administration

Administrative coordinator
Appeals reviewer
Arbitrator
Assistant clerk
Case flow manager
Case manager
Chief deputy clerk
Clerk of court

Court administrator
Court clerk
Court executive
Court magistrate
Court representative
Deputy clerk
Judicial assistant
Mediation specialist

Paralegal

Legal assistant

Paralegal

Legal Research

Analyst
Conflicts researcher
Court analyst
Court services analyst
Law librarian

Legal researcher
Researcher
Senior researcher
Sentencing analyst

Law

Adjudicator
Assistant district attorney

Law clerk
Lawyer

Attorney

District attorney

Expert witness

Judge

Litigation manager

Public defender

State's attorney

Trial lawyer

Related Occupations

Claims examiner

Contracts administrator

Medical transcriptionist

Patent agent

Title abstractor

Title examiner

Title searcher

Professional Associations

Listed in this section are some of the associations that relate to careers in the courts. For more information about these professional associations, either visit the websites listed or consult the *Encyclopedia of Associations*, published by Thomson Gale. Review the Members/Purpose notes for each organization to determine if it pertains to your interests. Membership in one or more of these organizations may gain you access to job listings, networking opportunities, and employment search services. Some provide information at no charge, but if you want to receive specific publications that list job opportunities, you may need to join. If you're still in college, check for student member rates.

American Bar Association

321 N. Clark St.

Chicago, IL 60610

abanet.org

Members/Purpose: The premier association for attorneys. Its mission is to be the national representative of the legal profession, serving the public and the profession by promoting justice, professional excellence, and respect for the law. The association provides extensive resources for its members, law students, the media, and the general public.

Publications: Numerous books, magazines, journals, and newsletters

Training: Midyear and annual meetings; sponsors the Center for Continuing Legal Education

American Correctional Association

4380 Forbes Blvd.

Lanham, MD 20706-4322

aca.org

Members/Purpose: For more than 125 years, the American Correctional Association has championed the cause of corrections and correctional effectiveness. Founded in 1870 as the National Prison Association, ACA is the oldest association developed specifically for practitioners in the correctional profession.

Publications: *Corrections Today* magazine; *Corrections Compendium* journal; publications catalog from which you can choose books, videos, or products; online job bank

Training: Online training workshops; training sessions throughout the year on specific topics; video library

American Probation and Parole Association

P.O. Box 11910

Lexington, KY 40578-1910

appa-net.org

Members/Purpose: Established to serve, challenge, and empower members and constituents from the United States and Canada by educating, communicating, and training; advocating and influencing; acting as a resource and conduit for information, ideas, and support; developing standards and models; and collaborating with other disciplines.

Publications: Issue papers on topics facing the field of community corrections; *Perspectives*, a quarterly journal; variety of books and manuscripts, many of which are aimed at career building

Training: Training institutes; national/regional training seminars and technical assistance; professional development program

Canadian Bar Association

500-865 Carling Ave.

Ottawa, ON K1S 5S8

cba.org

Members/Purpose: A professional, voluntary organization that promotes the legal profession in Canada.

Publications: *Canada Bar Review, National* magazine, newsletters, and books

Training: Continuing legal education; national and international conferences

Conference of State Court Administrators

National Center for State Courts

300 Newport Ave.

Williamsburg, VA 23185

http://cosca.ncsc.dni.us/

Members/Purpose: Dedicated to the improvement of state court systems. Membership consists of the state court administrator or the equivalent official in each of the fifty states, the District of Columbia, Puerto Rico, American Samoa, Guam, Northern Mariana Islands, and the Virgin Islands.

Publications: Variety of monographs; many online publications such as court technology bulletins, jury news, and job announcements

Training: None offered

National Association for Court Management

c/o Association Management
National Center for State Courts
300 Newport Ave.
Williamsburg, VA 23185-4147
nacmnet.org

Members/Purpose: Committed to improving the administration of justice and promoting the interdependence of court managers and judges.

Publications: *Court Manager; Comminique*

Training: Annual conference

National Association of Legal Assistants

1516 S. Boston, #200
Tulsa, OK 74119
nala.org

Members/Purpose: A leading professional association for legal assistants, providing continuing education and professional certification programs for paralegals.

Publications: Variety of manuals

Training: Seminars; workshops; online educational programs

National Court Reporters Association

8224 Old Courthouse Rd.
Vienna, VA 22182-3808
ncraonline.org

Members/Purpose: To create an understanding of the role of information/court reporters among customers, legislators, and regulators and to ensure that they are professionals who capture and manage the record through education, training, and state-of-the-art technology.

Publications: *Journal of Court Reporting; The Job Bank;* membership directory

Training: Annual conferences; seminars; extensive professional development opportunities, including certification programs; also offers a Virtual Mentors program to bring court reporters and students together

National Federation of Paralegal Associations
P.O. Box 2016
Edmonds, WA 98020
paralegals.org
Members/Purpose: To advance, foster, and promote the paralegal concept; to monitor and participate in the developments affecting the paralegal profession; and to maintain a nationwide communications network among paralegal associations and other members of the legal community.
Publications: *National Paralegal Reporter*; directory of member associations; informational brochures; online job listings
Training: Annual conventions and seminars

National Organization for Victim Assistance
510 King St., Suite 424
Alexandria, VA 22314
trynova.org
Members/Purpose: A private nonprofit organization of victim and witness assistance programs and practitioners, criminal justice agencies and professionals, mental health professionals, researchers, former victims and survivors, and others committed to the recognition and implementation of victim rights and services.
Publications: Information packets and bulletins; articles; training materials on selected topics
Training: Crisis response training using selected topics and training methods

National Paralegal Association
Box 406
Solebury, PA 18963
nationalparalegal.org
Members/Purpose: An international organization offering benefits and services to individuals, law firms, corporate legal departments, independent paralegals, and paralegal training schools and colleges, as well as vendors of services or products to the paralegal profession.
Publications: Material directed to people exploring entry into the profession and to established paralegals, either employed by a firm or in independent practice
Training: None offered

Pretrial Services Resource Center
927 15th St. NW, 3rd floor
Washington, DC 20005
pretrial.org
Members/Purpose: To improve the quality, fairness, and efficiency of the criminal justice system at the pretrial stage by promoting systemic strategies that improve court appearance rates, reduce recidivism, provide appropriate and effective services, and enhance community safety.
Publications: *The Pretrial Reporter*, monographs and reports
Training: Pretrial Justice Institute

Victim Offender Mediation Association
c/o Center for Policy, Planning, and Performance
2233 University Ave. W, Suite 300
St. Paul, MN 55114
voma.org
Members/Purpose: To provide greater networking among practitioners and other interested individuals to enhance the overall credibility of victim/offender mediation and reconciliation programs within the justice community.
Publications: *VOMA Connections* newsletter; numerous articles
Training: Training institute and conference (annual meeting)

Path 3: Corrections

Lock Up Your Future

A recurring theme in this book is the changing role of criminal justice careers in society. As a nation, we are paying more attention to all aspects of criminal justice; we are more demanding of our police and federal officers, our courts are under intensive scrutiny for fairness and cost efficiencies, and our jails and prisons are no longer warehouses for criminals. The result is that a criminal justice degree has never been as valued as it is today, and graduates holding that degree have never had as many opportunities to make a difference. This chapter deals with an aspect of the criminal justice system that society sometimes wants to forget but that features largely in the criminal justice curriculum: the field of corrections.

Perhaps the biggest change—and the most important one for you as a criminal justice major—is that the field of corrections is increasingly populated by people like you: graduates who are choosing the field knowing they can apply their education and training to an area of criminal justice that is in the process of major reforms even as it continues to struggle with the age-old problems of budgets and overcrowding. Sure, the problems are there, but so are the opportunities. If one of your goals is to make a difference, corrections is worthy of your interest!

Criminal justice jobs have been a prime target for movies, novels, and television shows. Police, FBI agents, judges and lawyers, and, of course, prison and jail personnel have been depicted in numerous ways—some accurate, many not. On the whole, the image of personnel in corrections that is projected by the popular media is way off. Brutalization of inmates by abusive staff (almost always male) is the stuff of fantasy and not today's reality.

Today's corrections professionals are typically dedicated, service-oriented men and women with a college education whose dual duty is to house lawbreakers away from society and to provide those same lawbreakers with an environment that offers tools for positive change to those wishing to access them before their return to society.

The Corrections Situation Today

According to the most recent statistics from the Bureau of Justice Statistics, in 2004 the number of state and federal prisoners approached 1.5 million. In one year, the Federal Bureau of Prisons grew by more than 9,500 inmates; state prisons grew by about 20,000 inmates. That kind of growth continues today and has largely been responsible for the arrival of private prison management firms, some of which have developed modular construction programs that can erect, outfit, and staff a prison faster than the public sector. On top of the overpopulation problem, we have prisons now charged with increasingly sophisticated missions of a combination of punishment, treatment, or rehabilitation, depending on the sentence meted out and the nature of the criminal and the crime.

Women in Corrections

The typical inmate is male, under thirty, and without a high school diploma; however, the number of women who are incarcerated is increasing at a faster rate than the number of men. Though women currently make up less than 10 percent of the total inmate population, this number is expected to continue to multiply. During 2003, the number of female prisoners grew 3.6 percent, which was higher than the 2.0 percent increase in male prisoners. As of December 31, 2003, there were 101,179 females under state or federal jurisdiction, accounting for 6.9 percent of all prisoners.

More women inmates mean more women corrections staff and more facilities to house this growing population. Traditionally, women performed a limited role in corrections. Inmate teachers, nurses, clerical positions, arsenal staff, information desk service, and gun tower duty were the principal occupational areas for women. The tide began to turn in 1982, when a federal court decision declared that women could not be barred from other duties and provided compensation to women corrections officers previously restricted from these assignments and to those who had been denied promotional advancement for lack of experience that they could not obtain. Female officers thus began to receive the training they had been denied and took up their positions in the housing units without incident.

The Corrections Setting: Prisons and Jails

Most members of the general public are not aware of the distinction that the criminal justice field makes between prisons and jails. *Prisons* are operated by the federal government or state governments; they are often large facilities with large staffs and many inmates. Sizable populations of inmates generally mean that men and women can be segregated in separate facilities and that a variety of programs and instruction for rehabilitation and treatment is available. These prisons house individuals convicted of felonies carrying a sentence of more than one year.

The small facilities run by counties, cities, and towns and that generally house only up to about fifty people are correctly termed *jails.* Prisoners in these facilities are serving shorter sentences, generally for smaller crimes or misdemeanors, or they may be awaiting a trial date for a crime for which either there is no bail or they could not post the required dollar amount. Increasingly, these jails also may be housing convicted felons who have been sentenced to a prison facility but must wait for a spot to open. Since jails are not designed for extended use and many are not used consistently or even frequently, many are in disrepair. Support programs are not offered because turnover is intended to be rapid. Likewise, staff may have no special training and may be charged with many other duties in the county or city facilities that house the jail.

The jail facilities that we toured during our research for this book, even those that were new, were at best, functional. We were struck by how basic the cells were, and, of course, there is no privacy whatever. Cell design and preventing vandalism by angry offenders dictate a certain sterility in the furniture and heavily influence the cost of even the most spartan lockup unit. Open stainless-steel toilets that we saw cost more than $600 apiece. Consequently, budgets of small cities or localities can rarely extend to jail modifications and upgrades.

Prison Populations

The Web is a handy source for corrections information, and every state has a state corrections site. The site for Connecticut, state.ct.us/doc/facts/facts_body.htm, provides a good picture of the staff and population of one state's corrections facilities:

- Eighteen facilities (seventeen for male offenders; one for females)
- Total staff of 6,279

- An incarcerated population of 17,928, of which 1,296 are women
- 863 prisoners under transitional supervision
- 1,048 in halfway houses
- 139 on reentry furloughs
- Total expenditures of $573,839,097 in fiscal year 2004–05.

Connecticut has separate facilities for men and women. Several of its state facilities serve as jails and as intake facilities for unsentenced males, though these jails will also process and confine convicted males for sentences of less than two years. Special facilities exist for sentenced and unsentenced males between the ages of fourteen and twenty-one. Five security levels have been established: level 5 is maximum security, level 4 is high security, level 3 is medium security, level 2 is low security, and level 1 comprises prisoners who have been released into the community but remain under departmental supervision.

Each state has its own complement of prisons, and they vary in age, architecture, size, and amenities. What they share is a special world of extreme regimentation and detailed structure. Within this structure exist any number of subcultures built around offenses, personalities, education, goals—even anger. These subcultures display hierarchies, leaders, values, codes, and behavioral patterns that can be remarkably similar from prison to prison. Some of these subcultures can exert tremendous pressure on individuals as well as groups of prisoners. It is within and between these groups that conflict often arises and violations of prison protocols occur. Some of the country's most dangerous and violent prison breakouts and hostage situations have had their beginnings within these subcultures. As a corrections officer, you'll develop a specialized antenna for the nuances of group behavior, membership, codes, and interactions.

Corrections Officer

The corrections officer is the mainstay and principal employment figure of the corrections system.

Definition of the Career Path

Also called correctional officer, the role of this professional is to oversee individuals who have been arrested and are awaiting trial or who have been convicted and sentenced to a jail, reformatory, or penitentiary. They maintain security and inmate accountability to prevent disturbances, assaults, or escapes. These officers have no law enforcement powers outside the institutions where they work.

Occasionally corrections officer jobs are found in county jails or precinct station houses, and the people holding these posts are known as detention officers. These jobs, too, pose serious physical threats, especially in the period immediately following an individual's arrest, when the suspect may be violent and his or her background (and even name) may be unknown. This is a dangerous phase of the incarceration process.

In addition to prisons and jails, a smaller number of corrections officers may also find employment with the Immigration and Naturalization Service, which holds noncitizens and permanent residents before they are released or deported.

Regardless of the work setting, the duties and responsibilities of corrections officers are generally similar. They include:

- Ensuring that inmates are orderly and obey rules
- Monitoring inmate activities and work assignments
- On occasion, searching inmates and their living quarters for contraband and weapons
- Settling disputes between inmates
- Enforcing discipline
- Inspecting the facility for unsanitary conditions, fire hazards, or any infractions of the rules
- Reporting orally and in writing on inmate conduct
- Reporting security breaches, disturbances, and any unusual occurrences
- Keeping a daily log of corrections facility activities
- If the situation arises, helping other law enforcement officials to investigate crimes or search for escapees

Most corrections officers work unarmed if they are in facilities with direct-supervision cell blocks, although they do carry communication devices to summon help. Generally, officers work alone or in pairs in cell blocks of fifty to a hundred inmates. Order is maintained through interpersonal skills on the part of the officer and progressive sanctioning, including loss of some privileges. Corrections officers walk a fine line between being friendly and being firm. They must gain the respect of prisoners but not encourage a familiarity that could prove dangerous.

Working Conditions

Make no mistake about it—working conditions are stressful and hazardous. Each year, corrections officers are injured in the line of duty. Work is indoors and outdoors, and not all correctional facilities are up-to-date with modern equipment, lighting, plumbing, and climate control. Some facilities are modern, brightly lit, and well ventilated; others are noisy, dim, overcrowded, and unpleasant. Most corrections officers begin their careers working rotating eight-hour shifts, and since prisons must be staffed twenty-four hours a day, seven days a week, these shifts are bound to coincide with holidays, special occasions, family celebrations, and other important events. Again, due to staffing imperatives, overtime may be required.

Training and Qualifications

As with many other jobs in the criminal justice area, becoming a corrections officer now generally requires a postsecondary education of some kind, either an associate's degree or a bachelor's degree, and your criminal justice major means you'll be highly competitive in this field. Likewise, your degree in criminal justice enhances your promotional prospects as you advance in your career. Other postsecondary degrees of bearing include psychology, sociology, police science, and criminology.

Although the application process varies from state to state, you can expect a battery of tests and interviews to determine your suitability for this work. The ability to think and act quickly in the corrections environment is paramount. You'll be screened for drug use, and in addition to undergoing a background check, you'll generally have to pass a written examination. Many states or clusters of states have training academies that you may be required to attend, and all state and local agencies provide on-the-job training that covers legal elements as well as interpersonal skills. Certain systems also require firearms proficiency and self-defense skills. In some employment settings, the officer candidate participates in months of probationary on-the-job training alongside a more experienced officer.

The following is an actual job advertisement for an entry-level corrections officer posted by the state of Massachusetts. Note the education incentive for those with a degree.

Correctional Officer. Salary Range: $36,000–$44,000. The Essex County Sheriff's Department is seeking individuals interested in joining a multitalented and multicultural department of correctional professionals. Correctional officers provide care, custody, and control for both sentenced inmates and pretrial detainees. Starting salary: $36,016.14, shift differential: $2,881.00, roll call: $1,428.00, uniform allowance and cleaning: $1,000.00, physical fitness incentive: $750.00, education incentive: $1,500.00, performance: $1,250.00. Maximum starting compensation: $44,825.14. Excellent benefits plan. Required Qualifications: Associate's degree or sixty credits toward a bachelor's degree, and/or two years military experience, U.S. citizen, minimum twenty-one years old, valid driver's license. Applicants are subjected to physical fitness test, written examination, intensive background investigation, interview process, psychological testing, drug screening, medical clearance, and Basic Training Academy. All new officers are appointed as Reserve Correctional Officers. Full-time positions are filled from the reserve ranks.

Federal corrections officers must have 200 hours of formal training within the first year of employment. They also complete a 120-hour course at the federal Bureau of Prisons training center in Glynco, Georgia, within sixty days after they are appointed. Some officers will receive additional, specialized training for assignments on tactical response teams so that they can deal with weapons, forced entries, chemical agents, crisis management, hostage events, forced cell moves, and other highly charged situations.

Corrections Counselor/Caseworker

Corrections provides many varied fields through which you can help others, as the listing of possible job titles later in this chapter attests.

Definition of the Career Path

One classification of corrections worker is corrections counselor, sometimes called corrections caseworker. Other titles apply as well, such as for positions in prerelease programs and halfway houses. Because the training and day-to-day work among these jobs share the counselor/client relationship, they are discussed collectively in this section, using some of the different job titles possible in the examples and applications to give you a sense of the variety of settings possible for a corrections counselor.

The following excerpt from an actual advertisement for a counselor in the Georgia Department of Corrections makes clear the variety of potential work settings and the importance of your criminal justice degree.

Counselor. Under general supervision, provides professional counseling services to offenders at a correctional facility such as an institution, boot camp, probation detention center, transitional center, division center, or office. Completion of an undergraduate degree in criminal justice, social work, counseling, or sociology.

Corrections counselors provide intensive case management and counseling to adult offenders in corrections facilities and outreach settings (such as halfway houses). They may be employed by the state, by the county sheriff, or by their community department of justice. Basic duties may include intensive case management, counseling, alcohol and drug evaluations, and needs assessments. You may also lead and facilitate therapeutic and educational group sessions. In addition, you will frequently coordinate your work with related departments such as family services, alcohol and drug treatment programs, and other departmental staff. Programs with which you may be involved include probation, alternative detention, release on own recognizance, supervised release, DWI assessment, deferred prosecution, restitution, work crews, jail programs, employment, and alternative service.

The duties of corrections counselors vary by size of institution and employer (federal, state, county, or local). Following are typical key tasks and responsibilities of the corrections counselor/caseworker:

- Supervise the distribution of caseload functions and court referrals among staff members within the assigned unit
- Prepare the unit budget and grant applications, monitor services expenditures for program participants, and provide summary statements
- Review program changes and policy mandates, assist in evaluation of unit programs, evaluate contract performance, and develop new proposals for contract work
- Visit work crews and special project sites
- Maintain unit records and case files in accordance with applicable laws
- May represent the department at boards or meetings
- Prepare a variety of reports for the courts

Rehabilitation or prerelease program counselors plan and coordinate rehabilitation treatment services for adult offenders. They work with offenders during and immediately following their incarceration. While offenders are in custody, the counselor assists with programming, monitoring of behavior, and preparation of release plans. Upon their release, the counselor continues to work with the offenders during the initial transition from custody to community supervision, perhaps in a halfway house.

Halfway house managers and counselors perform duties similar to those of rehabilitation counselors. Halfway houses are facilities designed to hold offenders for a limited period prior to their independent release into the community. Referrals of offenders to halfway houses are accepted from the courts, probation officers, case managers, and jail and prison staff; also, many residents are self-referred. These programs accept individuals with a history of criminal offense who are motivated to make positive changes in their lives, remain drug and alcohol free, and accept program rules and policies while living as law-abiding members of the community. Helping clients with their individual needs is a highly collaborative process involving other professional staff in order to tailor an appropriate treatment plan.

The program of services that you devise for each client is individually planned and incorporates a variety of academic and vocational studies, work assignments, recreational activities, and psychological and medical services. Counselors must also maintain extensive documentation on offenders' progress in their specific plans. Other typical functions of this type of counselor include:

- Supervise activities of subordinate staff on assigned shift; assign duties, schedule workloads, and authorize time off
- Ensure that proper security, sanitation, and safety requirements are met, maintain surveillance of residents, supervise resident counts, search for contraband, and distribute medications
- Supervise the orientation of all new facility residents; ensure that residents have been informed of rules and regulations of the facility
- Coordinate transportation of residents to and from work locations, medical appointments, and recreational activities; maintain accurate vehicle records and reports
- Review reports prepared by subordinate staff, such as resident count sheets, medication logs, and sign-out sheets; prepare and maintain records and reports of any unusual resident activities
- Provide instruction to residents and staff on emergency procedures
- May provide direct paraprofessional guidance to residents on grooming, public transportation, parole requirements, and other areas as indicated

Working Conditions

Candidates may take jobs as lead counselor or senior staff for any of a variety of functional units (educational, recreation, therapeutic, residential, and so on). Work is performed primarily in an office setting. However, stress comes with the territory, as counselors are frequently mandated to resolve problems of a serious and immediate nature arising from staff or offenders. You may have to defuse potentially hazardous situations involving offenders and may be pressed to carry out your assignments within extremely short time frames.

Training and Qualifications

Most supervisory jobs go to candidates with four-year degrees in criminal justice, social work, sociology, or psychology. Additionally, most of these jobs, even at the entry level, require at least a year's experience in adult corrections casework, probation or parole, or substance abuse counseling. Some graduate work may be substituted for that work experience. In some instances, additional but less-related work experience (employment interviewing, social casework) may substitute for the education and experience requirements. More senior positions in the pay scale require commensurate experience or education.

Depending on the level of position for which you are applying, here are some of the skills and attributes you would be expected to possess to qualify as a candidate:

- Use of diagnostic criteria
- Understanding of the basic factors that reduce recidivism
- Developing, implementing, and facilitating groups
- Familiarity with cognitive restructuring techniques
- Dealing with noncompliant and mandated clients
- Ability to establish effective and appropriate boundaries with offenders
- Ability to work in a jail, prison, or other part of the criminal justice system
- Experience working with difficult populations, including offenders with mental disabilities, sex offenders, and substance abusers

The ability to pass a security clearance and a thorough background investigation as well as possession of a valid driver's license are also common criteria for this position. Bilingual candidates are highly valued.

Warden

Although the distinguished position of warden would be the culmination of most people's careers in corrections, it has a definite place in a career guide devoted primarily to entry-level positions.

Definition of the Career Path
The résumés and biographies of the country's wardens today reveal that this is a profession that truly promotes from within. The men and women serving as wardens of prison complexes almost always detail a job history beginning with corrections officer. As these individuals advanced in their careers, they typically held the job titles of corrections counselor, program supervisor, and corrections administrator. Some were selected, after several

assignments, to return to teach at a corrections officers training academy or to work in staff development and training before moving into the ranks of deputy warden and warden.

Working Conditions

Several websites feature wardens from large corrections institutions in various states showcasing their facilities. An outstanding site is that of Marvin Polk of the North Carolina Department of Correction, Division of Prisons (doc.state.nc.us/dop/cptour). Central Prison, depicted in his site, is the oldest corrections facility in the state, and the warden supervises eight hundred professionals in this complex prison facility.

What is especially attractive about this site is that it provides a virtual tour of the prison, beginning with arrival at the gatehouse and continuing on to receiving and processing, records, the cell block, the cell, and work assignments (license plate manufacture). Touring the prison with Warden Polk gives you an excellent sense of the multiple departments and varied concerns of the warden, from equipment maintenance to food service management, health and safety issues, and the time-consuming area of staff management. It's a big job, and you can understand why it's best done by someone who has come up through the ranks and understands intimately every aspect of prison life.

Just how involved prison life can be is well illustrated by some facts about the California State Prison at Sacramento. The warden of this facility presides over a site that covers 1,200 acres and has 839 professional staff and 298 support staff, with an annual operating budget for the year 2003 of more than $125 million. The prison was designed for a capacity of 1,728 inmates and currently houses 2,967, so you can appreciate the scope of cell and cell-block redesign necessary to accommodate such an overflow. This particular prison is a maximum-security facility for inmates who are serving long sentences or who exhibited behavior management problems at other institutions. It also has one minimum-security unit. The warden here has a variety of inmate work programs, including furniture assembly, reupholstery, and refinishing; paper products; printing; and a warehouse. Some prisoners even do computer refurbishing. Adult basic education programs, G.E.D. programs, English as a second language, computer-assisted education, and many other academic and service-related programs are available for inmate participation. You can view this facility at cdc.state.ca.us/facility/instsac.htm.

Training and Qualifications

Corrections institutions increasingly seek officers and top management with collegiate and graduate education, particularly in criminal justice, psychology, political science, criminology, and related fields. A number of wardens cite having a master's degree in business administration (M.B.A.) as particularly helpful in dealing with the complex facilities management, budgetary, and staffing concerns involved in maintaining a corrections facility.

The following actual advertisement for a warden of a midwestern corrections facility clearly demonstrates how the job is the culmination of a wide variety of work experiences in corrections combined with business, analytical, and management skills. This ad was posted (among other places) on the largest online resource for news and information on prisons and corrections departments, the Corrections Connection, at http://database.corrections.com.

Warden. This is a highly responsible position managing a large adult state correctional facility (security level minimum and high medium). The selected candidate will formulate all operating and security functions and all program functions of the institution, and interpret and carry out state and agency policies. The selected candidate will supervise a large staff in maintaining and enforcing disciplinary, safety, security, and custodial measures. Qualifications: Applicants must possess at least a bachelor's degree from an accredited college or university. Applicants must also possess at least five years of professional/managerial experience in correctional or related work. A comprehensive benefit package includes medical, dental, vision, life insurance, retirement plans, and accrued leave. Salary range: $56,000–$88,000.

Earnings

If you are considering a career in corrections, try to determine what corrections staff are being paid in the geographic location in which you're interested. Average salaries across the country are presented in this section to give you a base from which to work; however, salaries in corrections can vary tremendously from one state or region to the next. This type of variability occurs in most professions, but it is especially applicable in corrections. In fact, a survey conducted by the American Correctional Association concluded that there is no common pattern or trend in corrections salaries and that vast differences between low and high starting salaries existed across all positions and personnel at all experience levels.

The employment field in corrections is volatile, and salary levels in any given area can change quickly as state or local governments try to come up with innovative ways to fill the ever-growing number of positions they have available. Ratcheting up salaries is one of the strategies that many are closely evaluating.

So, do some homework. Consult state human resources pages on the Web; visit your town hall personnel office or county jail; check regional newspapers for current corrections job announcements. Even salaries for federal positions will vary based on locality pay, as explained in Chapter 6. Here's some information to get you started.

Corrections Officer

The most recent government labor statistics indicate that corrections officers earned a median salary of $33,600 in 2004. While most earned between $26,560 and $44,200, the differences from state to state were considerable. The lowest 10 percent of officers earned less than $22,630, while some in other states earned more than $54,820. The variance wasn't quite as great among officers at different levels of government. Average salaries at the federal level were highest at $44,700, followed by state government, (where most officers are in fact employed) with average earnings of $33,750, and finally the state level with an average of $33,080. Remember that these are average salaries for all corrections officers and that starting salaries will be less. Also, a small number of corrections officers are employed by privately operated prisons, and their median salary is the lowest at $21,490.

Entry-level federal corrections officers are hired at the GS-5 level, which pays $25,195 to $32,755, excluding locality pay. In addition, officers assigned to night duty are paid a percentage of their basic hourly rate above regular pay, and officers earn 25 percent above regular pay for all work on Sundays.

Employees of the government also receive a good benefits package and usually an allowance to purchase uniforms if they are not already provided. Tuition reimbursement may also be included, which can be a tremendous financial help if you intend to further your education. And don't forget the federal retirement coverage, whereby if you enter employment in your twenties, then you may be able to retire in your forties.

Corrections Counselor/Caseworker

Counselors in the field of corrections can be generalists, such as case managers, or they can be specialists, such as substance abuse counselors. They can even be a combination of a corrections officer and a counselor. Given this range of possible job responsibilities, it is not surprising that salaries can vary widely depending on the job description and geographic location.

Take an example from Massachusetts:

Correctional Program Officer. Maintain a dual function by performing casework while providing custodial care and control of inmates. Conduct counseling interviews with inmates, inform them about rehabilitative services available, and confer with agency staff regarding treatment plans. Salary: $31,542.

We sampled listings from around the country for a variety of counseling positions in corrections. Advertised salaries ranged from a low of $21,000 to a high of $39,785. A new graduate with a bachelor's degree will most likely qualify for positions with average salaries in the middle $20,000s. The higher salaries generally require some experience and graduate study; in some situations certification is also needed. Let's take a look at some recent ads to illustrate this:

Correctional Center Rehabilitation Counselor. Conducts initial classification interviews. Provides individual counseling to each inmate on caseload. Facilitates inmate treatment program(s). Prepares annual/parole progress reports. Qualifications: Bachelor's degree from a college or university in a field related to social services. Salary: $25,881.

Here's one for a substance abuse counselor. Notice the two pay ranges depending on the degree you hold.

Addictions Counselor. Responsibilities include management and individual and group counseling. For those with a B.S. or B.A., pay range will be $23,000–$29,000; master's level is $25,000–$33,000. We offer a competitive salary and an excellent paid benefits package.

And finally, with a little experience, you could qualify for the following position:

Corrections Counselor, Department of Community Justice and Sheriff's Office. Provide intensive case management and counseling to adult offenders in the county's correctional facilities and in community outreach settings. Basic duties include counseling; alcohol and drug evaluations; needs assessments; and leading and facilitating process and educational groups. Minimum of two years of social counseling and/or case management experience; specific experience with the criminal justice system is preferred. Bachelor's degree with major course work in criminal justice, psychology, or sociology. Salary: $31,737–$45,998.

Salaries are somewhat higher in federal government, but the qualifications are higher as well. The Bureau of Prisons, which oversees all federal corrections facilities, requires that "correctional treatment specialists" (case managers) and "drug treatment specialists" have two full years of graduate study in behavioral or social sciences, or one year of supervised casework experience, or an equivalent combination. Entry-level salaries for these positions are at the GS-9 level, $39,175 to $43,267, not including locality pay increases where applicable.

Warden

Most wardens are promoted from within, so by the time you reach the position, assuming this is part of your career plan, you will have received multiple promotions and salary increases. Wardens are the chief operating officers in corrections facilities and are, in almost all cases, the highest wage earners as well. Recent ads for wardens cited salaries in the $50,000 range, continuing upward to $98,999.

Career Outlook

Corrections facilities process more than 22 million people a year, and that figure is expected to rise. As inmate populations grow and mandatory sentencing guidelines calling for longer sentences are adopted, the need for corrections facilities and workers to staff them will grow as well. Employment growth is also anticipated in the private sector as government authorities contract with private industry to create and staff additional facilities. Moreover, the government continues to fund community-based corrections programs such as halfway houses and alternative sentencing programs to ease overcrowding and better accommodate and rehabilitate certain types of offenders. Because of this employment growth, you can also expect layoffs to be rare and job security to be strong.

Corrections Officer

Job opportunities for corrections officers are expected to be excellent over the next several years. The need to replace officers who transfer to other occupations, retire, or leave the labor force, coupled with rising employment demand, will generate thousands of job openings each year. In the past, some local and state corrections agencies have experienced difficulty in attracting and keeping qualified applicants, largely because of lower salaries, shift work, and the concentration of jobs in rural locations. This situation is expected to continue, resulting in many opportunities in these areas.

Reduced parole for inmates and the expansion and new construction of corrections facilities should also spur job growth. However, mandatory sentencing guidelines are being reconsidered in many states because of a combination of budgetary constraints, court decisions, and doubts about their effectiveness. Instead, there may be more emphasis on reducing sentences or putting offenders on probation or in rehabilitation programs in many states. As a result, the prison population, and employment of correctional officers, will probably grow at a slower rate than in the past. Some employment opportunities also will arise in the private sector, as public authorities contract with private companies to provide and staff corrections facilities. Layoffs of correctional officers are rare because of increasing offender populations. Officers are allowed to join bargaining units, but they are not allowed to strike.

Although this overall employment growth rate is one reason for the positive outlook, another reason cannot be ignored: the high turnover rate for corrections officers. This is a tough job. Corrections officers wear multiple hats and put their lives on the line every time they go to work. Not only are they required to work different shifts, but also, because of staffing shortages, they may need to work extra shifts to maintain appropriate security levels. You can see, then, how stress can affect a corrections officer's decision to transfer into other areas, retire, or change careers altogether.

For those who stay in the field, there are many opportunities for promotion and advancement. A corrections officer with experience, education, and additional training can move up to corrections sergeant, directing the activities of corrections officers. This path could extend all the way up to warden.

Corrections Counselor/Caseworker

As new facilities are built and community corrections efforts expand, employment for counselors and caseworkers will remain favorable. Here too are opportunities for promotion and advancement, provided that you continue your training and education. You may start as a counselor and go on to become a unit manager, case management coordinator, or director of therapeutic services. Or perhaps you'll decide to specialize in alcohol and substance abuse, in vocational guidance, or in juvenile rehabilitation. If you're more interested in working in a community-based facility, maybe you'll become the program's director or regional administrator. In summary, not only is the outlook good for entering the career, but also, once you're there, many and diverse options are available to you.

Warden

Wardens will be hired mainly as new facilities are built or, in some cases, to replace wardens who retire. A salient difference between this occupation and the others that have been mentioned is that the field is much narrower. Each institution has one chief administrator, and at the federal level, for example, there are only ninety-six institutions. Wardens and superintendents do have assistants, who usually have moved up through the ranks of the corrections system and are in line for a warden position. Wardens themselves may go on to become state corrections administrators, overseeing entire state systems.

Strategy for Finding the Jobs

Because the vast majority of positions are with the government, an ideal place to start looking is online at the Corrections Connection website, corrections.com. When you click on "Jobs," you can select links to federal agencies and state departments of correction as well as local resources. Pretty much all the information you'll need is in one place. Some states include employment opportunities on their department of corrections websites. For others, you may need to visit the state's home page to obtain personnel information. Some county sheriff's offices also list openings directly on their sites; at the very least, you'll be given contact information such as phone numbers, mailing address, and e-mail addresses so that you can check with prospective employers personally.

Many positions require civil service testing, so don't forget to inquire about that as well. Books and guides to help you prepare for this exam can be ordered online at amazon.com or barnesandnoble.com or through your local bookstore.

If you are interested in working in a federal corrections facility, you will need to follow these application guidelines:

- Visit the federal government website, usajobs.com, to locate the position you are interested in. Each position announcement will tell you how to apply for that specific job. In many cases, applications are only accepted online.
- If required, submit form OF 612, Optional Application for Federal Employment, or a résumé. The form is downloadable from the Bureau of Prisons website at bop.gov/recruit.html. Keep your original application or résumé in case you are contacted for an interview because applications and résumés received in the Examining Section (where your application is evaluated and rated against the required and preferred eligibility) are not retrievable by the candidate.
- Have your official college transcript sent.

Additional paperwork may be required if you have served in the military. For complete application information, visit the Bureau of Prisons website.

If you are seeking a position in a community-based facility or program, don't neglect to look in the local newspapers or contact one of your state's unemployment offices. You can locate the office closest to you by checking the white pages in the phone book or online. In the state's listing of offices, you will usually find them under "Employment Security Department."

You can also visit America's Job Bank at ajb.dni.us, which connects you to all state employment offices. You will be asked to select a job category; choose "Community and Social Services." Then you enter the zip code of the area you want to search (the site will help you identify a zip code if you're not sure), and the service will display jobs that meet your criteria. You can view complete job descriptions and even some benefit information. This is a helpful site to review on a regular basis.

As you begin to interview for jobs in corrections, heed these words of advice from corrections officials who conduct interviews and review applications for employment: Arrive for the interview on time. It shows dependability, which is imperative in this field. Be able to articulate your goals, and be proud of the profession you have chosen. Prepare for the interview by doing basic research on the institution. Know something about the facility. Know what forms of testing your state requires.

A bachelor's degree will help not only because the applicant pool is big and your degree makes you more competitive but also because it reflects a willingness to commit to and complete responsibilities.

Possible Employers

Employees in the field of corrections are most likely working for the government at some level, be it local, county, state, or federal. More than half of all corrections officers work at state corrections institutions such as prisons, detention centers, prison camps, and youth corrections facilities. Most of the remainder work for city and county jails or other local corrections programs and centers. Some are employed by the federal Bureau of Prisons and work in a federal penitentiary, corrections institution, prison camp, or medical center.

Some corrections workers are employed by community corrections centers or detention facilities that contract with the Bureau of Prisons to provide these services. State departments of corrections also fund such programs. So, even if you are working in a social service agency providing substance abuse counseling services to prerelease inmates, your employer may be a local agency, but your position is in all likelihood ultimately funded by the government. As noted, a small but growing number of privately owned and managed prisons also employ corrections workers.

Possible Job Titles

As you read through this list, remember that different job titles can mean very different job responsibilities, and job responsibilities may not be reflected in the job title. This is particularly true in the case of the corrections officer, who sometimes has responsibilities similar to those of a counselor, teacher, or work supervisor. Although the job titles here are grouped into three categories—Corrections Officer (protective/security services), Counselor (social services), and Administrator (management services)—titles may sometimes overlap categories.

Corrections Officer

Classification officer
Correctional officer
Correctional officer trainer
Correctional program officer
Correctional sergeant
Corrections officer trainee

Detention officer
Guard
Jailer
Prison tactical response team
Transport officer

Counselor

Addictions counselor
Alcohol and substance
  abuse counselor
Case manager
Caseworker
Community service caseworker
Correctional rehabilitation
  counselor
Correctional treatment
  specialist
Corrections counselor
Drug treatment specialist

Education counselor
HIV specialist
Prerelease program correctional
  counselor
Prerelease program employment
  counselor
Recreational counselor
Release counselor
Social worker
Substance abuse specialist
Vocational counselor

Administrator

Chief of programs
Classification and treatment
  director
Corrections facilities manager
Inmate records coordinator

Penologist
Prerelease program halfway
  house manager
Superintendent
Warden

Related Occupations

Academic teacher
Director of community education
Education specialist

Private security specialist
Recreation leader
Store detective

Professional Associations

Listed in this section are some of the associations that relate to careers in the field of corrections. For more information about these professional associations, either check the websites listed or consult the *Encyclopedia of Associations*, published by Thomson Gale. Review the Members/Purpose notes for each organization to determine if it pertains to your interests. Membership in one or more of these organizations may gain you access to job listings, networking opportunities, and employment search services. Some provide information at no charge, but if you want to receive specific publications that list job opportunities, you may need to join. If you're still in college, check for student member rates.

American Correctional Association
4380 Forbes Blvd.
Lanham, MD 20706-4322
aca.org
Members/Purpose: A multidisciplinary organization of professionals representing all facets of corrections and criminal justice, including federal, state, and military correctional facilities and prisons, county jails and detention centers, probation/parole agencies, and community corrections/halfway houses in the United States and Canada.
Publications: *Corrections Today* magazine; *Corrections Compendium: The National Journal for Corrections*; major catalog of additional publications
Training: National training conventions; certification seminars; online workshops; video lending library

American Jail Association
1135 Professional Ct.
Hagerstown, MD 21740-5853
corrections.com/aja
Members/Purpose: A national nonprofit organization dedicated to supporting those who work in and operate our nation's jails.
Publications: *American Jails* magazine; *Write It Right* quarterly; *Jail Operations Bulletin*
Training: Annual conferences; Jail Manager Certification Program; online national training schedule

American Probation and Parole Association

P.O. Box 11910

Lexington, KY 40578-1910

appa-net.org

Members/Purpose: An international association of individuals from the United States and Canada actively involved with probation, parole, and community-based corrections, in both adult and juvenile sectors, at all levels of government.

Publications: *Perspectives* quarterly journal; complete library of books, magazines, and periodicals

Training: Training institutes; national/regional training seminars and technical assistance; professional development program

Association for the Treatment of Sexual Abuse

4900 S.W. Griffith Dr., Suite 274

Beaverton, OR 97005

atsa.com

Members/Purpose: To foster research, facilitate information exchange, further professional education, and provide for the advancement of professional standards and practices in the field of sex offender evaluation and treatment.

Publication: *Sexual Abuse: A Journal of Research and Treatment,* quarterly

Training: Annual conference

Association of Halfway House Alcoholism Programs

860 N. Center St.

Mesa, AZ 85201

ahhap.org

Members/Purpose: Represents more than 1,500 residential facilities providing long-term, cost-effective recovery services to more than 120,000 individuals each year. AHHAP members have positively affected millions of lives for almost thirty years, returning individuals to sober, productive living within their families and communities.

Publication: Online newsletter

Training: National Certified Recovery Specialist Certification program

Correctional Education Association

8182 Lark Brown Rd., Suite 202

Elkridge, MD 21075

ceanational.org

Members/Purpose: To increase the effectiveness, expertise, and skills of its members and to represent the collective interest of corrections education before the government, the press, and the public on the national as well as on the state, provincial, and local levels.

Publications: *The Journal of Correctional Education; CEA News and Notes; Directory of Continuing Educators*

Training: Annual national conference

Council of Juvenile Correctional Administrators
170 Forbes Rd., Suite 106
Braintree, MA 02184
cjca.net

Members/Purpose: Dedicated to the improvement of juvenile corrections services and practices. The CJCA promotes and facilitates three major activities: the exchange of ideas and philosophies at the top administrative level of juvenile corrections planning and policy making, the advancement of juvenile corrections and juvenile justice techniques, and the education of the public about juvenile justice and corrections systems.

Publications: Quarterly newsletter; yearbook survey

Training: Summer meetings

International Community Corrections Association
1730 Rhode Island Ave. NW, Suite 403
Washington, DC 20006
iccaweb.org

Members/Purpose: To promote and enhance the development of community corrections programs. It also provides information and training to enhance the quality of services, to promote effective management practices, and to promote the effectiveness of community corrections programming.

Publications: *ICCA Journal on Community Corrections; ICCA Justice Committee News; Research Conference Proceedings;* membership newsletter

Training: Extensive year-round conference schedule

Mental Health in Corrections Consortium
2885 W. Battlefield
Springfield, MO 65807
http://forest.edu/mhcca/index.html

Members/Purpose: A leading voice for mental health providers within the criminal justice system, primarily corrections, providing high-quality training related to mental health issues in criminal justice.

Publications: Members share publications with the American Association for Corrections Psychologists and receive the journal *Criminal Justice and Behavior* and the newsletter *The Correctional Psychologist*

Training: Annual conference

National Correctional Industries Association
1202 N. Charles St.
Baltimore, MD 21201
http://nationalcia.org

Members/Purpose: Provides, promotes, aids, serves, and encourages individuals and agencies, both public and private, engaged in and concerned with correctional industries as a meaningful employment program for inmates of correctional institutions.

Publications: *CIA Newsletter, Executive Director's Report*

Training: Prison Industries Enhancement (PIE) Certification; training conferences and regional meetings

National Institute of Corrections
320 First St. NW
Washington, DC 20534
nicic.org

Members/Purpose: To advance and shape effective corrections practice and public policy that respond to the needs of corrections, through collaboration and leadership and by providing assistance, information, education, and training.

Publications: Extensive online publication database of more than 1,200 titles in jails, prisons, community corrections, and general-interest categories

Training: Corrections staff training; regional training events and teleconferences

9

Path 4: Juvenile Justice

Your Future Is Their Future

The current dilemma of whether to try adolescents as children or adults is just one symptom of the complexities and difficulties that surround and infuse the area of juvenile justice. The previous three chapters outlined various career paths that also apply to juvenile justice. For example, certain police and federal law enforcement positions offer specialties in areas of juvenile justice. The career paths of corrections officer, probation officer, parole officer, and counselor also can focus on the activities germane to juvenile court.

This chapter is devoted to two broad categories of employment that represent the challenging and rewarding career opportunities in juvenile justice. First we will review positions that are involved with the daily rehabilitation of juveniles in a particular setting, including caseworkers, counselors, group home workers, juvenile justice counselors, and child, youth, and runaway counselors. The second employment category discussed is that of juvenile probation officers, who are responsible for case management of juvenile offenders in conforming and fulfilling the probationary dictates of the court.

Background

The juvenile justice process varies from community to community, depending on local practice and tradition, but the justice process for juveniles in general is distinguished by some common decision points, regardless of the system. The first decision point pertains to the question that opened this chapter: youth or adult? At the time of the arrest of a juvenile, a decision is made by the courts to either send the matter on to the justice system or divert the case out of the justice system to some alternative program. This decision incorporates the youth's criminal record (if any), conversations with parents or caregivers, and a review of any past contact with the law enforcement system. About a third of juvenile subjects are released by the police back to the parents or caregivers, while the remainder are sent to juvenile court. Law enforcement referrals account for 85 percent of all delinquency cases referred to juvenile court. Other referrals are made by parents, caregivers, victims, schools, and probation officers.

Federal law has traditionally frowned on holding juveniles with adults, so there have been strict guidelines on where and for how long a juvenile can be detained in a nonjuvenile detention facility. However, the number of people under eighteen years old who are sentenced to adult state prisons each year continues to rise. According to the Justice Department's Bureau of Justice Statistics, at the end of 2002 (the most recent year for which data are available), more than 3,000 of the 1.2 million state prisoners were younger than eighteen; in addition, adult jails held more than 7,200 prisoners under eighteen.

Generally, the court intake function is the responsibility of the juvenile probation department or the state prosecutor's office, who decide either to handle the situation informally and dismiss the case or take it to juvenile court. Generally this decision involves the degree of sufficiency of evidence in the case, although half of all cases referred to juvenile court are handled informally by dismissal.

Those who are not dismissed outright may still be handled informally by setting some specific conditions that the juvenile voluntarily agrees to observe for a specific time. This set of conditions is formally drafted and signed and is often termed a consent decree. Conditions may include restitution to the victim, school attendance, drug counseling, or curfew restrictions. In most cases, no informal disposition is possible unless the juvenile admits to having committed the act. Though informal, the decree may still be monitored by a juvenile probation officer, a procedure often referred to as informal probation. If the juvenile complies with this consent decree, the case is dismissed. If the juvenile fails to meet the conditions of the consent decree, then the case reverts to the other option: formally prosecuting the juvenile. The case would then be referred for an adjudicatory hearing.

While awaiting the hearing, the juvenile may be held in the nearest local juvenile detention facility (if that action is determined by the court to be in the best interest of the community). Juvenile probation officers or detention workers review the case to decide if the juvenile should be held pending a hearing by the judge. In all fifty states, a detention hearing must be held within twenty-four hours. A judge decides between continued detention and release. About one-fifth of cases remain in detention. If a juvenile facility is not available (usually because of crowded conditions), the detention may extend beyond the adjudicatory and dispositional hearings.

Prosecutors may file a case in either juvenile or criminal court. Of course, debates over which court should hear such cases have been much in the news. In some states, the legislature has determined that certain crimes are so egregious that the perpetrator will be treated as a criminal offender. Some states have given the prosecutor discretionary power to decide which court will hear the case of a juvenile.

Juvenile Court

If the case is handled in juvenile court, two types of petitions may be filed, a delinquency petition or a waiver petition. If a delinquency petition is filed, the allegations are stated, and the prosecutor requests that the juvenile become a ward of the court and requests the judge to adjudicate the juvenile as a delinquent. This language and the disposition of the case are very different from criminal court, where an offender is convicted and sentenced.

The response to the delinquency petition is a hearing with a judge, at which the facts of the case are presented and witnesses may be called. In most of these cases, the judge makes the final determination of responsibility for the offense, although in some states the juvenile has the right to a jury trial. In 1999, about 60 percent of juveniles were judged delinquent in cases petitioned to juvenile court for criminal violations.

Waiver petitions can result in a case being transferred to criminal court.

Criminal Court

A waiver petition is filed when the prosecutor or intake officers feel that the case is more appropriate for criminal court. If probable cause that the juvenile committed the act is determined by the court, the court will then decide if the matter should be waived and transferred to criminal court.

Generally, in making this decision the court is concerned with how amenable to treatment the offender would be in the juvenile court system. Arguments against staying in the juvenile court system (by the prosecutor) may be based on a record of past offenses in juvenile court or the seriousness of the current offense. If the judge approves the waiver, the case is filed in criminal court and the offender is charged as an adult.

Possible Disposition Recommendations from Juvenile Court for Young Offenders

If a case stays in juvenile court and a petition of delinquency is adjudicated, several possible recommendations may be put before the bench either by probation staff or by the prosecutor. The court may also entertain proposals by the offender. Before this disposition plan is presented, probation staff have usually thoroughly interviewed the youth; ordered diagnostic evaluations, including psychological evaluations; and assessed available support systems. Possible outcomes include:

- **Probation and other provisions.** Most dispositions are a combination of requirements that may incorporate drug counseling, weekend confinement, victim restitution, or community restitution in addition to probation. Probation itself may be either for a specific period or open ended. Once probation conditions are met in full, the case is terminated by the judge.
- **Commitment to residential placement.** This, too, may be either for a specific period or open ended. About a third of adjudicated delinquents are assigned to residential placement, which may be publicly or privately operated, and conditions vary from a prisonlike setting to more homelike atmospheres. In some states, the state department of juvenile corrections determines the placement; in other states, it is the judge's decision.
- **Juvenile aftercare.** Following release from detention, confinement, or a residential facility, the juvenile is ordered to court-supervised aftercare, which is, in effect, no different from adult parole conditions. Violation of the aftercare conditions may result in recommitment.

Corrections Officer/Corrections Counselor

In juvenile justice employment, you will often encounter variations on the job title of corrections officer, some with varying duties.

Definition of the Career Path

Frequently this position is referred to as counselor, corrections caseworker, corrections residence counselor, or some variant of those. These may, in fact, be different positions, depending on the setting. The corrections officer in a detention facility, for example, has different duties from those of the corrections officer in a residential unit for juvenile delinquents. To add to the confusion, one residential unit may call that position corrections officer, and another residential unit (in a different state or county) may term the very same position juvenile counselor. Make it a practice to read job descriptions for any of these positions carefully to understand what the job is, regardless of what it is named. Here's a good example of this nomenclature confusion. Both of the ads quoted are seeking two- and four-year college graduates in criminal justice or other social science majors.

Youth Corrections Officer (Arizona). Interact daily, on a face-to-face basis with youth; provide supervision in a therapeutic role; facilitate behavior management groups; maintain security and discipline; check units for safety hazards or security violations; assist teachers with classroom management.

Juvenile Services Officer (California). Supervise and counsel juveniles in custody in accordance with established procedures; organize and direct services that support the juvenile's physical, emotional, and social development, including education, recreation, counseling, nutrition, hygiene, reading, visitation, transportation, communication, and continuous supervision; use force to ensure a safe environment, in accordance with established policy, including the use of physical, mechanical, and chemical restraints; book minors into custody in accordance with procedures; perform strip searches as necessary; transport minors.

Though the titles are different, the jobs sound very similar, both have the same requirements, and both indicate salaries in the same range ($30,000 to $40,000). So, as you read the job descriptions provided in this chapter, be aware that what's important is the job and not the title of that job. Increasingly, residential treatment centers are staffed by counselors, caseworkers, and teachers, and all function as disciplinarians when called upon, but technically no positions are labeled "corrections officer."

Here's a job ad for a youth worker at a private rehabilitation center for young boys in Montana structured in a military format:

Responsible for the supervision of cadets during their daily activities, to include all aspects of daily living, treatment, and education. Provides daily structure for the platoon cadets, provides discipline, and holds cadets accountable for their actions. Follows strategies as established to assist the teachers in the classroom. Responsible for the safety and security of cadets. Supervises barracks maintenance and recreational activities and is responsible for teaching the cadets hygiene and cleanliness. Issues instructions and provides direction to cadets. Provides on-the-spot counseling and correction to cadets, implements intervention strategies, and completes programmatic reports as necessary.

Though couched in the language of the military setting, the functions of this position are representative of the juvenile corrections counselor whose main role is to provide a combination of care, treatment, and custody for juvenile offenders.

One essential part of your job is daily hands-on implementation of the programs designed to habilitate, remediate, and divert young offenders from a life that has included some dysfunctional or maladaptive behavior, which has led to their involvement with the juvenile justice system.

A second area of responsibility is to attend to juveniles with overtly negative rehabilitative records and to provide programs for their personal growth and social development. Generally, juvenile corrections officers working with offenders with more serious rehabilitative issues would be sited at a medium-security facility. These inmates might have done poorly in their previous placements or escaped from a lower-security site and been assigned to the medium-security facility by the juvenile justice authorities.

A third aspect of this job embraces a larger context. As you grow in your position and develop experience in juvenile justice, you will participate in a variety of cooperative ventures. These may be collaborations among state, local, and county agencies and private concerns to share your combined resources and perhaps develop new initiatives to prevent or inhibit juvenile crime. Juvenile justice experts like you will be called on to share age-appropriate strategies with school, child welfare, medical, and mental health professionals to assist at-risk children in mastering key development tasks. Experts agree that fostering the strengths of at-risk children as they progress from birth to adulthood holds the greatest promise for reducing juvenile crime. As your own expertise develops, you will become skilled in helping others to explore better ways of delivering treatment and aftercare programs to juvenile offenders.

Following are some of the services for which you may be responsible.

Academic Services. Depending on your population's age, you may be helping students earn a G.E.D. certificate or high school diploma in a cooperative program with a local public school. You may also be helping teaching staff to implement an I.E.P. (individualized educational plan) for students with special educational needs.

Vocational Services. Most rehabilitative settings provide some vocational work experience as a mechanism for learning cooperative behavior and team responsibility, building trust, and, of course, developing workplace skills. Typical program offerings include upholstery, horticulture, welding, optical lab work, graphic design, auto body and mechanics, electrical and building trades, machine shop, small engine repair, and radio and television communications.

All of these programs help the resident population learn to set realistic life and career goals for themselves.

Social Services. You may be required to provide individual, group, and crisis counseling. Substance abuse services are often contracted out to Alcoholics Anonymous or Narcotics Anonymous trainers, either in-house or off-site. Some residential programs offer specialized housing units for residents needing treatment for substance abuse.

Aftercare. Aftercare is the term used for the treatment plan that begins almost immediately upon the offender's arrival at the facility. The goal is to ensure that all the ingredients of a successful rehabilitative stay are met and that the offender is fulfilling his or her responsibility to commit to the program. A team approach is standard, often involving the offender's family and all support staff, who meet regularly to plan and prepare for the eventual return of the juvenile to his or her home and community.

Medium-Security Sites

The difference for corrections officers working at medium-security sites is that the population tends to be youths with more serious emotional and behavioral disorders who require a more structured and secure environment. Within this structure, many of the services previously described are the same, although the supervision of residents is more intensive. The goal is still rehabilitative, with efforts directed to returning the juveniles to the community.

Counseling in the medium-security setting is also more intensive, and counseling services are provided most often by licensed clinical social workers supervised by a clinical psychologist, in recognition of the population's more complex emotional and behavioral profile.

Voluntary Sites

Some states offer juveniles the opportunity to sign (with the court's recommendation and approval) a voluntary agreement to participate in a structured residential program of limited duration designed to rehabilitate juvenile offenders whose histories do not warrant a lengthy sentence in a corrections facility.

These voluntary reintegration programs usually take less than six months to complete and involve many of the services previously detailed, including drug and alcohol counseling, general counseling services, educational programs, and an emphasis on a highly regimented daily routine, involving considerable physical activity.

Because these programs are of limited duration, aftercare planning is pivotal and begins right after the offender's arrival to help ensure a successful transition back to the community. Usually, corrections staff, family, teachers, social workers, and the juvenile's probation officer would all be involved in monthly team meetings.

Working Conditions

You have a wide choice of work settings in this position. Correctional facilities range from an almost summer camp atmosphere to relatively restrictive institutional settings. You could work in a juvenile "boot camp," a probation detention center, a transitional center, or an office. In working with troubled youth, you might prefer to be in an outdoor setting, perhaps riding horses and doing some farming. Check out the website of the Idaho Youth Ranch at youthranch.org. This remarkable institution provides residential treatment, group homes, adoption, and other services to troubled, disturbed, delinquent, or abused children and adolescents. It's unique as a facility, but it exemplifies the variety of settings possible in working with juveniles.

Regardless of the setting, your job as a juvenile correctional worker is a hands-on, energy-intensive, patience-demanding role that will put enormous physical and emotional demands on you and deliver comparable rewards for your efforts. You are, first and foremost, a role model. You become a teacher through your day-to-day conduct, your behavior toward your charges, your language, and your reactions to situations. It's not a job for those who want to stand back and observe nor for those with defensive personalities or who have not achieved some level of stability in their lives. To do this job well, you need to be focused, natural, versatile, and able to communicate.

Each day, you'll share confidences and concerns, provide advice, and help solve a wide assortment of problems. Since many of the settings for juveniles involve some degree of structure and rule setting, your ability to work within those rules and remain consistent will be fundamental to your efforts to exert leadership over your charges.

Because these facilities operate twenty-four hours, you will work in shifts, and entry-level job holders generally do not have shift preference until they achieve some seniority. More frequently, your personal schedule will be subjected to some buffeting as your shifts vary from 8 A.M. to 5 P.M., 4 P.M. to 1 A.M., and midnight to 9 A.M. Shifts frequently overlap an hour so that incoming staff can be thoroughly briefed and updated by the previous shift to ensure continuity of treatment. Though these jobs generally offer excellent benefits, including holidays, because of the year-round nature of the work, you will frequently work holidays that others (friends and family) have off.

It is important to note here that depending on where you work and the background of the offenders under your supervision, there can be some physical risk. Among older adolescents and in medium-security facilities, particularly, inmates may expose corrections staff to a considerable degree of danger of injury or assault.

Training and Qualifications

Many job ads indicate that they are seeking criminal justice majors. Occasionally, you will see a corrections position requesting previous work with a juvenile population in any capacity. Those employers know that if you have served in a parks and recreation program, coached junior or senior high school sports teams, or worked at a summer camp, you will have a better appreciation of the developmental dynamics of this population. It's a legitimate job demand and one that you may want to take into account when you are pursuing part-time or summer jobs if you feel that a career in juvenile justice is in your future.

In some positions, you will start as a trainee in corrections counseling and be promoted from trainee status after a two-year period of satisfactory work and training experience.

Juvenile Probation Officer

The juvenile probation officer works directly with youthful offenders who have completed their sentences.

Definition of the Career Path

The previous discussion of juvenile correctional officers stressed that the job title is undergoing a "softening" and being replaced more frequently by titles such as juvenile counselor, juvenile caseworker, corrections counselor, and other terms that may read more supportively and therapeutically than the word **corrections**. In reviewing job postings in the career path of a juvenile probation officer, however, it is not the job title that demands your caution but the description (if any) of the duties and responsibilities of the position.

Let's begin with one of the briefest job ads:

Juvenile Probation Officer (Ohio). Bachelor's degree in criminal justice or other behavioral science area. Must be twenty-one years old and have a valid Ohio driver's license.

Not a very illuminating job description, is it? And since there are some significant differences in the duties and responsibilities possible within this classification, you'll want to have a sense of the specific job before you apply, if possible.

Let's look at a more complete job advertisement—this one from Arizona:

Juvenile Probation Officer: Bachelor's degree in criminal justice or related field with one year of work experience with youth. Bilingual (Spanish/English) a plus. No criminal background. Must successfully complete a criminal history check relevant to employment since persons convicted of a felony may not be child-care workers in Arizona. Must be twenty-one, have a valid Arizona driver's license, and be able to work some flexible hours. Final job offer will be contingent upon a satisfactory five-year Arizona Motor Vehicle Report.

Duties: Under general supervision performs social investigations and evaluation of assigned offenders, including interviews with relatives, members of social agencies, employers, and others; prepares required reports and assessments and makes recommendations to the court; advises and supervises offenders as ordered by the court in order to enforce compliance with court directives; develops and implements client-based programs and refers offenders for placement in needed services; appears and testifies in court; conducts visits with offenders at the office and at various sites; performs searches, makes arrests, and provides crisis intervention; enters data and provides statistical data for computer-based management; maintains written and computerized records, runs reports, and verifies statistics with central records; keeps track of client payments; consults with attorneys and works with victims and community agencies; may transport offenders; may counsel offenders; works in partnership with the community for input, planning, and accountability (Restorative Justice); trains other officers; makes most case decisions independently.

Essential functions of this position include: searching for files, etc.; working with and around other clients, community contacts, child-care advocates, and staff; dealing with interruptions; repetitive motion (hand-wrist) for report writing, computer input, and documentation; vision acuity (near) for reading and computer input; vision acuity (far) for surveillance and driving; hearing and speech (ordinary conversation) for interviews, fieldwork, and communicating with staff and the public.

While states often publish detailed job specifications, we cite this example from Arizona because it is among the most detailed. More important, it offers a very helpful set of clues to the criminal justice job seeker interested in juvenile justice because it so thoroughly delineates the different tasks and occupations of the probation officer's job. Using this particular position as a basis, here's a breakdown of the different tasks and skills required of a juvenile probation officer:

- Interviewing (clients, parents, social service personnel, employers, and others)
- Report writing
- Making assessments and recommendations
- Knowledge of court directives and protocols
- Developing and implementing client-based programs
- Serving as a court witness
- Transporting offenders
- Performing searches; making arrests
- Counseling, including crisis intervention
- Computer proficiency (data entry, report writing, database management)
- Consulting (with attorneys, victims, and social agencies)

If you are strongly interested in juvenile justice, and especially in the position of parole/probation officer, and reading this job description and the list of skills required inspires both excitement and a bit of apprehension, that's OK! You've just come to the realization that the job is a highly responsible position with significant demands. Even more good news, as you will see in the following section on earnings, is that the salary for these positions tends to be among the best for entry-level jobs and is commensurate with the demands of the work.

You will be managing a caseload of probationers. What this means in your day-to-day work is that you assess each client to identify and monitor what risks the individual may present, you attempt to ensure his or her compliance with the judge's sentence, and you do all you can to encourage positive behavior changes.

Behind the scenes, you act as one of many probationary consultants to the courts, providing direction, services, and information on possible treatment plans, sentencing protocols, and alternatives for each offender. Because of this relationship to the court, many of the ads for juvenile probation officers require that you submit your application packet directly to the judge or the judge's administrative aide.

Working Conditions

Though some "desk time" is required with this job, you probably aren't delivering the best service if you are behind a desk much of the time. This job carries intensely competing demands of paperwork and record keeping and personal contact with offenders and members of their support systems.

You may be transporting your client to the doctor or to a job interview or to a group counseling session with parents and social workers. There will be conferences with lawyers, judges, and other court officials. You will have a full calendar of your own court dates as a witness as well as appointments to visit treatment and residential centers.

In any job this busy and this hectic, organizational skills are the key to successful performance. Your own skills and how you employ them will directly affect the quality of your working conditions. Good time management and record keeping; clear communications with others; and follow-up, follow-up, follow-up will go far in keeping your stress level down and the job manageable.

Training and Qualifications

Because of the responsibilities (and the good salary) that this job offers, the position is not as readily available as many others. Review the self-assessment exercises in Chapter 1, and be honest with yourself about your skills and experience. Can you demonstrate competency in oral and written communication technique? How can you assure prospective employers that you have the required ability to work independently and exercise good judgment? Many of these positions (though not all) demand some familiarity and work experience with a youth population. If you are still in school and have not had this kind of experience, through either summer camp counseling, church or community youth groups, or parks and recreation programming, then consider an internship in some area of juvenile justice before you graduate. Not only will it allow you to meet the requirements of working with youth, but also it will give you the advantage of insight into the criminal justice system through the experiences you will have enjoyed.

Each job and each employer will have unique demands. The lengthy job ad quoted in this section, for example, put particular emphasis on your state driving record, specifying evidence of five years of blemish-free driving. Other employers will require firearms experience or some training in self-defense. All of them will require that you undergo a thorough background investigation and will not consider any candidate with a felony conviction or evidence of any past moral turpitude.

Earnings

The juvenile justice system parallels the adult judicial process, with salary levels among correctional officers and counselors/case managers at juvenile facilities similar to those at adult prisons. The same can be said for probation officers in juvenile courts, whose salaries correspond to their counterparts associated with adults in the criminal court system throughout the country.

Corrections Officer/Corrections Counselor

As noted in Chapter 8, the median annual salary for all corrections officers in 2004 was $33,600. In other words, among all officers employed in the field, in both adult and juvenile facilities and at the entry level as well as after many years of experience, half earned above that amount and half earned below it. Our informal sampling of current employment ads for just entry-level juvenile corrections officer positions tends to support this earnings level. An ad for a residential treatment officer in Texas specified a salary of $21,500. However, this position did not require a college degree. At the opposite end of the spectrum, an opening for a group supervisor in Nevada was advertised at a high starting salary of $32,000. Here a college degree was required, and you could expect to earn more than $40,000 depending on your level of education and experience. The majority of positions carried minimum salaries in the upper $27,000 to $35,000.

Juvenile Probation Officer

Based on a survey of job postings and information available from states, starting salaries for juvenile probation officers range from $30,000 to $60,000, depending on geographic location, education, and experience. Beginning salaries are generally higher in state government than in systems run by county or local government.

Because salaries in one state or region of the country can differ vastly from those in another, you may want to check out the website maintained by the National Center for Juvenile Justice at ncjj.org/stateprofiles. This is one of the best sites on the Web for up-to-date, comprehensive information at the local level. Select a state, and you will be given a complete profile of the juvenile justice system in that state, including information on probation, detention, and state institutions, along with beginning salaries and caseload averages for probation officers. It is definitely worth investigating whether you want to learn about your area or explore other locations. If that's not enough, the site gives you contact information and, in most instances, directly links you to the juvenile departments or agencies responsible for hiring probation and other youth workers.

Career Outlook

As long as there are juveniles being arrested, there will be a need for corrections officers, probation officers, youth workers, and other professionals to provide services for them. Sadly, those numbers are rising. According to the most recent statistics from the U.S. Department of Justice's Office of Juvenile Justice and Delinquency Prevention, juvenile courts handled 1.6 million delinquency cases in 2002, up from 1.1 million in 1985 (a delinquency case is defined as an offense for which an adult could be prosecuted in criminal court). The volume of delinquency cases handled by juvenile courts rose 41 percent between 1985 and 2002. While statistics for male offenders have declined, the opposite is true for females. In 2002, more than four hundred thousand delinquency cases involved females, representing just over one-quarter of all juvenile offenders.

These figures have bearing for employment prospects because virtually every one of those cases would have had contact with a probation officer at some point. Moreover, this increase in juvenile court cases has not occurred just since 1985; in fact, the 2000 juvenile court delinquency caseload was more than four times what it was in 1960! You can easily see how marked increases such as these necessitate an increase in staffing as well.

As explained previously, juvenile courts sometimes hold youths in secure detention facilities while the court is processing their cases. Depending on the specific mission and the types of services offered, these facilities need some combination of counselors, caseworkers, instructors, trainers, security officers, recreation leaders, treatment specialists, and managers and other administrators. If your career goal is in the field of juvenile justice, the odds are very good that you will find a job that matches your interests and skills.

Strategy for Finding the Jobs

An important point to keep in mind as you begin your job search is that there is no comprehensive juvenile justice system in this country. Instead, there are separate, individual systems in each state and the District of Columbia. In some states, for example, probation is administered by local juvenile courts; in others, state executive agencies oversee probation services. Most often, these executive agencies are separate juvenile corrections agencies. However, they may also be welfare/social service agencies, children and youth agencies, or, in a few instances, adult corrections agencies. Probation services can also be run by the judicial agency of the state, such as a court administrator's office, or by a local executive agency. Some states even employ a combination of the foregoing, whereby local courts administer probation services in some parts of the state while the state oversees services in other parts, usually the more rural areas. So, to find out where the jobs are within a given state, you must first determine how the state's juvenile justice system is organized.

The best way to do this is through the National Center for Juvenile Justice website (ncjj.org/stateprofiles). There you will be able to view complete profiles of juvenile justice systems by state and can determine which agencies to target. You'll be provided with resources and contact information and, in the majority of cases, direct links to those agencies and organizations. Many of the linked sites clearly list job openings and application procedures, while for others you may need to navigate around a bit to find the human resources Web page. You may not always be able to locate employment announcements, but you should find enough information to guide you in the right direction.

Paperwork Tip

The application and hiring process in public employment is often heavily dependent, especially in the early stages, on the careful submission of paperwork. Therefore, pay particular attention to the application forms and their completion. Make several copies of every form you receive, and use them to work up a preliminary draft before submission. You'll discover that many application forms demand frustratingly long responses in very small spaces, often requiring you to attach additional sheets. You'll want to work out your responses on a copy of the original form before completing the finished product. Remember that appearance is important, as is the thoroughness of your information.

Other Sources of Job Leads

Not all positions in juvenile justice are with government agencies. Many opportunities are available in private and nonprofit youth agencies that contract with government agencies to administer and operate juvenile justice programs. To find these positions, you will need to go to other sources, some of which have already been mentioned, such as local and regional newspapers and local employment offices. Others are described here.

Your College's Career Office. Almost all college career offices maintain some system of posting the job advertisements that they receive daily via fax, phone, mail, or e-mail. Ads may be posted on a website (either the school's own or a national jobs database aimed at college students, such as Job Direct at jobdirect.com), in three-ring binders, or on job boards. Most of the jobs will be entry level and targeted to recent college graduates. These postings change quickly as new ones arrive each day, so be sure to check the site or office at least weekly. You may also want to check with the criminal justice department at your college or university. Sometimes employers send postings to the relevant academic department, where they may be maintained on a bulletin board.

Internet Job Searching. Chapter 3 emphasized the importance of developing a list of employment websites to monitor. Two of the most popular employment sites are monster.com and careerbuilder.com. Don't forget to also include any state or local sites you've found, along with online newspaper classifieds in your area; careerpath.com is a link to newspaper classifieds nationwide. You may want to prepare an activity log, with the name of each site listed in one column and dates to check across the top of the page. This will help to organize your Internet job search and ensure that you check each site at least once a week. Develop a list of keywords for searches based on your areas of interest, such as youth counselor, youth worker, juvenile probation officer, and juvenile corrections.

Another worthwhile Web-based search function is the Web yellow pages found on many search engines (dogpile.com is one service). Using keywords more suited to employers, such as juvenile, social service, or youth centers, you can search your own locale and surrounding areas where these hiring organizations may be listed.

Professional Associations. Associations are the best-kept secret of the job search. A listing of some that are appropriate to the field of juvenile justice is included at the close of this chapter. Some of these associations will provide you with actual job listings; others may provide links to related sites with employment information. For the most part, you will have to join an association to take full advantage of its services, such as professional journals and newsletters. Some may offer a student membership rate. Consider any expense an investment in your future. It's worth it! This book lists national associations, but many have local affiliates that may be cheaper to join and more in line with your needs.

A Final Tip: Build Skills and Gain Some Direct Experience with Youth

Many, if not most, of the want ads for juvenile justice worker that you encounter will ask for some kind of documented experience dealing with youth. Be sure to include the camp counselor job you had during your summer breaks in college on your résumé and highlight any responsibilities that involved supervision, leadership, program or activity planning, or counseling support. Volunteer work counts as well. Are you a Big Brother or Big Sister? Have you coached youth sports teams? How about any involvement with youth church groups? Record any of these on your résumé, and be prepared to discuss them in an interview.

If you haven't had any experience with youth programs, now is the time to get some. An internship would be the best way. These professional experiences give you an opportunity to test the reality and see if juvenile justice work is a good fit given your interests and abilities. Sometimes you can earn academic credit for an internship if it fits into your curriculum. Check with your criminal justice academic department or college career office to find out what opportunities are available to you. Start the process early, as internships can be very competitive. Once you complete an internship, you'll have that all-important experience to put on your résumé, and you will have established some professional contacts in the field.

If an internship is not possible, consider volunteer work. Many nonprofit and government agencies are short-staffed and would welcome the additional support. You can also contact youth organizations in your area and ask what their volunteer needs are. Find out what kind of training they may provide. This can be a great way to enhance your skill base at no cost. These same organizations may even offer part-time or summer opportunities.

Possible Employers

State and local governments are the primary employers of juvenile justice workers. Unlike some of the other careers already discussed, the federal government is not a major employer here. That's because very few juvenile offenders are processed through the federal criminal justice system. Almost all juvenile offenders go through state and local courts.

Because each state has its own system for handling juvenile delinquency, how services are organized and, therefore, who does the hiring will depend on the state. Nevertheless, some generalities apply. To understand the system, it's helpful to break down juvenile delinquency services into front end and back end. The front end includes probation, defined as intake, investigation, and supervision of delinquents, and detention, which refers to the temporary custody of juveniles awaiting final court disposition. The back end includes delinquency institutions, sometimes called training schools, where delinquents are securely housed, and aftercare services, when the juvenile has been conditionally released but is being supervised in the community.

Generally speaking, front-end services (probation and detention) tend to be local responsibilities, while those at the back end (delinquency institutions and aftercare) tend to be state responsibilities. Most state systems, however, are hybrids, with some services being the responsibility of local government and others administered at the state level. The hiring agencies, therefore, may be the local courts (often the case with probation services), local executive agencies (most often a county juvenile bureau), or state-level executive agencies (for example, a state's department of youth services or office of court administration).

In every state, delinquency (residential) institutions and aftercare services are administered by a state executive agency, such as a department of youth services. In most cases, the agency that oversees the delinquency institutions is the same one that oversees aftercare services. As you look from state to state, you will notice varying names for these agencies. The ones most often seen are Department of Youth Services, Department of Juvenile Corrections, Youth Authority, Department of Children and Families, Juvenile Justice Authority, and Department of Health and Human Services (usually with a specific division for handling youth services). Sometimes the state's department of corrections will handle both adult and juvenile cases.

Although state and local authorities may be charged with administering juvenile delinquency services, that doesn't mean they always provide these services directly. Many states contract with private providers to operate detention centers, residential sites, and aftercare services. Nonprofit agencies and organizations also receive funding for residential and nonresidential services such as education programs, wilderness camps, recreation programs, vocational training, and treatment-specific programs for alcohol and substance abuse and sexual misconduct, to name a few.

Possible Job Titles

This career path is directed at a specific target population, so you will often see the words *youth* or *juvenile* in the job title. Sometimes the word *counselor* is in the title, and these jobs are often considered entry-level positions. Once you gain some related experience, you may begin to qualify for positions with *coordinator* or *supervisor* in the title. With additional years in the field and increased administrative responsibilities, such as training and supervising new workers, monitoring overall caseloads, and preparing and maintaining budgets, your options for jobs will include terms such as *director* and *executive director*.

Corrections Officer/Corrections Counselor

Aftercare counselor	Program/project director
Alcohol and substance abuse counselor	Reentry counselor
	Residential facilities manager
Case manager	Residential treatment counselor
Corrections residence counselor	Runaway counselor
Cottage manager	Support services coordinator
Counselor	Team leader
Detention officer	Training specialist

Employment specialist
Group counselor
Juvenile detention counselor
Juvenile rehabilitation
  coordinator

Youth advocate
Youth counselor
Youth services group worker
Youth worker

Probation Officer

Chief juvenile probation officer
Community program specialist
Court advocate
Deputy probation officer
Director of juvenile court
  service
Intervention officer

Juvenile probation officer
Juvenile services assistant
Juvenile services officer
Parole officer, juvenile justice
Probation officer

Related Occupations

Beyond the preceding list, your educational background and interest in working with youth can be combined with other skills or interests you may possess. Some positions of this type may be found within the corrections system; some may support the system in some way. Examples include:

Adoption caseworker
Recreation center director
School attendance officer
School resource officer

Teacher
Vocational instructor/
  specialist
Wilderness instructor

Professional Associations

Listed in this section are some of the associations that relate to careers in the field of juvenile justice. For more information about these professional associations, either check the websites listed or consult the *Encyclopedia of Associations*, published by Thomson Gale. Review the Members/Purpose notes for each organization to determine if it pertains to your interests. Membership in one or more of these organizations may gain you access to job listings, networking opportunities, and employment search services. Some provide information at no charge, but if you want to receive specific publications that list job opportunities, you may need to join. If you're still in college, check for student member rates.

American Bar Association
Juvenile Justice Committee
321 N. Clark St.
Chicago, IL 60610
abanet.org/crimjust/juvjus
Members/Purpose: Dedicated to monitoring legislative, fiscal, policy, and
administrative changes emerging in juvenile justice systems across the
nation. The website contains more than five hundred links to other
juvenile justice sites.
Publications: *ABA Journal;* various topical publications
Training: Midyear and annual meetings; also sponsors the Center for
Continuing Legal Education

American Correctional Association
4380 Forbes Blvd.
Lanham, MD 20706-4322
aca.org
Members/Purpose: A multidisciplinary organization of professionals
representing all facets of corrections and criminal justice, including
federal, state, and military corrections facilities and prisons; county jails
and detention centers; probation/parole agencies; and community
corrections/halfway houses in the United States and Canada.
Publications: *Corrections Today* magazine; *Corrections Compendium: The
National Journal for Corrections;* major catalog of additional publications
Training: National training conventions; certification seminars; online
workshops; video lending library

American Jail Association
1135 Professional Ct.
Hagerstown, MD 21740-5853
corrections.com/aja
Members/Purpose: A national nonprofit organization dedicated to
supporting those who work in and operate our nation's jails.
Publications: *American Jails* magazine; *Write It Right* quarterly; *Jail
Operations Bulletin*
Training: Annual conferences; training seminars throughout the year on a
variety of topics; Jail Manager Certification Program

Canadian Bar Association
500-865 Carling Ave.
Ottawa, ON K1S 5S8

Canada

cba.org

Members/Purpose: A professional, voluntary organization that promotes the legal profession in Canada.

Publications: *Canada Bar Review, National* magazine, newsletters, and books

Training: Continuing legal education; national and international conferences

Community Action Partnership

1100 17th St. NW, Suite 500

Washington, DC 20036

communityactionpartnership.com

Members/Purpose: National organization representing the interests of the one thousand community action agencies working to fight poverty at the local level. The partnership's mission is to be a national forum for policy on poverty and to strengthen, promote, represent, and serve its network of member agencies to assure that the issues of the poor are effectively heard and addressed.

Publications: *The Promise* quarterly magazine; *Community Action Directory;* research reports

Training: Specialized training classes and certification

Council of Juvenile Correctional Administrators

170 Forbes Rd., Suite 106

Braintree, MA 02184

cjca.net

Members/Purpose: Dedicated to the improvement of juvenile correctional services and practices. The CJCA promotes and facilitates three major activities: the exchange of ideas and philosophies at the top administrative level of juvenile corrections planning and policy making, the advancement of juvenile corrections and juvenile justice techniques, and the education of the public about juvenile justice and corrections systems.

Publications: Quarterly newsletter; yearbook survey

Training: Summer meetings

Juvenile Justice Trainers Association

7509 Waterlily Way

Columbia, MD 21046

jjta.org

Members/Purpose: Provides a structure for collaboration on initiatives and projects for improved services to at-risk youth throughout the nation; devoted to the development and advancement of a specialized system of education and training for juvenile justice professionals.
Publications: *Juvenile Justice Training Notes*; newsletter
Training: Annual conferences

National Center for Juvenile Justice
3700 S. Water St., Suite 200
Pittsburgh, PA 15203
ncjj.org
Members/Purpose: To improve the quality of justice for children and families by conducting research and providing objective, factual information that is used to increase the juvenile and family justice systems' effectiveness.
Publications: Numerous publications available for download on topics such as juvenile protection, juvenile and family courts, substance abuse, and statistical information
Training: Resource center for telephone consultation, technical assistance, preparation of informational packets, and custom database searches/bibliographies of the center; on-site visits

National Center for Youth Law
405 14th St., 15th floor
Oakland, CA 94612-2701
youthlaw.org
Members/Purpose: To use the law to protect children from the harms caused by poverty and to improve the lives of children living in poverty. An advocacy group, it aims to protect abused and neglected children, expand access to health care for children and youths, secure public benefits to meet the special needs of children and youths, and improve child support collection.
Publications: Articles; manuals; books; bimonthly journal, *Youth Law News*
Training: Technical assistance and training

National Council of Juvenile and Family Court Judges
P.O. Box 8970
Reno, NV 89507
ncjfcj.org

Members/Purpose: Focuses attention on the concept of a separate tribunal for children and encourages the development of essential treatment programs for children with special needs.

Publication: *Juvenile and Family Court Journal*

Training: Annual conferences, institutes, and training sessions; technical assistance

National Council on Crime and Delinquency

1970 Broadway, Suite 500

Oakland, CA 94612

nccd-crc.org

Members/Purpose: Promotes effective, humane, and economically sound solutions and criminal justice strategies for family, community, and justice problems. The group conducts research, promotes reform initiatives, and seeks to work with public and private organizations and the media to prevent and reduce crime and delinquency.

Publications: Quarterly journal; crime and delinquency special reports

Training: Conferences

National Juvenile Detention Association

Eastern Kentucky University

301 Perkins Building

521 Lancaster Ave.

Richmond, KY 40475-3102

njda.com

Members/Purpose: To promote adequate detention services for juveniles through such means as delivery of first-class products to the field of juvenile justice and detention services; interpreting and promoting the concepts of juvenile detention services at the national, state, and local levels; and defining the mission of and interpreting the detention services process.

Publications: *The Journal for Juvenile Justice and Detention Services*; *Juvenile Detention Careworker Curriculum*; videos such as *Services to Female Juvenile Offenders*, *Communicating the Write Way*, *Implementing Medication in Youthcare Correction Settings*, and *Explosion of Gang Violence in the United States*

Training: Annual conference; training and technical assistance provided through the association's Center for Research and Professional Development

10

Path 5: Allied Business

Careers for the Criminal Justice Entrepreneur

Criminal justice has been a great major for you: hard work, demanding faculty, but lots of fun and interesting areas of study. You've enjoyed school, and you've liked the people you've met in the classroom (both teachers and students) and out in the field. You believe in the field of criminal justice and you've grown to appreciate its vital role in our social fabric. You have no doubts that criminal justice is the career field for you, but you are still wondering just where you may fit in.

Perhaps the career paths described in the preceding chapters all have their appeal, but none of them completely satisfies your career interests and demands. Perhaps you have high income aspirations, or through your work experience you've learned that you have strong management or business skills that you would like to put to use. Maybe you are a highly creative systems-thinker, always coming up with new and better ways to do things. You may be wondering, "Can I stay in the criminal justice work arena if I don't see myself as a law enforcement officer, or a corrections professional, or a court or juvenile justice worker?" Of course! A career in one of the many possible businesses outlined in this chapter may be the blend that satisfies you.

Every job in the areas examined in this path brings its own environment and its own "package" of associated values. If you've worked through some of the self-assessment exercises in Chapter 1, you likely have begun to build a mental picture of your particular personality dimensions, work attributes, and values. When you combine that growing self-awareness with your work experience, you begin to realize that different jobs deliver different atmospheres and interactions with others; varying degrees of remuneration; and often exceedingly different work experiences in terms of pace, location, and energy.

So, while this may all sound intriguing and attractive, you may be asking yourself, "What's the catch? What else do I need to know about working in the area of private enterprise?" You're correct in thinking that there will be other expectations beyond your criminal justice expertise. Other attributes that will be helpful include, but are not limited to, the following:

- Interest in and familiarity with the commercial marketplace
- Appreciation for the competitiveness of the marketplace
- Willingness to assume management responsibilities, including staff supervision, budgets, and hiring and evaluation of employees
- As your career progresses and you start to be promoted, willingness to shed your technical abilities (sales skills, technical writing, and so forth) and take on the increasingly conceptual responsibilities of management for strategic concerns, planning, and evaluation

This is a career path in which you are hired for your criminal justice degree and "something more"; you will use your degree every day, but you'll use many other aptitudes as well. In these jobs, you may be expected to assume the mantle of management responsibility in your preparation of business reports, memorandums, and other correspondence; in your training and supervision of employees; and in your representation of the organization in a responsible and professional manner.

Private Security

Many insurance companies, banks, and other businesses use private security to protect private property above and beyond what can be easily safeguarded by the police. Many corporations and virtually all banks use private firms to guard and patrol their premises. In some instances, representatives of these firms may be called on to investigate crimes by employees and customers. Independent private security companies also hire investigators for work on a contract basis.

Definition of the Career Path

The field of private security is reflecting the same changes and upgrades in professionalism that are influencing the entire field of criminal justice. There was a time in the not too distant past when a book such as this would probably not have included private security as a possible employment field. Firms were small and not particularly well managed, and the jobs were just that—jobs—not careers.

Much has changed for private security, both as an industry and as an individual career path for criminal justice graduates, most notably in the "blurring" of private security into a sometimes public law enforcement job. Private security professionals are now seen working in the public sector, specifically townships, counties, and smaller towns where the fiscal authorities find it more economical to supplement the regular police department with private security professionals instead of hiring, training, and permanently employing a larger public workforce.

Each of the jobs featured here falls into one of the many broad occupational areas within the general rubric of private security. In addition to the job of security services, those occupational areas include the following:

- **Consulting and investigation.** Consulting services available to clients can include help in the areas of competitive intelligence; computer and systems intelligence; crisis management; disaster preparedness; engineering services; intellectual property programs; threat analysis and security surveys; kidnap, extortion, and incident management; product contamination protection; and workplace violence.
- **Systems integration.** This growing area includes closed-circuit television (CCTV) systems, intrusion detection, access-control systems (using the latest access card and "open architecture platform" technology), electronic imaging (badging), optical turnstiles, and custom security consoles.
- **Global intelligence.** Professionals in this specialty monitor and report on international security threats and events related to terrorism, crime, and civil unrest and help protect executives, office staff, and property around the world.

Working Conditions

Working conditions in private security vary by assignment. Although security officers spend considerable time on their feet and frequently work different shifts, growing numbers sit at large electronic consoles to monitor security or surveillance devices. The only general statement that can be made about security officer positions is that they tend to be relatively routine in terms of duties and responsibilities, but the person fulfilling this role must be ever vigilant. Even in the case of uniforms, there is little consensus anymore. The types of duties as well as the environments in which officers work are changing. Some employers seek a military look, while others prefer the "soft" look, whereby officers blend less conspicuously into the social milieu.

But security officer is not the only entry-level position available, especially for a bachelor's degree graduate of a criminal justice program. The range of private security occupations makes generalizations about working conditions almost meaningless.

Training and Qualifications

Good judgment, common sense, physical fitness, observational skills, leadership, conscientious application of company principles and policies, ability to provide credible testimony in a courtroom, professional appearance and attitude, and strong interpersonal skills are some of the general qualities employers look for when hiring private security professionals.

Most states require private security officials to be licensed. If you enter this work as a security officer—a typical entry-level position for a criminal justice graduate—you must pass a background check and complete classroom training in areas such as property rights, emergency procedures, and detention of suspected criminals. Drug testing is frequently required and may be ongoing and random. The Montana Department of Commerce, Division of Professional and Occupational Licensing, has a Board of Private Security Patrol Officers and Investigators licensing unit (http://mt.gov/dli/bsd/license/bsd_boards/ psp_board/board_page.asp) that provides an excellent example of licensing requirements for a variety of private security positions, including:

- Private investigator
- Private security guard
- Security alarm installer

Many jobs also require a driver's license. In addition, if your position mandates that you carry a firearm, you will be required to be licensed by the appropriate authority; frequently, you will be required to be certified additionally as a special police officer so that you are empowered to make arrests while on duty. Obviously, armed positions have more stringent background checks and entry requirements due to the potential liability to the hiring organization.

As an indication that private security is rapidly becoming as demanding and professional as every other criminal justice occupation, many states are making ongoing training for private security professionals a legal requirement for the retention of certification. This training encompasses topics such as protection, public relations, report writing, crisis deterrence, and first aid, as well as any specialized training relevant to the individual's assignments.

Private Investigator

This employment field is difficult to categorize. It is not law enforcement, and it is not criminal justice, nor is it, strictly speaking, private security. It is, however, a possible employment option for criminal justice majors in the private sector.

Definition of the Career Path

Because most private investigators operate alone as independent agents, they come to this work with considerable experience gained elsewhere. Only the larger private investigatory hiring organizations offer entry-level jobs and will provide the training necessary. Since most of the firms that offer investigative services are small (often entrepreneurships) and their time is contracted in discrete units for pricing purposes, this field can be grouped within the category of products and services.

Let's dispel the myths about this job right now. It's not about glamour; it's mostly about divorces and missing people, generally family members. A considerable amount of detective work is done on the computer, and that is why many private investigators successfully advertise their services on the Internet—they can work from anywhere.

Your days are spent researching birth and death records, marriage licenses, real estate transactions, tax filings, news reports, and legal findings. You investigate, produce results, and write up a report. If you are working for yourself, you will also need to spend considerable time generating clients in order to maintain a steady stream of income.

If you are associated with a large private investigatory firm, you may be involved in investigations of internal security or other internal problems of large organizations whose potential risk or dollar loss is such that they can afford to contract with your employer.

Working Conditions

Working conditions for "private eyes" are generally solitary. You'll spend considerable time on the computer searching records, spend some time on telephone work, and travel rarely—generally, only in the final stages of an investigation. A high degree of isolation exists in this job, in which many practitioners are self-employed or employed by very small agencies. Income can be unpredictable if you are self-employed or work on a contingency basis.

Many independent private investigators describe a situation in which they have a full roster of clients and are so busy that they can't take on any more clients, and then, one by one, they resolve all of their clients' business only to find that they have no new clients. They then must spend precious time recruiting new business, advertising, and telemarketing to get a full client load again. The cycle starts anew.

Much of your time may be occupied doing library research, or searching courthouse or city hall records, and writing reports for clients. Hours can be long, and most work is done behind the scenes.

In summary, the specific dynamics of the private investigator's work environment include the following:

- Solitary work
- Significant computer desk time
- Outside research of courthouses, city halls, large libraries
- Limited caseload (divorces, missing persons, credit checks, insurance fraud)
- High degree of interaction with lawyers and legal issues

Training and Qualifications

Most employers look for strong background in any specific field (law or business, for example). Most private investigators learned their skills in local law enforcement, the military, federal law enforcement, or private security firms.

Some states have specific licensing requirements, including examinations, and may require you to post a bond to ensure compliance with state regulations. The following attributes are also important:

- Appropriate demeanor. Can you work alone, think logically, react quickly to changing circumstances, use sound judgment, and keep professionally distant from your work? Maturity is a must.
- Excellent research skills, including familiarity with credit checks, Lexis/Nexis, and Dow Jones searches, and strong skills in Internet research.
- Strong work ethic, with an independent style.
- Good budgeting and record-keeping skills.
- Excellent client-relations skills.
- Ability to prioritize.

Cybercrime

As Internet use continues to grow at a rapid rate, so does the possibility of criminal activity involving Web technology.

Definition of the Career Path

The scene of the crime: a twelve-year-old girl is at home on her computer writing in a chat room to someone she thinks is a fifteen-year-old boy in the next town who wants her to meet him at a local mall . . .

The reality of this situation is that the "young boy" may, in fact, be an adult sexual offender trying to lure the girl out of her home and to a public place where her abduction would be less likely to be noticed.

The vulnerability of our children on the Web is not the only hot issue in computer crime. A review of just a week's worth of newspaper and television news brings items such as:

- Millions of bogus messages flooding websites or Internet service providers, blocking access to networks and servers and "freezing" systems
- Computer break-ins by malicious hackers who violate the confidentiality and integrity of data and systems by exploiting security holes or poor procedures, including lack of firewalls and passwords
- Internal computer attacks, often by disgruntled or dismissed employees
- Development and proliferation of destructive viruses
- Simple physical attacks on computer hardware in which criminals or terrorists damage or unplug critical components of a computer system to disrupt operations

As the United States and the world community begin to confront cyber-crime, efforts have begun to classify and codify these crimes. A basic break-down might look something like this:

Crimes Against Property
- **Hacking:** Using programming abilities with malicious intent
- **Cracking:** Using programs to gain unauthorized entry into a computer or network
- **Spreading viruses:** Creating and disseminating harmful computer programs
- **Software piracy:** Illegally copying and distributing software

Crimes Against Persons
- **Electronic dissemination of obscene material or pornography:** Trafficking in, posting, or distributing pornography, child pornography, or indecent-exposure materials over the Web
- **Cyber-harassment:** Using e-mail, chat rooms, or programs to harass individuals
- **Cyber-stalking:** Using the Internet to track the movements and behavior of individuals

Cyber-Terrorism
- Most cryptographic systems depend on secrecy because it is not yet a crime to break those codes; however, the U.S. government has set standards for the strength of encryption programs. Hackers breaking these cryptographic codes remain a threat to some governments and private businesses that employ them.

- As our lives become more involved with and recorded by computers, the possibility of "crackers" using this collective information to terrorize governments, businesses, or groups of individuals becomes ever more a reality.

The investigation of any crime involves the painstaking collection of clues and forensic evidence and requires attention to detail. This is particularly true of today's "white-collar crime," in which computer-linked evidence frequently plays a pivotal role as documentary evidence. With the advancing number of households now using computers and the reliance on computers by businesses large and small, coupled with easy Internet access, it is almost inevitable that at least one electronic device will be found during a crime investigation. It could be a computer, but it could also be a printer, mobile phone, personal organizer, or other item. The electronic device may figure prominently as evidence in the investigation, or it may be on the periphery. No matter which, the information must be retrieved and investigated in the proper manner, especially if any of this evidence is to be relied on in a court of law.

Examples of the evidence you may find on a computer system that could assist the prosecution or defense of a case include:

- Use or abuse of the Internet
- Production of false documents and accounts
- Encrypted or password-protected material
- Theft of computer time
- Abuse of systems
- E-mail contact between suspects or conspirators
- Theft of commercial secrets
- Unauthorized transmission of information
- Records of movements
- Malicious attacks on computer systems
- Names and addresses of contacts

Roles you might play in an entry-level career investigating computer crime include advising on how to initiate an investigation in which computers are involved and, related to this, advising on how best to secure any possible evidence. In other situations, investigators visit sites to secure data, either overtly or covertly, using the latest in forensically sound imaging techniques. Investigators detecting criminals become skilled in examining data captured and retrieved from the deepest files and lowest levels of discs that the owner or operator might have thought were long discarded. They also must record, report, and summarize all of this information in a professional format.

Working Conditions

Because cyber-crimes can be committed from almost anywhere, they present an interesting variety of working conditions. Here are a few examples of possible working situations.

> **Case:** Your client suspects misuse of its computer system. Your job is a covert, on-site examination of more than one hundred machines to uncover use of the employer's equipment for downloading child pornography. Result: the ultimate conviction of an employee and disciplinary action of others for related offenses.
>
> **Case:** Sensitive files are missing from a central computer system. Your work uncovers a former employee dialing in, using a long disused (but not deleted) phone access code, to delete these files.
>
> **Case:** An insurance company has received a huge claim for the loss of all data on an insured firm's mainframe computer due to interaction with an industrial magnet. While you confirm major damage to the motherboard and casing by magnetic interaction, you are able to reclaim all data from the hard disk and thus nullify the claim.
>
> **Case:** In the course of only a couple of days of consulting time, you are able to establish that an employee is downloading valuable client information to start his own company. Resulting savings to your client could be in the millions of dollars.
>
> **Case:** You are called as an expert witness in a court case to testify to specific facts regarding your knowledge and examination of specific technology and to state your opinion as to why certain events did or did not occur.

This is real detective work, and on many of your assignments you will be on-site at the client's place of business. Other times, you can work from your own terminal and patch into the client's system on a shared drive. From the few sample scenarios described, you can see that each day, each client, and each investigation is very different. Of course, each client's hardware and software will be different as well. So, while there are few overriding similarities in working conditions, one constant is that this is not a boring nine-to-five desk job!

Because some of your work will be on-site and your presence is sometimes acknowledged and other times hidden, you will need to be conscious of your appearance and demeanor. At times, you may have to make subtle adjustments in your wardrobe and manner to more easily go unnoticed as you collect evidence.

Training and Qualifications

The field of cybercrime represents new territory in law enforcement, and many procedures, jurisdictions, laws, and even investigative and evidentiary techniques have yet to be worked out. That's compelling because we are seldom offered an opportunity to get in on the emergence of some aspect of our chosen calling. Look around at some of the other majors graduating with you. Psychology, foreign language, social work, accounting—all are good and worthwhile majors leading to productive jobs and satisfying lives but, perhaps, with fewer chances than you have to experience the cutting edge of a career.

Right now, the ideal qualifications for entry-level positions in the cybercrime field would be a dual major in criminal justice and accounting. Accounting courses (which involve considerable and sophisticated computer use) teach students how a business is structured, and that knowledge combined with your investigative-procedures course work in criminal justice can be a powerful combination. A close second is a criminal justice major with a computer science minor. A third and also viable combination is a criminal justice major with significant electives in computer science and perhaps some strong work experience with computer systems.

If you can take advantage in any way of the courses offered at your college or university in the computer science department, do so. Focus on courses in information technology, which would include the functioning and workings of hardware and software systems in an organizational setting. This is just what you'll need on your résumé for an entry-level position in computer crime work.

In addition to your academics in criminal justice and your computer skills, you'll want to be able to document either internships, practicums, or solid work experience using either or both of these specialties. Through these experiences, you will be able to meet and interact with the computer professionals on staff. By all means, tell them about your career plans and ask them to share as many insights as they can about systems analysis and information retrieval. This kind of on-the-job training will prove invaluable, and you may develop enough of a relationship with those professionals to request a recommendation at some point in your job search. Even better, if your part-time employer has some deleted files that need to be rescued, or hidden files that need to be found, or data in free space that may contain deleted or overwritten files to be retrieved, you may be asked to undertake this project. What great experience for your future career!

Other important skills and attributes for this job include report writing, systems analysis, patience, and enjoyment of problems. In this career you need to wrestle with the problem and see it from different perspectives to find a creative way to acquire your evidence. You can't be the kind of person who finds tough challenges defeating; rather, you need to approach solving problems as intriguing and fun.

An additional requisite is interviewing skills. Working with clients in a variety of office and corporate settings, you need to become skilled at understanding how their systems function and how people perform their duties and interact so that you can get inside the situation for yourself and deduce where evidence might lie. Good questioning, probing, and restatement skills are what put you on the right evidentiary trail.

Earnings

This career path tends to present the greatest variance in earnings among occupations. Much of the reason for this is that options in the private sector are so diverse that they cover a wide stretch of income levels. The two specific occupational areas highlighted in this chapter will provide you with a good sense of just how wide the ranges can be. On the lower end of earnings, you have many private security jobs. On the higher end, you have one of the highest-paying fields among all occupations: computer specialists. These, of course, are all general statements. Many private security jobs pay quite well, but computer security specialists represent the one area for which the general statement may apply across the board; salaries for those with computer expertise rank relatively high. Let's take a look inside each of these areas.

Private Security

Most men and women who choose this career begin as security or protection officers. Entry-level salaries can be somewhat low compared with other criminal justice occupations. The latest Bureau of Labor Statistics figures show that in 2004, most security officers earned an annual salary of $16,640 to $25,510. While this level of remuneration may be discouraging to aspirants who are working toward or have completed a bachelor's degree, some additional factors should be brought to bear before you dismiss private security as a viable career option.

First, the field has been experiencing a rapid upgrade in professionalism. As our society becomes more and more security conscious, and as private industry responds with demands for increased and sophisticated security in its operations and systems, this trend is expected to continue. Add to this the fact that the private security field is continually expanding and taking on roles and responsibilities previously held by public law enforcement officials, and you can see why the level of professionalism has been elevated. In fact, special certification such as the certified protection professional (CPP) is now preferred or required for some positions. As the need for security professionals to become more sophisticated, better educated, and specially trained increases, so will the salaries.

Salaries vary with the type of employer. Many security officers are employed by private security agencies that then contract with companies or organizations to provide security services for them. The hiring organization benefits by having a dedicated security force without having to recruit, hire, train, and supervise personnel. The downside for you is that it may mean less income than you might receive if the company employed you directly. Because your employer (the security firm) is, in effect, a middleman, you sacrifice some income for the firm's profit margin.

Many companies and organizations do hire their own security staff. In these cases, salaries (and the opportunity for advancement) may be higher. The American Society for Industrial Security, online at asisonline.org, offers some relevant demographic information, including salary ranges, for security professionals based on various criteria. For example, in 2004 the average annual salary of a security professional between the ages of twenty and twenty-nine was $43,500.

The industry or specialty area itself can be a key determinant in salary levels. Those requiring higher levels of security, such as nuclear power plants, require higher standards in employment and involve longer and more intense periods of training, but salaries typically are higher as well. The size, location, and financial stability of the employer also influence salary levels. A large, established hospital in a major metropolitan area is more likely to pay its administrators and security staff a salary higher than a small, suburban community hospital will. Many larger organizations also offer a ranking system whereby opportunity for advancement in position and salary is clearly outlined.

Many who start as private security officers will go on to become investigators, earning considerably higher salaries. Some become protection specialists, guarding and protecting the lives of corporate executives or celebrities traveling around the country and the world, and meeting interesting people. Others are more entrepreneurial and eventually establish a business, such as a contract security agency or a security consulting firm, or even one that specializes in a particular product, such as security alarm systems. In all cases, you can expect your salary to grow as the demand for your experience, knowledge, and services increases.

Private Investigators

Most private detectives and investigators come to the profession with some work experience, usually in private security, the military, or the insurance industry. Your criminal justice degree may help you to become one of the few who enter the field without any related experience. Earnings will depend on the size of the employer, the area of specialty, and the geographic area. On average, you can expect to earn about $30,000. Here's a recent ad from Chicago that is a good example of what you may encounter.

Investigator. Working for a national insurance firm, the position requires strong skills in the following areas: computer and Internet use, writing skills, attention to detail, proofreading, and grammar. Investigators are required to have a suitable vehicle for surveillance, cellular telephone, laptop computer, Internet access, and a video camera. Qualified candidates will have two years of investigative, law enforcement, loss prevention, or military experience or a degree in a criminal justice–related field, and an in-depth knowledge of surveillance and insurance claims. Our investigators have a professional appearance, exceptional work ethic, and articulate communication skills, and are results oriented. Salary: $27,040–$37,440.

With experience, you may eventually establish your own private detective agency. One out of four detectives is self-employed. In most cases, pay is per project, with limitations on the time that any fee will cover. Incomes for self-employed detectives, therefore, are indexed to the number of projects they have at any given time. The number of projects they receive and accept is determined by the amount of time they are willing to work, their reputation for results, their areas of specialty, and their location.

Cybercrime

If you have the advanced computer skills required for entry into the cyber field, you can expect significant income. Among new college graduates, those with computer expertise are often the highest paid of all. Computer security is a growing specialty within the computer field, so future salary potential is difficult to predict. Although specific information for computer security specialists is difficult to find, the Bureau of Labor Statistics reports that in 2005, starting salaries ranged from $44,500 to $63,250 for more senior technical support specialists. For systems administrators, starting salaries ranged from $47,250 to $70,500.

Although those figures are impressive, the vast majority of job seekers will not be able to step into a position such as security administrator straight out of college with a degree in criminal justice. You'll need to demonstrate advanced computer skills, including network design and integration, and a working knowledge of state-of-the-art computer hardware and software technology (particularly technology used in information security). Careers in computer crime investigation will demand additional experience, such as computer investigative techniques, application, and legal aspects related to computer evidence recovery, including procedures for collection, preservation, and presentation of computer evidence.

This is not to imply that you aren't qualified for some positions in the field of cybercrime. Many entry-level positions are available to you if you can establish that you have technical aptitude and a desire to learn the employer's systems and software. Course work in computer science and mathematics that supplements your criminal justice curriculum will be extremely helpful, as will a summer job or internship in the field. Basically speaking, you can expect to earn a salary commensurate with your experience and technical skills. In entry-level support positions, you stand to earn somewhere between $26,250 to $53,750. And keep in mind that to attract good employees in the information technology industry, companies are sometimes willing to provide such benefits as stock options and equity incentives, as well as signing bonuses, flexible work schedules, and telecommuting opportunities.

Career Outlook

You read in the preceding chapters about the promising employment outlook for the majority of jobs presented in those four career paths. How encouraging to see such strong evidence of the value of your criminal justice degree as you plan your career. And the news for the occupations outlined in this path is the best of all! In every category, you can expect to witness employment growth.

In many other career fields, new employment is primarily a function of replacing workers in that field who retire or move on to other careers. In the case of the careers in this chapter, however, the growth in new employment is the result of explosive growth in the field itself. Much of it can be attributed to the development of new and more sophisticated technologies. The best example of this is the expansion of Internet technology, which, for many companies, has resulted in a whole new way of conducting business: e-commerce. As popular as it has become, e-commerce would not be viable without built-in security systems consumers trust. Workers are needed to develop, monitor, upgrade, and investigate failures in these systems. Beyond those functions are the personnel needed to promote and sell the systems to companies and organizations. The development of new technologies and products comes at a time when the public is experiencing a heightened awareness and fear of crime. These concerns are most often expressed by demands for increased security in all areas of people's lives. The private sector is listening and responding.

Private Security

The outlook for employment in this field is favorable. Within the next several years, employment of security officers is expected to grow by as much as 17 percent. Growth in this field shouldn't come as a surprise when you consider how important security has become in so many circumstances. One example is the extensive publicity about campus crime and the level of violence in and around all educational institutions, including elementary and secondary schools. This has naturally led to demands for increased security in all of these facilities. Hotel security similarly has greatly expanded in response to the flood of lawsuits filed against hotels based on charges of security breaches. As fears of terrorism grow, airlines and airports heighten security. These are just a few illustrations of how demand—in the form of crime and the fear of crime—affects supplies needed for additional security personnel.

Another driver of employment in this field is the necessity to staff multiple shifts. In many instances, security is a twenty-four-hour business, so that instead of one person to fill a position, you actually need three.

Private Investigators

It is projected that private detective agencies will grow in number and size during the next eight to ten years. The news is especially good for you, as opportunities for entry-level jobs will be the best. Through 2014, it's anticipated that employment of private detectives and investigators will increase by as much as 26 percent. The reasons for this expected growth include a demand for investigatory services related to increased litigation involving civil and criminal cases. Add to that a growing need to protect confidential information; a continuing focus on protecting property of all kinds; and increased efforts by companies to control internal and external financial losses, prevent industrial espionage, and monitor their competitors, and this growth is not surprising.

Although the employment outlook is healthy, the competition for these jobs will be equally strong. You will be in contention with other recent college graduates in addition to candidates who have experience in law enforcement, the military, private security, or a specialty area such as finance or insurance.

Cybercrime

The fastest growing of all occupations through 2014 will be those that involve computers. The expansion of computer applications and the development and integration of new technologies fuel the tremendous demand for skilled professionals, including those with expertise in communications security.

It's easy to see why the employment outlook is expected to be extremely strong in the area of computer crime when you consider that companies are increasingly using the Internet and intranet applications to expand business operations and make them more lucrative and efficient. As business in cyberspace grows, unfortunately the likelihood of cyber-attacks grows along with it. The Computer Security Institute, with participation from the San Francisco FBI Computer Intrusion Squad, released its tenth annual Computer Crime and Security Survey in March 2005, and the findings were discouraging. While the total dollar amount of financial losses resulting from security breaches has decreased 61 percent, 32 percent of overall losses reported were caused by virus attacks. Unauthorized access of systems increased, becoming the second most significant contributor to computer crime losses. In addition, respondents reported a significant increase in theft of proprietary information.

Cybercrimes and other information security breaches are widespread and diverse. . . . Clearly, more must be done in terms of adherence to sound practices, deployment of sophisticated technologies, and, most important, adequate staffing and training of information security practitioners in both the private sector and government. So long as the threat from computer crime and security breaches continues unabated, not only is the financial toll mounting but also businesses and organizations may witness disastrous results from loss of consumer confidence and downstream liability. How can they not continue to supplement staff and resources to protect assets?

Strategy for Finding the Jobs

In strategizing your job search, it's important to use a variety of tactics. For example, reading the help-wanted ads in the Sunday paper is a must, but not all job announcements are published. In fact, for most general employment openings, only 20 percent nationwide are published. If you were to rely on this method alone, you would be missing up to 80 percent of the opportunities. Devise a plan consisting of some general approaches as well as some more specific to your chosen field. The following general avenues are good ones to include.

Alumni Career Connections
Either the career office or the alumni office on your campus can put you in touch with former graduates of your college who are now working in the particular job markets that interest you. These alumni connections can be very helpful, offering informational interviews, background on the firms that

employ them, and general insights into the retail job market. Your school's alumni database may even be able to isolate those who are working in private security versus public law enforcement. When contacting these individuals, remember that you are representing your college and every other student who may someday want to make use of this valuable referral service. Be prepared with a list of questions, and use their time wisely. You could make a good friend and will have increased insight into your chosen career field. Many alumni will invite you to visit their places of business, and some may even offer to assist with your résumé or job search strategy.

On-Campus Recruiting

Employers who visit your campus are giving you a strong indication of their interest in your school's students. Sign up for every recruitment interview that seems appropriate. On-campus interviewing can and does lead to actual job offers. Even when it doesn't, it's excellent interview practice. Most important, you will begin to develop a sense of what each employer is offering to make distinctions about what would be the best fit for you in a criminal justice career offering. Unlike job fairs, these are private interviews, one-on-one with a senior representative from the organization. Even better, the interviews are held on campus in familiar surroundings, which should help you in controlling those interview jitters. Your campus career office probably maintains files on all the recruiting firms to allow you to thoroughly prepare for your session.

Job Fairs

Job fairs are valuable job search tools for students. First, they are very efficient. How else would you be able to meet and talk with so many possible job contacts in one day? In addition, the process of walking up to employment representatives, greeting them, and giving them a one-minute "infomercial" about who you are and what you have to offer is a perfect example of the specific people skills that security employers seek. Most of these employers are looking for evidence of assertiveness, confidence, ingenuity, and persistence. They're seeking candidates with solid communication skills who aren't afraid of confrontation. The job fair provides you with an opportunity to demonstrate all of these.

Recently, you may have noticed "virtual job fairs" advertised at your college or on the Internet. These are becoming more popular, as they offer job candidates access to many more employers than they would be able to meet in a specific physical space. Plus, they usually run for a week or longer, giving you more time to explore and communicate with employers of interest to you.

Your Career Office

Your college career office not only will hold subscriptions to numerous job posting newsletters offering entry-level jobs but also will be on the mailing lists of many employers that recruit on college campuses to fill these positions. Employers looking for graduates with criminal justice backgrounds naturally target their recruitment efforts to colleges or universities that offer criminal justice programs.

Your Résumé and Cover Letter

Be sure that your résumé and cover letter reflect the skills and capabilities that employers in your field are looking for. This means that you'll have to spend some time reviewing actual ads for your field. For example, if you continually see ads that state the need for excellent people skills, be sure to highlight any previous jobs in which you had significant contact with customers or coworkers, or experience working as part of a team. Likewise, if you see that computer knowledge is often required (and you most definitely will), be sure to list your level of expertise with various hardware and software.

These are only a few of the general aids that you should consider putting to use in your venture. Other resources that have been mentioned elsewhere in this book are Internet searching, state employment offices, newspapers, and even the phone book. Now let's move on to ideas for your particular area of interest.

Private Security

You don't have to wait until you graduate to find a job in private security. Opportunities abound for part-time or seasonal work while you are still in college. Your campus security force can be a good place to start. You could also contact a security service agency in your area. They're easy to find— just look under "Security" in the yellow pages—and they almost always have part-time assignments to fill. Another possibility is a nearby department store, often a great training ground for a career in security. While security personnel are hired year-round, typically there is a need for increased staffing starting in late October as stores gear up for the holiday shopping season.

Whichever you choose, the point is that you can begin to establish a résumé for a career in security now. Working part-time or during the summer will enable you to try out the job to see if it's really the direction you want to go. You'll build the valuable experience needed for more advanced positions, and you'll meet people working in the field who can be instrumental to you when you graduate.

Remember that for most security positions, you will need to undergo a complete background check; be vigilant about keeping your record clean. You'll be expected to provide solid character references. Think carefully about people in your life who can attest to your dependability, trustworthiness, maturity, work ethic, and emotional stability, such as professors, your faculty adviser, former supervisors, or religious leaders. Usually, you'll need to provide three to five references. Be sure to ask your prospective references first if they would be willing to speak on your behalf, and let them know whenever you have provided their names to a potential employer.

Private Investigators

The National Association of Investigative Specialists (NAIS) provides a top-notch resource on how to become a private investigator. On the Web at pimall.com/nais/beapi.html you can find almost everything you need to know, including what the licensing requirements are in your state and how to contact your state's licensing authority, with direct links in most cases. While you're at it, learn about the latest trends in the field and even review a short, online course on private investigation. If that's not enough, you can search by state for NAIS member investigative agencies and pull up names, contact information including websites where available, and any specialty areas of the agency. The site also contains an online bookstore where you can order manuals such as *The Private Investigative Agency Business Start-Up Manual* and *PINA Self-Study Guide*. This is definitely a site to peruse if private investigation is in your future.

You may want to conduct an informational interview with a private investigator, maybe one chosen from the NAIS site. This is a great way to really get the inside story on a specific occupation. Most people are flattered that you're interested in their work and are happy to consent to the interview. But remember to keep the meeting brief, since time is money, especially in the case of self-employed investigators. Come prepared with a list of questions (your college career office may have a handout or other resource on informational interviewing), and be open to learning about both the good and the bad aspects of the job. You are, after all, looking for the "real" story.

Because almost all private detectives and investigators have some experience in a related field, the same advice offered earlier for private security applies here. Get some experience as soon as you can by working in private security or perhaps an insurance or collections agency. Another option is a position as a department store detective in which you can develop investigative and observation skills and acquire real-world experience in conducting surveillance and apprehending and prosecuting suspects.

Cybercrime

The most important strategy for finding employment in the cybercrime field is to gain, strengthen, and be prepared to demonstrate strong computer skills. You can do that by adding a minor in computer science, selecting a significant number of electives in that area, or gaining hands-on experience through part-time and summer jobs, internships, and practicums. This is not to say that other skills you have developed as a criminal justice major won't be valued. In fact, a survey of chief information officers indicates that "soft" skills such as business acumen and interpersonal skills were very important. When asked which capabilities they considered most important for reaching management levels in the information technology profession, respondents cited interpersonal skills most often, followed by advanced technical skills. It makes sense in a field where project teams predominate and technical staff need to be able to communicate complex information to employees at all levels with varying degrees of sophistication.

The point is that you need both of these skill areas, along with the investigative skills that you have developed in your major, to best position yourself in the cybercrime job market. Be patient and willing to accept a more entry-level technical or customer support position as you continue to learn and develop the skills that will be necessary. You will be entering a career field that is still in its developing stages. Think of how bright the future is!

Possible Employers

While this chapter features the private sector, don't think that the only opportunities for these positions are in the business arena. Many local governments employ private security to supplement their law enforcement staffs, and the federal government is in the forefront of cybercrime. Also, public and private utility companies must provide security services, particularly in the event of a natural disaster, resource shortage, or civil disturbance.

In contrast to the previous paths, for which the bulk of employment possibilities presented is within the public sector, the purpose of this chapter is to give you a better sense of the other, very broad side of the employment picture—the private sector.

Private Security

If you are working in the private security field, chances are that you are either employed by a security services agency or industrial security firm, or directly employed by the organization whose building or property you're responsible for securing. The difference lies in who your actual employer is—who issues your paycheck and assigns and supervises your work—not the actual location to which you report every day or the kind of work you do. For example, if you are a security officer at a community hospital, your work is the same whether you're employed by the hospital or by an agency that contracts with the hospital to provide security services.

The variety of industries that utilize security services include:

Construction	Manufacturing
Crisis management	Nuclear plants
Education	Office building management
Entertainment	Pharmaceutical
Executive protection	Proprietary/information
Government operations	Real estate management
Health care	Retail
High tech	Special events
Hotel/hospitality	Terrorism counteraction
Insurance	Transportation

Within these industries are numerous possibilities, yielding a wide variety of employment options. For example, transportation includes positions in airports and airplane hangars, trucking, rail terminals, armored cars, and sea operations. Entertainment includes shopping malls, museums, art galleries, theaters, parks, nightclubs, restaurants, gambling casinos, and sporting events. And for each of these, you have a variety of security services. In addition to protective services, there are opportunities for security consulting, design and engineering, education and training, investigations, and, of course, sales of products and services.

Private Investigators

One out of four private investigators and detectives is self-employed, whether as a full-time career or part-time second job. Of the rest, around 27 percent worked for investigation and security services, including private detective agencies, while another 15 percent were in department or other general merchandise stores. The rest worked mostly in state and local government, legal services firms, employment services companies, insurance agencies, and banks.

Many private investigators have an expertise and interest in a specific area that will determine who their employer is. A lawyer or law firm will hire an investigator who specializes in cases involving the courts. A corporation may employ a private investigator to do preemployment background checks, to conduct internal (such as drug use in the workplace) and external (such as billing fraud) investigations, or to provide protection for the corporation's chief executive. Private detective agencies often specialize in one or several areas. The National Association of Investigative Specialists lists the following top twenty private investigative specializations as of 2004:

1. Locating missing heirs
2. Preemployment screening
3. Mystery shopping (covert videotaped visit to stores or other businesses)
4. Bodyguard services and executive protection
5. Service of process (serving legal papers)
6. Nursing home abuse investigation
7. Professional judgment recovery
8. Complex legal investigation
9. Online searching and the Internet
10. Piracy investigation
11. E-mail tracing services
12. Vehicle repossession
13. GPS auto tracking services
14. Physical surveillance
15. Covert video specialist
16. Countermeasures and information security
17. Vehicle accident investigation
18. Business security consulting
19. Locating missing persons
20. Domestic investigations

While much of the work involved in private investigation is computer or research based, with limited opportunities (except for some types of investigations) for fieldwork, the foregoing list and descriptions of possible specializations suggest that the most effective and cost-efficient detectives would be those who develop a specific area of expertise. Through actual experience in the field, you will gain exposure to many of these specializations and be better able to gauge the best fit for you.

Cybercrime

Any company, organization, or government agency that does any business online is a potential employer. From a corporation conducting e-commerce to a small nonprofit organization using e-mail as a communication tool to the Federal Bureau of Investigation, the lead agency for a variety of the nation's security concerns, and everywhere in between, lies potential for employment in this field.

Additionally, there are firms that specialize in computer security or crime investigation, many of which are referenced on criminal justice and law enforcement websites, such as crimespider.com, and in the library at talkjustice.com. A growing number of computer-savvy professionals are self-employed, consulting with organizations or providing direct services to businesses on a contract basis. They may, for example, set up a new communications security system for a company and train the in-house information technology staff to monitor it. They may also handle any troubleshooting or upgrading that needs to be done.

At one time, you would almost always find the responsibility for computer security tacked on to the systems administrator's job duties, and it is still that way in many cases. However, as concern for information security grows in scope and as incidents of cyber-attacks continue to mount, more and more employers are turning to hiring full-time computer security and crime investigative specialists or contracting with firms to provide that service.

Possible Job Titles

Because the scope of employment is so large in the private sector, the list of potential job titles could never be exhausted on these few pages, but this sampling should give you a good idea of the possibilities:

Private Security

Armored car guard	Protection specialist
Bank officer	Security agent
Bodyguard	Security alarm installer
Corporate security specialist	Security consultant
Hotel security director	Security officer
Loss prevention agent	Security systems technician
Plant protection officer	Special police
Private security specialist	Store detective
Protection officer	Undercover investigative trainee

Private Investigator

Corporate investigator	Store detective
Legal investigator	Surveillance specialist
Private detective	Undercover investigator
Private investigator	

Cybercrime

Computer crime investigator	Malicious code lab analyst
Computer forensics operator	Manager of information systems security
Computer security specialist	Product developer
Customer support specialist	Security architect
Firewall and VPN lab analyst	Security systems technician
Information security analyst	Systems analyst
Information security specialist	Systems developer
Internet enforcement officer	Technical consultant
Investigations manager	Technical support specialist

Professional Associations

Listed in this section are some of the associations that relate to careers in businesses allied to criminal justice. For more information about these professional associations, either check the websites listed or consult the *Encyclopedia of Associations*, published by Thomson Gale. Review the Members/Purpose notes for each organization to determine if it pertains to your interests. Membership in one or more of these organizations may gain you access to job listings, networking opportunities, and employment search services. Some provide information at no charge, but if you want to receive specific publications that list job opportunities, you may need to join. If you're still in college, check for student member rates.

American Society for Industrial Security
1625 Prince St.
Alexandria, VA 22314-2818
asisonline.org
Members/Purpose: An international organization for professionals responsible for security, including managers and directors of security; attorneys; and federal, state, and local law enforcement.
Publications: *Security Management Daily, Dynamics* newsletter; buyer's guide
Training: Annual seminar; professional development programs

Computer Security Institute
600 Harrison St.
San Francisco, CA 94107
gocsi.com
Members/Purpose: Dedicated to serving and training information, computer, and network security professionals.

Publications: *The Computer Security Journal; Computer Security Alert;* CSI Blog

Training: Numerous information security seminars, annual conferences, and sessions

High Technology Crime Investigation Association

4021 Woodcreek Oaks Blvd., Suite 156, #209

Roseville, CA 95747

htcia.org

Members/Purpose: Designed to encourage, promote, aid, and effect the voluntary interchange of data, information, experience, ideas, and knowledge about methods, processes, and techniques relating to investigations and security in advanced technologies among members.

Publications: Online job postings; newsletter; *Legislative and Legal Update*

Training: International conference; local chapters sponsor training opportunities

Independent Armored Car Operators Association, Inc.

102 E. Avenue J

Lancaster, CA 93535-3521

iacoa.com

Members/Purpose: An association for the growing number of privately owned armored car companies. The organization's purpose is to establish high standards of operation and insurance.

Publication: Online newsletter

Training: Annual convention

International Association of Computer Investigative Specialists

P.O. Box 1728

Fairmont, WV 26555

iacis.info/iacisv2/pages/home.php

Members/Purpose: Dedicated to the education and certification of law enforcement professionals in the field of computer forensic science. IACIS exists to create and establish procedures, train personnel, and certify forensic examiners in the recovery of evidence from computer systems.

Publications: Newsletter; software

Training: Forensic examiner course; forensic issues course

National Association of Investigative Specialists, Inc.

P.O. Box 82148

Austin, TX 78705

pimall.com/nais

Members/Purpose: An American trade association of private investigative professionals that focuses on marketing investigative services, developing new investigative techniques, and providing training and resources to members.

Publications: Books; hundreds of manuals on a variety of topics and software; articles

Training: Interactive CD-ROM programs; numerous training packages and courses

National Association of Legal Investigators

nalionline.org

Members/Purpose: To conduct investigations related to litigation. NALI is open to all professional legal investigators who are actively engaged in negligence investigations for the plaintiff and/or criminal defense.

Publication: *The Legal Investigator*

Training: National conferences; certification program

World Association of Detectives, Inc.

908 21st St.

Sacramento, CA 95814

wad.net

Members/Purpose: To promote and maintain the highest ethical practice in the profession and to foster and perpetuate a spirit of cooperation among members and similar organizations.

Publications: Newsletter

Training: Annual conference

Index